the NONVERBAL COMMUNICATION BOOK

JOSEPH A. DEVITO

Kendall Hunt
publishing company

Kendall Hunt
publishing company

www.kendallhunt.com
Send all inquiries to:
4050 Westmark Drive
Dubuque, IA 52004-1840

ISBN 978-1-4652-1898-8

Printed in the United States of America
10 9 8 7 6 5 4 3 2 1

Brief Contents

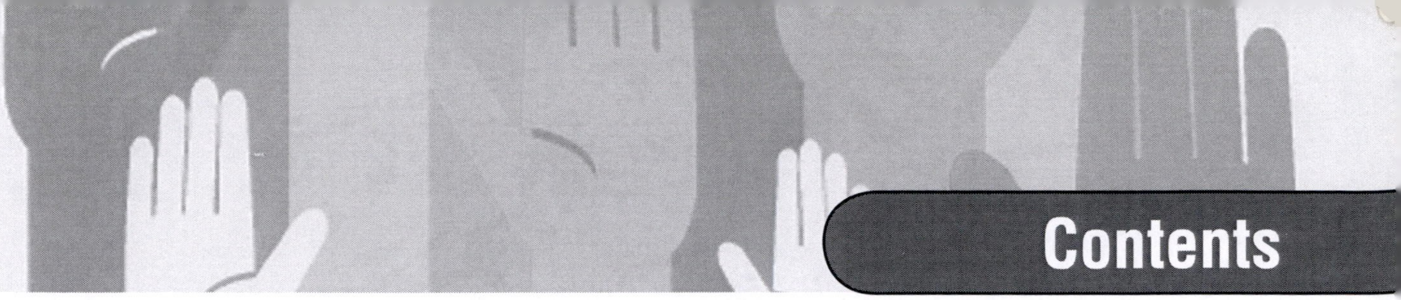

Contents

Features

Welcome to *The Nonverbal Communication Book*

The Nonverbal Communication Book is one of many textbooks currently available for the popular Nonverbal Communication course. This book, however, is different in several important respects. Here I explain the focus of the text, its plan and organization, and the ways it may be used.

FOCUS OF *THE NONVERBAL COMMUNICATION BOOK*

This text is designed to cover both the theory and research in nonverbal communication and to help you develop your nonverbal skills. More specifically, this text aims to:

- Explain the channels or codes of nonverbal communication and how you send and receive nonverbal messages.
- Explain the importance and the role of culture in both sending and receiving nonverbal messages.
- Increase awareness of the ways in which you interpret the nonverbal behaviors of others and the ways in which you use nonverbal behaviors yourself.
- Increase your accuracy in detecting nonverbal communication cues.
- Increase your effectiveness in your use of nonverbal cues.

PLAN OF *THE NONVERBAL COMMUNICATION BOOK*

The Nonverbal Communication Book is divided into three parts, consisting of 10 chapters, two appendixes, and a glossary of technical terms.

Part One (Foundations of Nonverbal Communication) consists of one chapter that presents an introduction to nonverbal communication, explaining the nature of nonverbal communication, the benefits to be derived from the study of nonverbal communication, and the major principles governing nonverbal communication. In addition, for those who are taking this course as their only or first course in communication, a brief and general introduction to human communication is provided.

Part Two (The Codes of Nonverbal Communication) consists of eight chapters (Chapters 2–9) that identify the codes of nonverbal communication—the channels you use in sending and receiving nonverbal messages—your body, face, eyes, artifacts such as jewelry and clothing, space, touch, paralanguage and silence, and time.

Part Three (Putting It All Together) consists of one chapter (Chapter 10) in which we put it all together and explain four areas that have been the focus of a great deal of nonverbal research and illustrate how all the channels work together: attraction, lying, immediacy, and power.

Appendix A provides some initial guidance in conducting a nonverbal research study and suggestions for completing this standard (and most exciting) term project.

Appendix B provides some suggestions for creating a video of some aspect of nonverbal communication and a list of sample videos that might be used as examples for this type of project. These videos may also prove useful in connection with the text. They do a great deal of what a printed text cannot do and so make really useful ancillaries.

A glossary of nonverbal concepts is included at the end of the text to clarify further the technical terms of this area of study.

Text and Exercises

Each chapter contains both text and exercises. After reading about a specific area of nonverbal communication, a variety of different types of exercises invite you to, for example, ensure your understanding of key concepts, explore your own nonverbal communication, or investigate ways to enhance your nonverbal competence and skill. The exercises are an essential part of this approach, which requires active learning throughout the course. In fact, you'll find it requires greater effort—more introspection, more soul searching, more self-interaction—than most of your courses. Some exercises are integrated into the text narrative. These are noted in brackets ([ ]) in the Table of Contents and in the chapter openers' list of Contents.

This book presents a three-step system for learning nonverbal communication:

- Step 1. Identification of objectives
- Step 2. Text explaining the content relative to the objectives
- Step 3. Exercises to encourage you to apply what was covered in Step 2 in order to achieve the objectives noted in Step 1. Depending on the nature and goals of your specific nonverbal communication course, some exercises (because of their focus or format) will prove more relevant than others. Consequently, a large number of exercises (60 in all) are included so that selections may be made appropriate to the specific course goals.

Each of the 10 chapters ends with a summary, a list of key terms presented as an exercise, and an exercise called "And in Addition" in which you're asked to add to the contents of the chapter and, if possible, share your additions with others in the course.

Chapter Objectives

Learning objectives open each of the chapters. These objectives spell out what you should be able to do after you read the chapter and complete the exercises. The objectives will help guide you in your reading and doing the exercises. Read these at the beginning of the chapter and, after reading the chapter, return to these and test yourself to make sure you understand the concepts and can apply the skills. These objectives highlight the major concepts and skills of the chapter. They do not include all the objectives a particular course may specify or that you'll gain from a given chapter. The learning objectives system used here—and there are a variety of these—identifies three major levels of thinking, each of which is included throughout the text:

- **Knowledge** (recalling, remembering, and comprehending), introduced by such specific verbs as *define*, *paraphrase*, *describe*, and *differentiate*.

- **Application** (applying a concept to a new situation), introduced by such specific verbs as *diagram*, *illustrate*, *use*, and *give examples.*
- **Problem solving** (analyzing/breaking a concept into its parts, synthesizing/combining elements into a new whole, and evaluating/making value or appropriateness judgments), introduced by such specific verbs as *assess*, *construct*, *organize*, and *evaluate.*

Each of the exercises is introduced by one of these learning objective terms.

Special Features

Each of the code chapters, the chapters in Part Two (Chapters 2–9), contain a number of special features.

- **Chapter-opening exercise.** Each of these chapters begins with a brief exercise that is designed to stimulate you to think about your own use of some aspect of nonverbal communication discussed in the chapter.
- **Nonverbal politeness.** Each of the code chapters contains a brief politeness note that points out some of the politeness implications of the particular nonverbal communication channel.
- **On the Job.** Boxes that highlight a variety of workplace situations involving nonverbal communication are included in Chapters 2–9; these boxes invite you to use your newly acquired nonverbal skills to help resolve (or at least manage) an array of different issues.
- **If you want to** items are included in these code chapters to illustrate that the codes (although covered in separate chapters) actually work together in communicating meaning and also to demonstrate how very practical the study of nonverbal communication is.

WAYS OF USING *THE NONVERBAL COMMUNICATION BOOK*

This book can be used in a variety of ways:

- **Offline and online.** The text can be used as any text in the "regular" classroom. With a hardcopy, students are able to respond to the exercises in the text and retain it as a record of the course and their own nonverbal communication behavior or scan or photocopy the pages to turn in to the instructor or share with other students. This text is also well suited to e-courses. In that case, students would be able to turn in the worksheets, share them with others taking the class, and discuss them online.
- **Alone or in a package**. The book provides thorough coverage of nonverbal communication and so could be used as the sole course textbook or it can be used in conjunction with a popular book such as *The Everything Body Language* (Hagen, 2011), *The Complete Idiot's Guide to Body Language* (Andersen, 2004), or *Body Language for Dummies* (Kuhnke, 2007)—all excellent books despite their popular appeal. Or, it could be used with a more focused popular book such as *Multicultural Manners* (Dresser, 2005), *Essential Do's and Taboos* (Axtell, 2007), or any of the inexpensive books on etiquette (most of which are primarily devoted to nonverbal behavior).

That pretty much explains the focus of the book, the plan of the book, and the ways in which it may be used. Now, we're ready to embark on what will prove to be an exciting journey into the world of nonverbal communication. Of course, it's a world that you've lived in all your lives. But, you may not have thought about it in the ways presented here. We'll bring to consciousness the ways nonverbal communication works with the ultimate aim of enabling you to control and manage this form of communication more effectively.

Joe DeVito
jadevito@earthlink.net
http://tcbdevito.blogspot.com

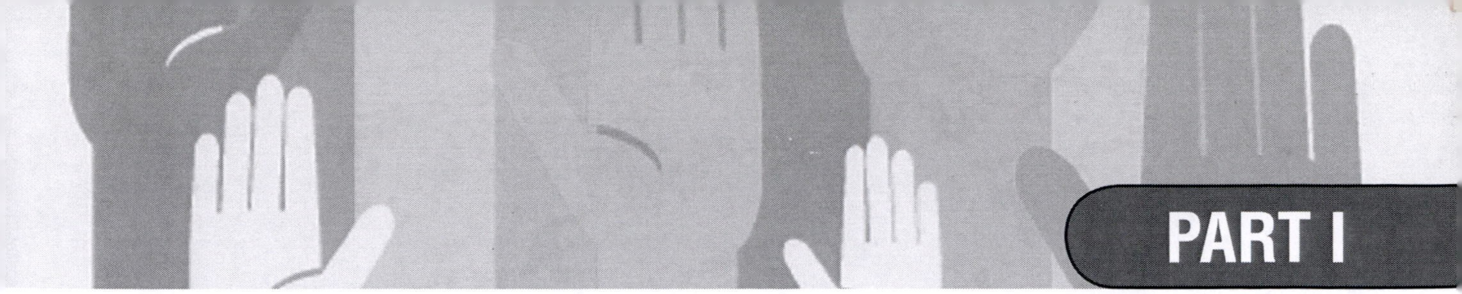

PART I

Foundations of Nonverbal Communication

This first part of *The Nonverbal Communication Book* (consisting of one chapter) introduces the field of nonverbal communication. Because nonverbal communication is a subdivision or part of the broader area of human communication, we begin by reviewing briefly some essential elements of human communication and then focus on our main topic, nonverbal communication. The topics in this part then include:

- The nature of human communication and especially its major components and processes.
- The nature of nonverbal communication where we identify the various codes or channels of nonverbal messages and some of the myths about nonverbal communication that we need to dispel right at the beginning.
- The benefits you'll derive from your study of nonverbal communication. After all, this course is going to involve a major investment of your time and energy; you should get something for it.
- Ten principles of nonverbal communication. These principles will further explain what nonverbal communication is and how it operates. These principles will provide a foundation for considering the various specific codes of nonverbal communication, beginning with the next chapter.

Chapter 1

Introducing Nonverbal Communication

CHAPTER TOPICS

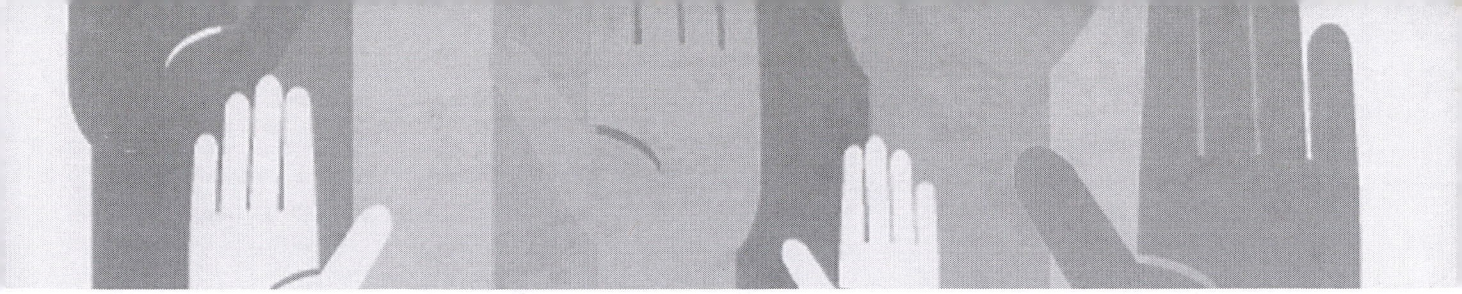

CHAPTER EXERCISES

Diagramming a Model of Human Communication
Identifying Nonverbal Communication
Explaining the Values of Nonverbal Communication Study
Paraphrasing and Identifying the Interaction of Verbal and Nonverbal Messages
Explaining "Getting to Know You"
[Identifying Gender Differences]
Paraphrasing and Illustrating the Principles of Nonverbal Messages

CHAPTER OBJECTIVES

After completing this chapter, you should be able to:

1. Define *human communication* and identify its essential elements.
2. Define *nonverbal communication* and identify the main codes or channels through which messages pass.
3. Identify the social and professional benefits of studying nonverbal communication.
4. Paraphrase and illustrate the 10 major principles of nonverbal communication.

Nonverbal communication is a branch or division of the broader field of human communication, so it would help us to look first at the general nature of human communication and see how nonverbal communication fits into this larger picture.

THE NATURE OF HUMAN COMMUNICATION

Human communication occurs when one person (or more) sends and receives messages that are distorted by noise, occur within a context, have some effect, and provide some opportunity for feedback. Figure 1.1 illustrates the elements present in all communication acts, whether verbal or nonverbal; whether intrapersonal, interpersonal, small group, public speaking, or mass communication; whether face-to-face, by telephone, or online: (1) context, (2) sources-receivers, (3) messages, (4) channels, and (5) noise.

Communication Context

All communication takes place in a **context** that has at least four dimensions: physical, social-psychological, temporal, and cultural.

- **The physical context** is the tangible or concrete environment in which communication takes place—the room or hallway or park, for example. This physical context is essentially nonverbal and encompasses many of the nonverbal channels we'll discuss in the chapters ahead. For example, if the context is a room, then its form, the colors the walls are painted, the type of accessories in the

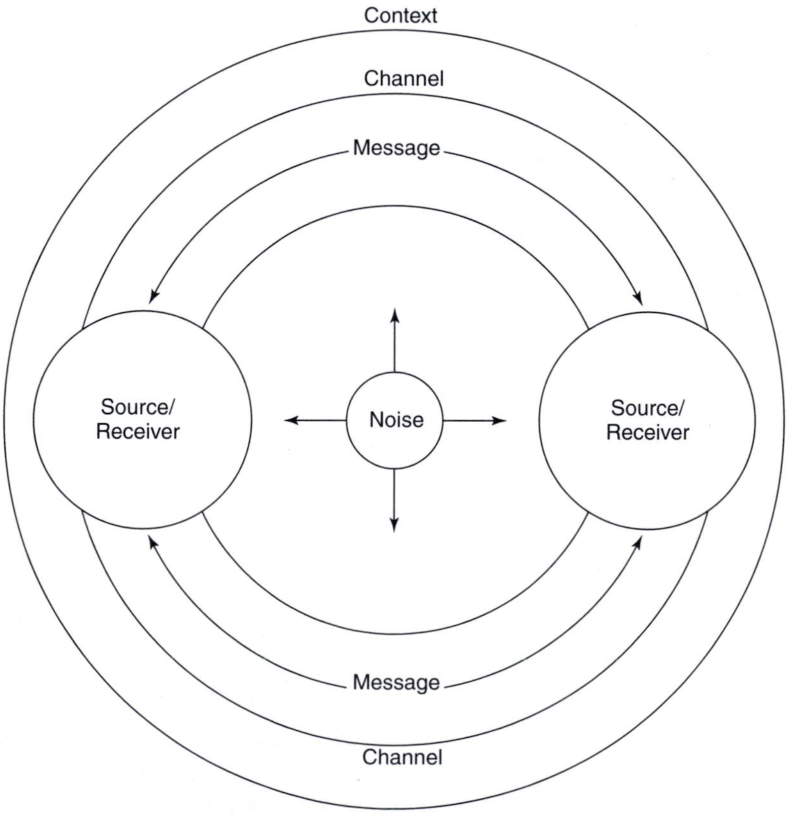

Figure 1.1 A Model of Human Communication

In what ways might the physical context shown here influence the communication? © 2013, AISPIX by Image Source, Shutterstock, Inc.

room, the number of windows, the lighting, the scent, and any number of other nonverbal elements come into play and exert influence on the content of your messages (what you say) as well as on the form (how you say it).

- **The social–psychological context** includes, for example, the status relationships among the participants, the roles and the games that people play, and the cultural rules of the society in which people are communicating. It also includes the friendliness or unfriendliness, formality or informality, and seriousness or humorousness of the participants (signaled in great part by facial expressions, eye contact, and body movements).
- **The temporal (or time) context** includes (1) the time of day (e.g., for some the morning is not a time for communication; for others, it's ideal), (2) the time in history in which the communication takes place (e.g., messages on racial, sexual, or religious attitudes cannot be fully understood outside of their time in history), and (3) how a message fits into the sequence of communication events (e.g., the meaning of a compliment would be greatly different depending on whether you said it immediately after your friend paid you a compliment, immediately before you asked your friend for a favor, or during an argument). Time is one of the major dimensions of nonverbal communication and Chapter 9 is devoted entirely to time and how it influences communication.
- **The cultural context** has to do with your (and others') culture: the beliefs, values, and ways of behaving that are shared by a group of people and passed down from one generation to the next. Cultural factors affect every interaction and influence what you say, how you say it, and how you respond to what others say. Many of these cultural ways of behaving are concerned with nonverbal communication—for example, how you greet people (do you bow, kiss, or shake hands?), whether or not you look them in the eye, how close you stand when interacting, and a host of other factors we'll talk about throughout the text.

These four dimensions of context interact with one another. For example, arriving inappropriately dressed for a scheduled dinner meeting with a prospective employer (*temporal* context) might violate a *cultural* rule, which might lead to changes in the *social–psychological* context, perhaps creating tension, annoyance, or discomfort, which in turn might lead to changes in the *physical* context—for example, choosing a less formal restaurant for your dinner.

How would you describe your culture's rules for say, greeting one of your professors who you meet in a restaurant? © 2013, Zunjeta, Shutterstock, Inc.

Senders and Receivers

You send messages when you speak, write, gesture, smile, or touch someone. You receive messages in listening, reading, smelling, and so on. As you send messages, however, you're also receiving messages. You're receiving your own messages (you hear yourself, you feel your own body movements, you feel your facial expressions, and you see many of your own gestures), and you're receiving the messages of the other person—visually, aurally, or even through touch or smell.

Messages

Communication **messages** take many forms. You send and receive messages through any one or any combination of sensory organs. Everything about you communicates. For example, the clothes you wear and the way you walk, shake hands, tilt your head, comb your hair, sit, and smile all communicate messages.

In face-to-face communication, the actual message signals (the movements in the air) are evanescent; they fade almost as they're uttered. Some written messages, especially computer-mediated messages such as those sent via e-mail or through social networking sites such as Facebook and Twitter, are virtually uneraseable.

Three special types of messages include metamessages, feedback messages, and feedforward messages.

- **Metamessages.** A message that refers to another message is known as a metamessage; it is communication about communication. For example, messages such as "This statement is false" or "Do you understand what I am trying to tell you?" refer to other messages and are therefore metacommunicational. Nonverbal behavior, as you probably guessed, is frequently metacommunicational. Obvious examples include crossing your fingers behind your back or winking when telling a lie. On a less obvious level, consider the blind date. As you say, "I had a really nice time," your nonverbal messages—the lack of a smile, the failure to maintain eye contact, the extra long pauses—metacommunicate and contradict the verbal "really nice time," suggesting that you did not enjoy the evening.

- **Feedback messages.** Throughout the listening process, a listener sends messages to the speaker in what is called feedback. Feedback tells the speaker what effect he or she is having on the listener(s). This can take many forms: A frown or a smile, a yea or a nay, a pat on the back or a punch in the mouth are all types of feedback. Another type of feedback is the feedback you get from listening to yourself: You hear what you say, you feel the way you move, you see what you write. On the basis of this self-feedback you adjust your verbal and nonverbal messages; for example, you may correct a mispronunciation, smile more, shorten your story, or increase your volume.
- **Feedforward messages.** Certain messages sent to the listener are known as feedforward—information you provide before sending your primary messages. Feedforward reveals something about the messages to come. Feedforward includes such diverse examples as the preface or table of contents in a book, the opening paragraph of a chapter, movie previews, magazine covers, and introductions in public speeches. Before you open your e-mail you get feedforward that tells you the sender's name and the subject matter. In communicating bad news, you might give verbal feedforward that aims to prepare the person to receive this news with something like, "I'm sorry I have to tell you this, but . . ." and nonverbal feedforward such as a sad expression.

Channels

The communication **channel** is the medium through which the message passes. Communication rarely takes place over only one channel; you may use two, three, or four different channels simultaneously. For example, in face-to-face interactions you speak and listen (vocal channel), but you also gesture and receive signals visually (visual channel). In social networking communication, you type and read words and use various symbols and abbreviations to communicate the emotional tone of the message and, in many cases, audio and video means as well. In addition, in face-to-face communication you emit and detect odors (olfactory channel). Often you touch another person, and this too communicates (tactile channel).

Noise

Noise is anything that interferes with your receiving a message, whether verbal or nonverbal. At one extreme, noise may prevent a message from getting from source to receiver. A roaring noise or line static can easily prevent entire messages from getting through to the receiver. At the other extreme, with virtually no noise interference, the message of the source and the message received are almost identical. Most often, however, noise distorts some portion of the message as it travels from source to receiver. Four types of noise are especially relevant:

- **Physical noise** is interference that is external to both speaker and listener; it interferes with the physical transmission of the signal or message. Examples include the screeching of passing cars, the hum of a computer, sunglasses, illegible handwriting, blurred type or fonts that are too small or difficult to read, misspellings and poor grammar, and popup ads.
- **Physiological noise** is created by barriers within the sender or receiver such as visual impairments, hearing loss, articulation problems, and memory loss.

- **Psychological noise** is mental interference in speaker or listener and includes preconceived ideas, wandering thoughts, biases and prejudices, closed-mindedness, and extreme emotionalism.
- **Semantic noise** is created when the speaker and listener have different meaning systems. With nonverbal messages semantic noise would include the varied meanings that people in different cultures give to various nonverbal gestures. In some cases, as we'll see, a gesture may be positive in one culture and insulting in another.

All communications contain noise. In fact, noise cannot be totally eliminated, but its effects can be reduced. Making your language more precise, sharpening your skills for sending and receiving nonverbal messages, and improving your listening and feedback skills are some ways to combat the influence of noise.

EXERCISE

DIAGRAMMING A MODEL OF HUMAN COMMUNICATION

Expand your perspective on human communication by drawing your own model of communication. In your model, include the communication context, senders and receivers, messages, channels, and noise. Your model may be a general communication act—such as that presented here—or a more specific communication act, for example, an interpersonal interaction between two friends, a small study group of four or five people, an employment interview situation, or a public-speaking situation. Create your diagram for face-to-face or computer-mediated communication.

THE NATURE OF NONVERBAL COMMUNICATION

Nonverbal communication is that part of human communication that does not include words. Nonverbal communication can, in fact, be defined simply as communication without words. You communicate nonverbally when you gesture, smile or frown, widen your eyes, move your chair closer to someone, wear jewelry, touch someone, raise your vocal volume, or even say nothing. The crucial aspect is that the message you send is in some way received by one or more other people. If you gesture while you're alone in your room and no one is there to see you, then, most theorists would argue, communication has not taken place. The same is true of verbal messages, of course; if you speak and no one hears you, then communication has not taken place.

What nonverbal messages can you identify in this photo?

As these examples illustrate, some nonverbal behaviors are large and some are small. Some, in fact, are so small that they cannot be seen with the unaided eye—slow-motion videos, for example, reveal small movements of the eyes and face, for example, that may, in some cases, reveal the real emotion a person is feeling rather than the emotion the person wants you to think he or she is experiencing. These are often referred to as **micromomentary expressions.**

Table 1.1 provides a variety of definitions used by nonverbal researchers.

The Areas of Nonverbal Communication

Another way to explain the nature of nonverbal communication is to identify the various channels through which messages are sent and received. As you'll see, this text is organized on the basis of these channels. Here's a brief preview of the areas of nonverbal communication and, at the same time, of this text and course:

Body communication (Chapter 2). This area is concerned with the messages that your body appearance communicates by its size, proportions, height, and skin and hair color, for example. It also includes the movements you make with your body, for example, the gestures you use. And less well known or talked about are the messages from your posture and the way you sit.

Facial communication (Chapter 3). This area is concerned with the messages that your facial expressions communicate. Especially important, as you can imagine, is your facial communication of emotion. And it is largely through

TABLE 1.1 Definitions of Nonverbal Communication

Here are some definitions of nonverbal communication by a variety of researchers and theorists. As you can see, the definitions boil down to "communication without words."
The use of interacting sets of visual, vocal, and invisible communication systems and subsystems by communicators with the systematic encoding and decoding of nonverbal symbols and signs for the purpose(s) of exchanging consensual meanings in specific communication contexts. (Leathers & Eaves, 2008, p. 11)
The process of one person stimulating meaning in the mind of another person (or persons) by means of nonverbal messages. (Richmond, McCroskey, & Hickson, 2012, p. 14)
Messages expressed by nonlinguistic means. (Adler, Rosenfeld, & Proctor, 2012, p. 175)
All aspects of communication other than words themselves. (Wood, 2012, p. 132)
The process of using messages that are not words to generate meaning. (Pearson, Nelson, Titsworth, & Harter, 2008, p. 86)
Communication other than written or spoken language that creates meaning for someone. (Ivy & Wahl, 2009, p. 3)
The transfer and exchange of messages in any and all modalities that do not involve words. (Matsumoto, Frank, & Hwang, 2013, p. 4)

facial expression that you communicate your attraction to and interest in another person.

Eye communication (Chapter 4). This area focuses on the messages that eye contact (the length and focus) and eye avoidance communicate as well as the meanings communicated by pupil dilation and constriction.

Artifactual communication (Chapter 5). This area concerns a wide variety of items that you make or arrange that communicate messages and includes, for example, your clothing selections, the colors you wear or paint your room, the ways in which you furnish your space (whether actual or virtual), and the way you wear your hair or display your tattoos or body piercings. Also included here is smell communication and your use of scent to communicate.

Spatial communication (Chapter 6). This area, known as proxemics, concerns your use of space in your interactions with others. It also concerns another aspect of nonverbal communication known as territoriality, which focuses on your ownership-like reactions to areas of space and how these influence your behaviors—how you may encroach upon the territory of others and how you react to encroachment on "your" territories.

Touch communication (Chapter 7). Known also as tactile communication or haptics, this area concerns the meanings that touch communicates—when they're constructive and when they may prove destructive, intimidating, or sexually offensive.

Paralanguage and silence communication (Chapter 8). Paralanguage focuses on the messages that you communicate with variations in your vocal qualities such as rate, pausing, volume, pitch, and hesitations whereas silence focuses on the messages and the many meanings that are communicated by the absence of speech.

Time communication (Chapter 9). The focus here is on the way you use time, known technically as chronemics, and the messages that your treatment of time communicates, which, as you'll see, varies widely from one culture to another.

Approaching nonverbal communication one channel at a time is useful for explaining the various dimensions of nonverbal communication but it obscures the very real fact that these channels most often operate together. For example, when you express love you use words, facial expressions, eye messages, and variations in your tone of voice all at the same time and all (generally) consistently supporting each other—your words of love are echoed in your nonverbal expressions. Because of this, Chapter 10 (**Putting It All Together**) focuses on several communication areas that nonverbal researchers have studied extensively to illustrate how the varied nonverbal channels work together. The areas discussed here are attraction, lying, immediacy, and power. The necessity of looking at the various nonverbal communication channels working together is also echoed in the "**If you want to**" feature that you'll find in each of the chapters devoted to the codes or channels of nonverbal communication (Chapters 2–9).

Traditionally many nonverbal communication courses include a final research project as a requirement. For that reason, two appendixes are included. Appendix A provides an introductory guide to designing and conducting a research project in nonverbal communication along with some discussion and exercises to help you master some of the essentials of communication research. Appendix B provides a brief introduction to creating a video in nonverbal communication and lots of examples.

The Myths and Truths of Nonverbal Communication

Consider each of the following statements about nonverbal communication. Which do you think are true?

1. With training, you can tell what a person is thinking from watching their nonverbal behaviors.
2. Lying is relatively easy to detect, especially with those with whom you have a close relationship.
3. Unlike verbal communication, which is learned, nonverbal communication is innate.
4. Unlike verbal communication, nonverbal communication is universal—members of all cultures have the same meaning for gestures, facial expressions, and eye movements, for example.
5. Nonverbal communication is more important than verbal communication.

Although we'll consider each of these assumptions as they become relevant in the course of our coverage of nonverbal communication, we should here examine what nonverbal communication is not. All of the five statements are more myth than fact. Briefly:

1. You can't tell what a person is thinking from their nonverbal behaviors, at least not generally. There are situations when you can tell—for example, you can often identify when a person is happy and when a person is sad. But, beyond these rather general meanings, you really can't read a person like a book.
2. Lying is actually extremely difficult to detect, especially when the liar is a person with whom you have a close relationship; the reason is that people in a close relationship have learned how to lie effectively to their relationship partner.
3. Some nonverbal behaviors are certainly innate—fear, for example, may be expressed similarly in different cultures. However, much nonverbal behavior is learned in much the same way as verbal behavior is learned—through imitating those with whom you grow up.
4. There are some nonverbal behaviors that are universal, the behaviors that are innate such as responses to fear. However, much nonverbal behavior varies widely in meaning from one culture to another. As we'll see the same hand gesture may mean very different things in different cultures.
5. This is perhaps the most popular myth about nonverbal communication. Certainly there are situations where nonverbal communication is more important than verbal communication—perhaps in first encounters or in expressing support or love—but certainly not in all. You'd be hard pressed to explain nonverbally theoretical concepts, complex directions, or what happened on your way to class today. So, the importance of one channel over another depends on the message and the unique communication situation you're talking about. Rather than thinking about verbal and nonverbal communication competing for importance with one another, think about these two signal systems working together—each communicating the information it communicates best.

EXERCISE

IDENTIFYING NONVERBAL COMMUNICATION

In order to personalize the material to come and to make sure you have a firm idea of the major nonverbal communication codes already identified and that we'll cover in more detail throughout this text, each of these codes is listed in Column 1. For 1, 2, 3, or all of the codes/channels, describe a specific behavior that you see, for example, on television, in online videos, in movies, or in your personal experiences. In Column 3 identify the meaning(s) that it communicated in the show or video.

Nonverbal Channel	Nonverbal Behavior Description	Possible Meanings Communicated
Body communication	*Jim slouches just about all the time*	*He's not energetic; he's tired and uninterested*
Facial communication		
Eye communication		
Artifactual communication		
Spatial communication		
Touch communication		
Paralanguage and silence communication		
Time communication		

Now that you have an idea of what nonverbal communication is, what it's not, and its various channels, consider the benefits in studying nonverbal communication.

THE BENEFITS OF STUDYING NONVERBAL COMMUNICATION

The ability to use nonverbal communication effectively can yield a variety of both general and specific benefits in your social and your workplace lives. First, let's identify some general benefits and then some more specific benefits.

Some General Benefits

The general benefits span the entire range of your communication life whether online or face-to-face, whether personal or workplace.

First, it will improve your accuracy in understanding others, those who are from your own or similar culture as well as those who are from cultures very different from your own. Increased accuracy in understanding others will yield obvious benefits in social and workplace situations—from understanding a coy smile from a date to the meaning of a supervisor's gestures.

Second, an increased knowledge of nonverbal communication will improve your own ability to communicate information and to persuade others. In many instances, it will help you reinforce your verbal messages. The greater your nonverbal skills, the more successful you're likely to be at informing as well as influencing others.

Third, it will increase your own perceived attractiveness; the greater your ability to send and receive nonverbal signals, the higher your popularity and psychosocial well-being are likely to be (Burgoon, Guerrero, & Floyd, 2010).

Fourth, it will enable you to make a more effective self-presentation. Consider, for example, that when you meet someone for the first time—at least in face-to-face meetings—you form impressions of the person largely on the basis of his or her nonverbal messages. Being able to more effectively understand and manage your nonverbal messages will enable you to present yourself in the way you want to be perceived. The **"If you want to"** feature is largely devoted to the skills of self-presentation. As you can appreciate, these benefits will prove especially valuable in the workplace. In fact, the workplace is emphasized throughout the next chapters with the **On the Job** feature, which presents a workplace issue, revolving around nonverbal communication, and asks you how you'd apply your nonverbal skills in dealing with the issue.

Each of these benefits and skills, unfortunately, can be used to help or support another, or, unfortunately, they can be used for less noble purposes. For example, a person adept at nonverbal communication will be more effective in persuading others to buy cars or sign a mortgage they can't afford or present themselves as competent when they aren't or increase their attractiveness before hitting you up for a loan.

Some Specific Benefits

In addition these general benefits, here are some specific benefits of studying and mastering the art of nonverbal communication. Of course, learning about an important area of human behavior—what it is, how it works, what influences it, and a variety of other dimensions we'll explore—is a benefit in itself. Increased knowledge is a benefit, pure and simple. However, there are additional, more immediately pragmatic, specific benefits that you can gain as a result for reading the text and completing the exercises. Here are 25:

1. Use nonverbal messages to interact with your verbal messages, thus creating meaningful packages of messages.
2. Use nonverbal messages to manage the impressions you give to others.
3. Use nonverbal messages to help form and maintain productive and meaningful interpersonal and work relationships.
4. Use nonverbal messages to help regulate conversations and to make them more effective and satisfying.
5. Use nonverbal messages to persuade—to influence the attitudes or behaviors of others.
6. Use nonverbal messages to help express and communicate your emotions.
7. Use nonverbal messages with sensitivity to cultural and gender differences and expectations.
8. Use hand and body gestures to communicate varied meanings.
9. Use body posture to reinforce your intended messages.
10. Manage your facial expressions to communicate the meanings you want to share.
11. Vary your facial styles to communicate a wide variety of messages.
12. Communicate different meanings with eye movements and with eye avoidance.
13. Use color, clothing, and other artifacts to communicate the meanings you wish.
14. Use spatial messages to reinforce your verbal messages and in ways appropriate to the purpose of the interaction.
15. Use territorial markers and respond to the markers of others appropriately.
16. Use touch appropriate to the relationship stage and avoid touch that may be considered overly intimate or intrusive.
17. Use paralanguage to signal conversational turns, your desire to speak or to continue listening, for example.
18. Use silence to communicate a wide variety of meanings.
19. Respond to the rules of interpersonal time that are maintained in the particular context, for example, the workplace or the classroom.
20. Manage your time effectively and efficiently; avoid wasting time.
21. Increase your own attractiveness in a variety of ways.
22. Increase your ability to detect lying (but with important limitations).
23. Increase your immediacy or closeness to others when you wish.
24. Increase your perceived power with nonverbal cues.
25. Use nonverbal cues in a civil and polite manner to further your purposes.

EXERCISE

EXPLAINING THE VALUES OF NONVERBAL COMMUNICATION STUDY

Continue personalizing the areas of nonverbal communication by examining the specific benefits you can derive from the study and mastery of nonverbal communication. In Column 1 are listed the areas of nonverbal communication. For 1, 2, 3, or all of the areas, record in Column 2 any potential values or benefits you might derive in your personal or business life from greater effectiveness in using each of the channels or codes. In Column 3 indicate how you specifically might go about achieving this benefit or value.

Nonverbal Channel	Personal/Business Value	Achieving the Value
Body messages	*Make a good first impression.*	*Avoid fidgeting and playing with my hair.*
Facial messages		
Body messages		
Facial messages		
Eye messages		
Artifactual messages		
Spatial messages		
Touch messages		
Paralanguage and silence messages		
Time messages		

TEN PRINCIPLES OF NONVERBAL COMMUNICATION

Perhaps the best way to begin the study of nonverbal communication is to examine several principles that nonverbal messages serve (Afifi, 2007; Burgoon & Bacue, 2003; Burgoon et al., 2010). These principles are in a sense an extended definition of nonverbal communication and its essential qualities and explain how nonverbal messages figure into the total communication act and into your life.

Nonverbal Messages Interact with Verbal Messages

Although nonverbal messages may be used alone, without any verbalization, often they occur together. Verbal and nonverbal messages usually form a package of signals and interact with each other in six major ways:

- **Accent.** Nonverbal communication is often used to accent or emphasize some part of the verbal message. You might, for example, raise your voice to underscore a particular word or phrase, bang your fist on the desk to stress your commitment, or look longingly into someone's eyes when saying "I love you."
- **Complement.** Nonverbal communication may be used to complement, to add nuances of meaning not communicated by your verbal message. Thus, you might smile when telling a story (to suggest that you find it humorous) or frown and shake your head when recounting someone's deceit (to suggest your disapproval).
- **Contradict.** You may deliberately contradict your verbal messages with nonverbal movements; for example, by crossing your fingers or winking to indicate that you're lying.
- **Control.** Nonverbal movements may be used to control, or to indicate your desire to control, the flow of verbal messages, as when you purse your lips, lean forward, or make hand movements to indicate that you want to speak. You might also put up your hand or vocalize your pauses (e.g., with "um") to indicate that you have not finished and aren't ready to relinquish the floor to the next speaker.
- **Repeat.** You can repeat or restate the verbal message nonverbally. You can, for example, follow your verbal "Is that all right?" with raised eyebrows and a questioning look, or you can motion with your head or hand to repeat your verbal "Let's go."
- **Substitute.** You may also use nonverbal communication to substitute for verbal messages. You can, for example, signal "OK" with a hand gesture. You can nod your head to indicate yes or shake your head to indicate no.

Think of a recent specific conversation that you had. How was control signaled?

With the exception of "substitute," these nonverbal messages may be viewed as metamessages or metasignals. For example, when you smile warmly when approaching someone you metacommunicate that the interaction will be friendly and pleasant. When you smile when saying "You old crow, I haven't seen you in years," your smile and your vocal expression metacommunicate that you're pleased to see the other person. When you argue with someone and you clench your fists and your pitch level rises, your nonverbals are metacommunicating your degree of intensity.

EXERCISE

PARAPHRASING AND IDENTIFYING THE INTERACTION OF VERBAL AND NONVERBAL MESSAGES

To explore further the ways in which verbal and nonverbal messages interact, consider the six functions just discussed (listed in Column 1). For each of these functions, explain in your own words what that function involves in Column 2. For one, two, three, or all of these functions, provide an example from your own experience, from the media, or from your imagination.

Verbal and Nonverbal Interaction	Paraphrase the Function	Examples
To accent	*to highlight, emphasize, give stress to some part of the verbal message*	*The witness on a recent* CSI *identifed the perp by pointing and scowling*
To complement		
To contradict		
To control		
To repeat		
To substitute		

When you communicate electronically, of course, your message is communicated by means of typed letters without facial expressions or gestures that normally accompany face-to-face communication and without the changes in rate and volume that are a part of normal telephone communication. To compensate for this lack of nonverbal behavior, the emoticon was created (see Table 1.2). Sometimes called a "smiley" after the ever-present :), the emoticon is a typed symbol that communicates through a keyboard the nuances of the message normally conveyed by nonverbal expression. The absence of the nonverbal channel through which you can clarify your message—for example, smiling or winking to communicate sarcasm or humor—make such typed symbols extremely helpful. As you'll see from Table 1.2, even something as simple and as stylized as the smiley varies from one culture to another.

TABLE 1.2 Emoticons

These are some of the emoticons used in computer communication. The first six are widely used in the United States; the last three are popular in Japan and illustrate how culture influences such symbols. Because Japanese culture considers it impolite for women to show their teeth when smiling, the emoticon for a woman's smile shows a dot signifying a closed mouth. Depending on your computer, these typed symbols are often on auto correct (as in the first two examples) and change into the graphic smileys. Additional emoticons, acronyms, and abbreviations—in varied cultures—are plentiful on the Internet.

Emoticon	Meaning	Emoticon	Meaning
:-) J	Smile: I'm kidding	{*****}	Hugs and kisses
:-(☺	Frown: I'm feeling down	^ . ^	Woman's smile
;-) ☹	Wink	^ _ ^	Man's smile
*	Kiss	^0^	Happy
{ }	Hug		

Nonverbal Messages Help Manage Impressions

It is largely through the nonverbal communications of others that you form impressions of them. Based on a person's body size, skin color, and dress, as well as on the way the person smiles, maintains eye contact, and expresses him- or herself facially, you form impressions—you judge who the person is and what the person is like. These first impressions are extremely important because they influence your perceptions of future interactions—a favorable first impression is likely to give you a template for interpreting the person's future behaviors. Ambiguous behaviors, for example, will be interpreted positively if your first impression was positive and negatively if your first impression was negative. These first impressions are also long-lasting and extremely resistant to change.

And, at the same time that you form impressions of others, you are also managing the impressions they form of you. You use different strategies to achieve different impressions. And, of course, many of these strategies involve nonverbal messages. For example:

- **To be liked** you might smile, pat another on the back, and shake hands warmly.
- **To be believed** you might use focused eye contact, a firm stance, and open gestures.
- **To excuse failure** you might look sad, cover your face with your hands, and shake your head.
- **To secure help** by indicating helplessness, you might use open hand gestures, a puzzled look, and inept movements.
- **To hide faults** you might avoid self-adaptors. Or you might cover your acne or dye your hair.

Look around your bedroom or living room. What impressions would this room communicate to someone who doesn't know you, say a new classmate? © 2013, Kasia Bialasiewicz, Shutterstock, Inc.

- **To be followed** you might dress the part of a leader or display your diploma or awards where others can see them.
- **To confirm self-image and to communicate it to others**, you might dress in certain ways or decorate your apartment with things that reflect your personality.

Because impression management is so important and so much a part of nonverbal communication, a recurring feature called **"If you want to"**—appearing in all the code chapters (Chapter 2–9)—contains essentially impression management strategies.

Nonverbal Messages Help Form and Define Relationships

Much of your relationship life is lived nonverbally. For example, you communicate your desire to form a relationship in part nonverbally by approaching the person, smiling, winking, or, if online, with verbal messages often accompanied by virtual cards or gifts and photos. And, alternatively, you also use nonverbal signals to communicate your desire to end the relationship or to signal displeasure with the relationship. Table 1.3 presents a model of relationships and some of the nonverbal behaviors that are likely to be displayed at each of the stages.

You also use nonverbal signals to communicate the nature of your relationship to another person; and you and that person communicate nonverbally with each other. These signals that communicate your relationship status are known as **tie signs**: They indicate the ways in which your relationship is tied together (Afifi & Johnson, 2005; Goffman, 1967; Knapp & Hall, 2010; Morris, 1977). Usually the relationship is with another person and so you might wear an engagement or wedding ring to show your relationship or you may walk hand in hand to show your connection. Sometimes the tie can be with a group or organization, for example, your relationship with a particular religion may be displayed with your jewelry or your relationship with your college or some organization with a ring or pin, for example.

Tie signs are also used to confirm the level of the relationship; for example, you might hold hands to see if this is responded to positively. And, of course, tie signs are often used to let others know that the two of you are tied together. Because tie signs are so often a form of touch communication, we return to these in Chapter 7 (pages 140–141).

TABLE 1.3 Nonverbal Communication in Relationships

Here is a simple list of relationship stages, the stages that a relationship might progress through. Certainly not all relationships go through dissolution or even deterioration and, of course, not all achieve intimacy. However, the six stages identified in Column 1 seem to describe the major stages that relationships can go through. In Column 2 are listed some of the nonverbal behaviors that are likely to take place at each relationship stage and that may well be considered inappropriate at other relationship stages. There are, as you can imagine, lots more nonverbal behaviors that could be identified for each stage. Add those you think especially important at each stage.

Relationship Stage	Nonverbal Behaviors
Contact: the initial meeting; you perceive the person and have some initial interaction	Smile Make eye contact View photo Approach
Involvement: the relationship becomes closer and you develop a sense of mutuality, of being connected	Touch More focused eye contact Time spent together increases
Intimacy: the relationship becomes a very important one; the other person becomes your best friend, lover, or companion	Kissing Hugging Intimate touching Sexual contact
Deterioration: the bonds holding you together seem to weaken; dissatisfactions increase	Eye contact avoidance Touch avoidance Time spent together decreases Larger distances are maintained Less smiling
Repair: special efforts are made to correct the problems with the relationship and to move it closer to intimacy	Increased contact Smile Eye contact Shorter distance
Dissolution: the relationship breaks up; the individuals separate	Physical separation Negative facial expressions Time spent apart

EXPLAINING "GETTING TO KNOW YOU"

EXERCISE

The purpose of this experience is to explore how we get to know each other and to appreciate the nonverbal cues that we use to form impressions. For this experience, form dyads with a person you have not spoken with before or, if that's not possible, with someone you know little about. For 3–5 minutes discuss a topic currently in the news—for example, politics, business, entertainment, sports, economic, or social media. Do this before reading on.

After these brief discussions, each person should complete the following table. In Column 1 are 10 questions about the other person. Record your best-guess answers to these questions in Column 2 and in Column 3 record the nonverbal cues you used in arriving at the answers you recorded in Column 2. You'll find it virtually impossible to not also base your impressions on the person's verbal messages as well. So include verbal cues where appropriate.

Once the tables are completed, discuss your answers, why you answered as you did, the nonverbal cues you used, the accuracy of your answers, and anything else that seems relevant to nonverbal communication and the perception of others.

Questions	Answers	Nonverbal Cues
Is this person normally an assertive person?	*Yes, probably.*	*She maintains great eye contact, speaks forcefully about what she believes, doesn't display any shyness cues.*
How would this person vote on the legalization of marijuana?		
Would this person enjoy giving public speeches?		
Would this person volunteer for the military?		
Does this person communicate on social media sites? If so, how often (in minutes/hours per day)?		
Would this person be relatively liberal or relatively conservative on social issues?		
Did this person vote in the last presidential election? If so, for whom?		
What type of music would this person be most likely to prefer?		
Would this person vote in favor or against same-sex marriage?		
What television shows would this person be likely to watch on a fairly regular basis?		

(Continued)

EXPLAINING "GETTING TO KNOW YOU"(CONTINUED)

After this discussion, you may find it helpful to reflect on or discuss the following possible implications of this brief experience.

- All communication is self-reflexive. Regardless of what you talk about (or do not talk about) you communicate something about yourself. You are forever telling others who you are, what you like and do not like, and a great deal more.
- You use a wide variety of nonverbal cues in forming impressions of others. Clothing, hair, gestures, jewelry, tone of voice, eye movements, facial expression, and many other cues are used to draw inferences about who this person is and what this person is like. At the same time, of course, others are forming impressions of you just as quickly.
- First impressions are formed very quickly. In this exercise, you formed impressions of another in 5 minutes or less. Often, impressions are formed even more quickly (sometimes in a matter of seconds) and are largely formed on the basis of nonverbal cues.

Nonverbal Messages Structure Conversation

When you're in conversation, you give and receive cues—signals that you're ready to speak, to listen, to comment on what the speaker just said. These cues regulate and structure the interaction. These **turn-taking cues** may be verbal (as when you say, "What do you think?" and thereby give the speaking turn over to the listener). Most often, however, they're nonverbal; a nod of the head in the direction of someone else, for example, signals that you're ready to give up your speaking turn and want this other person to say something. You also show that you're listening and that you want the conversation to continue (or that you're not listening and want the conversation to end), largely through nonverbal signals of posture and eye contact (or the lack thereof).

Nonverbal Messages Are Rule Governed

Verbal messages everyone knows follow the rules of grammar—at least generally. When it comes to nonverbal messages, the rules are not as clearly identified. Nevertheless, nonverbal messages are rule governed in a number of important ways. Some rules identify what nonverbal signals mean—green means "go" and red means "stop." Some rules tell you what you should or should not do in a given situation, for example, smile when someone smiles at you but don't pick your nose in public. Here are just a few rules that you probably follow without any real conscious attention to the concept of rules.

- Upon entering an elevator, turn to the door and stare at it or at the numbers indicating where the elevation is until your floor is reached.
- When sitting in a cafeteria, take a seat as far away from the next person as possible.
- When strangers are talking, do not enter their group.

- When sitting next to other people in a public space, don't invade their territory with your belongings.
- Avoiding staring at intimate parts of the bodies of strangers.

One of the most important sets of rules concerns politeness. We expect to be treated politely and we (generally at least) treat others politely. We can view politeness in terms of negative and positive types (Brown & Levinson, 1987; Goffman, 1967; Goldsmith, 2007; Holmes, 1995). Both of these types of politeness are responsive to two needs that we each have: (1) positive face—the desire to be viewed positively by others, to be thought of favorably and (2) negative face—the desire to be autonomous, to have the right to do as we wish.

What rules do you expect people to follow upon entering an elevator?

Politeness in nonverbal communication, then, refers to behavior that allows others to maintain both positive and negative face and impoliteness refers to behaviors that attack either positive face (e.g., you criticize someone) or negative face (e.g., you make demands on someone).

To help another person maintain **positive face**, you smile rather than scowl when greeting someone and you give the person your full attention. In short, you treat the person as you would want to be treated. In this way, you allow the person to maintain positive face through what is called *positive politeness.* You *attack* the person's positive face when you don't laugh at a colleagues "funny" story or avoid eye contact when someone is speaking.

To help another person maintain **negative face**, you respect the person's right to be autonomous and so you knock before entering another's office or wait to be invited into another's work cubicle. In this way, you enable the person to maintain negative face through what is called *negative politeness.*

As you can imagine politeness is very often signaled verbally and so, to communicate positive politeness, you speak respectfully to and about the person and you say "excuse me" when appropriate. To communicate negative politeness and allow the person to be autonomous, you request rather than demand that the person do something. You might also give the person a convenient "out" when making a request—"If this is a bad time to talk, we can do this another time."

Because politeness is so important in all forms of human communication (and little discussed in nonverbal communication) it is emphasized in this text with short boxes—called **Politeness in Nonverbal Communication**—appearing in all the code chapters, which identify some of the politeness implications of the various codes.

Nonverbal Messages Can Influence and Deceive

You can influence others not only through what you say but also through your nonverbal signals. A focused glance that says you're committed; gestures that further explain what you're saying; appropriate dress that says, "I'll easily fit in with this organization"—these are just a few examples of ways in which you can exert nonverbal influence.

And with the ability to influence, of course, comes the ability to deceive—to mislead another person into thinking something is true when it's false or that something is false when it's true. One common example of nonverbal deception is using your eyes and facial expressions to communicate a liking for other people when you're really interested only in gaining their support in some endeavor. Not surprisingly, you also use nonverbal signals to detect deception in others. For example, you may well suspect a person of lying if he or she avoids eye contact, fidgets, and conveys inconsistent verbal and nonverbal messages.

But be careful. Research shows that it is much more difficult to tell when someone is lying than you probably think it is. So, use caution in judging deception (Knapp, 2008). The topics of lying and lying detection, along with the cautions to observe in judging lying, are discussed in Chapter 10.

Another way of looking at this principle is to appreciate that nonverbal communication is often used strategically; we frequently use nonverbal messages to achieve a specific end. You may cry to get your way or give someone the silent treatment to win an argument, for example.

Nonverbal Messages Are Crucial for Expressing Emotions

Although people often explain and reveal emotions verbally, nonverbal signals communicate a great part of your emotional experience. For example, you reveal your level of happiness or sadness or confusion largely through facial expressions. Of course, you also reveal your feelings by posture (e.g., whether tense or relaxed), gestures, eye movements, and even the dilation of your pupils. Nonverbal messages often help people communicate unpleasant messages that they might feel uncomfortable putting into words (Infante, Rancer, & Avtgis, 2010). For example, you might avoid eye contact and maintain large distances between yourself and someone with whom you didn't want to interact or with whom you wanted to decrease the intensity of your relationship.

At the same time, you also use nonverbal messages to hide your emotions. You might, for example, smile even though you feel sad so as not to dampen the party spirit. Or you might laugh at someone's joke even though you think it silly.

Nonverbal Messages May Be Intentional or Unintentional

Some nonverbal behaviors are intentional and some are unintentional. For example, you may smile to show you're happy to see someone or you may extend your hand to greet someone. You dress in conservative business attire for a job interview and lower your voice when revealing a secret to a friend. These behaviors are largely intentional. Although you may not devote a great deal of time to thinking about whether to extend your hand or hug someone, for example, the behavior nevertheless has some intentionality. It's under your conscious control. Other nonverbal behaviors may be unintentional. For example, if you lie, many researchers claim that you leak cues that reveal your deception—small movements around the eyes and lips or perhaps a higher than normal vocal pitch. Similarly, when you're nervous or ill-at-ease you may shift your body posture or touch yourself more than normal. These behaviors are largely unintentional. In many cases you can bring these behaviors under conscious control and, for example, maintain a steady posture despite your nervousness. This is similar to the situation of the public speaker who learns to control the outward signs of apprehension or stage fright.

Nonverbal Messages Are Ambiguous

An ambiguous message is a message that you can interpret in more than one way; you can assign it more than one meaning. All communication, verbal and nonverbal, is ambiguous to some extent. Nonverbal communication, as you would imagine, can be a lot more ambiguous than verbal messages.

When you express an idea you never communicate your meaning exactly and totally; rather, you communicate your meaning with some reasonable accuracy—enough to give the other person a reasonably clear idea of what you mean. Sometimes, of course, you're less accurate than you anticipated. Perhaps your listener "gets the wrong idea" or "gets offended" when you only meant to be humorous, or the listener "misunderstands your emotional meaning." Because of this inevitable uncertainty, you may qualify what you're saying, give an example, or ask, "Do you know what I mean?" These additional explanations help the other person understand your meaning and reduce uncertainty (to some degree).

This quality of ambiguity makes it extremely important to resist jumping to conclusions about the motives of another person, especially, for example, assumptions that the person is lying on the basis of his or her avoidance of eye contact. Or, for example, if you e-mail or poke someone and the response time is overly long, it may mean that the person is not interested in communicating with you, or it may be a function of information overload, being away from the computer, or a lack of knowledge in how to poke back. Similarly, if someone unfollows you on Twitter or defriends you on Facebook, it may simply be a mistake.

The skills of nonverbal communication presented throughout this text may be looked at as means for appropriately reducing ambiguity and making your nonverbal meaning as unambiguous as possible (when you want it to be unambiguous).

A special type of ambiguity is found in what are called double-bind messages, in which verbal and nonverbal signals contradict each other. Consider the following interaction, an example I observed. A group of adults were playing poker for small change. In the next room two young girls—children of these adults—were also playing cards. After an hour or so the young girls asked their parents for some change so that they too could play cards for money. Almost with one voice, the parents began shouting that the girls should not gamble, gambling was wrong, and that they could have just as much fun without money. Clearly the girls were given mixed messages. The nonverbal message came in the form of their parents playing cards for money and the frequent injunction to act grown up and the contradictory verbal message "Don't play for money."

Here's another example:

Pat: You're never affectionate anymore. You never hug me like you used to. [These messages, in effect, tell Chris to be affectionate, to make loving advances.]
Chris: [Makes loving advances.]
Pat: [Nonverbal tenseness, failure to maintain eye contact, and, in general, nonverbal messages that say: Don't be affectionate.]
Chris: [Withdraws.]
Pat: See, you don't love me.

Here is a situation in which Chris can't win; whatever Chris does will violate one of the messages. If Chris makes loving advances, the nonverbal tenseness says this is wrong. If Chris does not make loving advances, the verbal messages are denied. So, Chris can't win. But, neither can Pat: Pat will be dissatisfied no matter what Chris does.

For messages to constitute significant double binds, several characteristics must be present:

- **Intense relationship.** The individuals must have a relatively intense relationship—lovers, best friends, and parent-child relationships are obvious examples.
- **Incompatible responses.** The two messages must ask for responses that are incompatible. The response to one message would contradict the other message.
- **Inability to escape.** At least one of the individuals in a double-bind situation must be unable to escape from the contradictory messages. This inability to escape may be in the form of a marriage license or an interpersonal understanding to be together. And, of course, children aren't able to escape double-binding parents.
- **Frequent occurrences.** For double-binding to be a serious communication problem, it must occur frequently. Such frequent explore has the effect of setting up a response pattern in the individual such that whatever is done will be incorrect; there is no escape from these confused and confusing communications, and that punishment will follow noncompliance (and since noncompliance is inevitable, punishment is inevitable).

Ernst Beier (1974) has argued that these double-bind messages—which he refers to as "discordance"—are the result of the desire of the individual to communicate two different emotions or feelings. For example, you may like a person and want to communicate this positive feeling, but you may also feel resentment toward this person and want to communicate this negative feeling as well. The result is that we communicate both feelings, one verbally and one nonverbally. Some researchers call double-binds "crazy-makers"—and, it seems, with good reason (Bach & Deutsch, 1990).

Nonverbal Messages Are Influenced by Culture, Gender, and Individual Differences

Throughout this text you find frequent references to culture, gender, and individual differences. As you'll see these factors will influence both the sending and the receiving of nonverbal messages.

Cultural Differences

Some nonverbal behaviors seem universal; they're common to all cultures. For example, the facial expressions of sadness or happiness are likely to be easily understood by members of widely differing cultures. These universal behaviors are basically biological expressions and so, not surprisingly, are common to all people. Other nonverbal behaviors may be universally understood (or nearly so) not because of biology but because of the media exposure. The nod meaning yes or the OK sign or the goodbye wave—although technically not universal—are understood by most of the world's population. In some parts of the world, however, the meanings for even these nonverbals would be different.

How would you describe this boy's nonverbal messages? Can you identify nonverbals in this photo that are universal and nonverbals that may be unique to a specific culture? © 2013, klohka, Shutterstock, Inc.

In addition to these widely understood nonverbals, there are many that vary greatly from one culture to another. For example, in some cultures direct eye communication expresses honesty and forthrightness but in others it may signal a lack of respect for the person with whom you're talking. Different cultures teach their members different display rules—the rules that dictate which nonverbal behaviors are appropriate and which aren't. In some cultures, men are permitted to cry at happy occasions or while watching a movie; in others, this would be considered inappropriate. Violation of such rules can result in a variety of negative effects, for example, being disliked or making a poor impression at a job interview. Cultural influences on all aspects of nonverbal communication are discussed throughout the text.

Gender Differences

Likewise, men and women use nonverbals and respond to the nonverbals of others differently. Here, for example, is a list of a dozen statements about gender. Respond to each of these by highlighting the correct term that appears in parentheses.

1. Two women in conversation, and even in silence, will gaze at each other (more than, less than, or the same as) men.
2. Women are (more than, less than, or the same as) men in their facial expressiveness.
3. Women are (better than, worse than, or the same as) men in expressing emotions.
4. Women smile (more than, less than, or the same as) men.
5. Women are approached (more closely, less closely, the same as) men.
6. Women, in sitting, take up (more, less, the same) space as men.
7. Women are (more than, less than, equally) likely to maintain short distances between themselves than men.
8. Women are (more likely, less likely, equally likely) to ignore/violate another's markers (e.g., a sweater placed over a chair to reserve it) than are men.

9. Women touch others (more than, less than, the same as) men.
10. Women are touched (more than, less than, the same as) men.
11. Women pause (more than, less than, the same as) men in their conversations.
12. Women interrupt (more than, less than, the same as) men in group communication.

As with culture, gender differences are discussed throughout this book.

Individual Differences

In addition to culture and gender influences, there are also numerous individual differences that influence nonverbal communication. Here are some of the more important ones that figure prominently in nonverbal communication and that will prove relevant in your mastering the skills of nonverbal communication.

- **The dyadic effect.** The dyadic effect refers to the imitation of another person's behavior when in an interaction. For example, some people will disclose in response to another person's disclosures; others will resist it. Some people (unfortunately most) have the tendency to lie in response to the lying of another (Tyler, Feldman, & Reichert, 2006). Generally, however, people have a tendency to imitate the communication style of the person with whom they're interacting. Sometimes called accommodation, mirroring, reciprocity, postural echo, or imitation, this effect, when done appropriately, can have positive effects—you'll be thought more attractive or friendlier, for example—and when done inappropriately can have negative effects—you may be seen as making fun of the other person.
- **The Pollyanna effect.** Some people are more optimistic than pessimistic and some are more pessimistic than optimistic. Some people do see the glass as half full and some people see the same glass as half empty. Generally, however, people have a tendency to assume the positive rather than the negative; they operate with a Pollyanna effect. For example, in a memory test, you'd be likely to remember more positive terms than negative ones. You're also more likely to recall positive experiences and interactions than negative ones.
- **Truth bias.** People vary in their degree to which they hold what is called a truth bias. Under most circumstances, most people assume a truth bias; you assume the person you're communicating with is telling the truth. Most people operate with what is called the "principle of cooperation"; you assume that in conversation each person cooperates by telling the truth. Some people, however, are suspicious (by nature?) and often operate with a deception bias and assume that the other person is hiding something or not being totally honest. In some situations, this deception bias is job related; for example, if you were a police officer interviewing suspects, you might operate with a deception bias and assume the suspects are lying.
- **Primacy effect.** People seem to vary in terms of whether they give primary influence to what occurs first, middle, or last. Some people (perhaps most) are influenced by what they see first; initial impressions for them last long and don't change. Perhaps more important is that these first impressions often serve as filters through which new information is viewed. And so if your first impression is that the person is a snob, then subsequent behaviors will be viewed as confirming this "snob" first impression. Other people will remember best what they hear last or most recently (a recency effect) and will forget what was heard earlier. Few people

will give primary attention to what occurs in the middle; this is the reason public speakers are advised to put their weakest argument in the middle of the speech rather than at the beginning or end. Whether you remember best what occurs first or last, research is clear that first impressions are important for everyone (more important for some than others but important for all); they are extremely long-lasting and are highly resistant to change. And because first impressions are largely based on nonverbal messages, they become especially important in all kinds of interactions—making friends, getting a job, or leading a group, for example.

How would you describe this woman's personality solely on the basis of her nonverbals? What specific nonverbal element leads you to your specific personality assessment?

- **Image management.** Most people are concerned with the image they communicate; some are obsessive about the image they communicate, most are concerned, and some are unconcerned. Most people engage in what is called *impression management* (they try to manage the impressions they give to others), although they vary in the extent to which they desire to manage impressions and in the skills they possess to do so. As you can imagine much of this impression management is accomplished through nonverbal communication. And, as you can also imagine, some of this impression management is honest and fair and some of it is dishonest and unfair.
- **Personality.** Your personality will influence your nonverbal communication style. If you take the "big five" personality traits (Extraversion, Agreeableness, Conscientiousness, Neuroticism, and Openness) you can easily appreciate their influence on nonverbal communication. Although you can learn new nonverbal styles and skills, your nonverbal communication style—as your verbal communication style—will be in some part a reflection of your personality. A person who is shy is not going to feel comfortable with the same nonverbal behaviors that an outgoing, highly social individual will. They have different personalities and they'll have different nonverbals.
- **Anatomy and physiology.** In a way somewhat similar to the influence of personality, people vary greatly in their anatomy and physiology, which in turn influences their nonverbal communication. People differ in body shape and size and this shape and size communicates in similar ways what your gestures or words communicate; they send messages to others. The shape and size of one's vocal cords will influence vocal pitch; nasal structure will influence the tone of voice, making the sound nasal or not. Becoming aware of these anatomical and physiological influences will help you anticipate reactions of others and perhaps mitigate any negative effects that your own anatomy and physiology might impose.
- **Skills level.** Perhaps the most obvious individual difference is seen in the level of skill that people possess. Some people have great skill and are seen generally as smooth, convincing, interesting, and attractive. Others have fewer skills and are often seen more negatively. At any point in time, you're at a particular skills level. And, of course, your skills level will vary depending on the nature of the task. In some things your skill level is high and in others, not so much. All this is simply to say that your nonverbal communication—as all your communications—is governed by your present skills level. Ideally, this skill level, what you might call your nonverbal competence, will grow and increase.

- **Self-monitoring/openness.** People vary greatly in the degree to which they self-monitor, the degree to which they consciously monitor what they say or what they do. Some monitor themselves very closely and are guarded in what they say to whom and when. They edit out the bad things (or the things that are likely to give others a negative impression) and emphasize the good things (the things they expect will give others a positive impression). The degree to which people are open with others will vary greatly on the basis of their culture and gender as well as on their personality, self-esteem, and lots of the individual differences discussed here.
- **Willingness to communicate/apprehension.** People vary in their willingness to communicate. Some people enjoy interacting with others—friends as well as strangers—whereas others are more apprehensive or fearful about communicating. What is true of verbal communication is equally true of nonverbal communication. An unwillingness to engage in small talk in an elevator, for example, is likely the same unwillingness that prevents direct eye contact or maintaining a face-to-face posture.
- **Self-esteem.** Some people have high self-esteem; they think very highly of themselves. Other people see themselves as failures. Most of us, of course, differ from these extremes in varying degrees. The degree of your self-esteem, as you can imagine, will influence a wide variety of nonverbal communication behaviors. For example, we often think of a high self-esteem person engaging in direct eye contact, walking tall with shoulders squared, and with an open facial expression. The low self-esteem person, in contrast, seems to avoid direct eye contact, walks with head down and shoulders slumped, and with a facial scowl. Whether these behaviors are a true reflection of a person's self-esteem or just a popular belief is not always clear. What does seem clear is that self-esteem will influence your nonverbal behavior and very likely your nonverbal behavior will influence your self-esteem.

EXERCISE

PARAPHRASING AND ILLUSTRATING THE PRINCIPLES OF NONVERBAL MESSAGES

To reinforce the principles of nonverbal communication, provide, in Column 2, a paraphrase of each of the principles listed in Column 1. In Column 3, for one, two, three, or all of the principles, provide a positive or negative example of the use of the principle. Use personal examples or examples you've witnessed among your acquaintances or in the media or that you can imagine.

Principles	Paraphrase	Illustration
Interacting with verbal messages	*Nonverbal messages work together with verbal messages to convey meaning.*	*Jill raised her voice and banged her fist when she said "the plan can't work," communicating her conviction with both words and gestures.*
Managing impressions		
Forming relationships		
Structuring conversations		
Rule governed		
Influencing and deceiving		
Expressing emotions		
Intentional and unintentional		
Ambiguous		
Influenced by culture, gender, individual differences		

Summary

1. Human communication occurs when one person (or more) sends and receives messages that are distorted by noise, occur within a context, and provide some opportunity for feedback. Among the essentials of human communication are communication context, senders and receivers, messages (metamessages, feedback messages, and feedforward messages), channels, and noise.
2. Nonverbal communication is a subdivision of human communication, consists of messages from a variety of channels, and includes body communication, facial communication, eye communication, artifactual communication, spatial communication, touch communication, paralanguage and silence communication, and time communication.
3. The benefits of studying nonverbal communication are many for both your social and your professional lives.
4. Among the principles of nonverbal communication are nonverbal messages interact with verbal messages, help manage impressions, help form and define relationships, structure conversation, are rule governed, can influence and deceive, are crucial for expressing emotions, can be intentional or unintentional, are ambiguous, and are influenced by culture, gender, and individual differences.

Key Terms

Supply a definition for each of the following terms. Once you've formulated these "standard" definitions, consider the following ideas for further defining and understanding. Not all will work for all key terms, but some will work for some terms and some will work for others.

- Find a quotation that illustrates the term.
- Provide an example from personal interaction, television, film, novels, or plays.
- Create a short dialogue to illustrate the operation of the key term.
- Locate a research study investigating the key term and report its findings.
- Illustrate the concept nonverbally.
- Find a video that illustrates the key term.
- Find images—photos or graphics, abstract or specific, literal or metaphorical.
- Diagram the concept.
- Explain the negative, what the concept is not.
- State a skill that centers on the concept.

Key Concept	Definition
Communication context (physical, social–psychological, temporal, cultural)	
Senders and receivers	
Messages (metamessages, feedback, feedforward)	
Channels	
Noise (physical, physiological, psychological, semantic)	
Body communication	
Facial communication	
Eye communication	
Artifactual communication	
Spatial communication	
Touch communication	
Paralanguage communication	
Silence communication	
Time communication	

AND IN ADDITION

Of course, no textbook can cover any topic completely and certainly this text is no exception. There's always more to say and more to learn. Therefore, add to this chapter's discussion. If you have the opportunity, share your additions so that all may profit from the new materials and especially from the different ways of adding to understanding.

Using your favorite search engine (in addition, use Google Scholar or the databases in your college library for the more scientific research articles) search for **human communication**, **nonverbal communication**, **myths about nonverbal communication**, **nonverbal ambiguity**, **nonverbal rules**, **nonverbal communication**, and **culture or gender**, or any of the other terms and topics considered in this chapter and add to the chapter contents. Depending on the structure of the course and the facilities available, you may want to post these additions to a course website; to a social media site such as Twitter, Facebook, or Google+; or to a listserv or through e-mail, for example. Here are a few ways in which you might make your addition:

- Write a paragraph that adds to the discussion of a particular concept.
- Provide a new, contradictory, or intercultural example of a concept.
- Create a figure or table to illustrate or organize a particular topic.
- Illustrate with an image or two or a 10- to 15-second video a particular concept of nonverbal behavior.
- Summarize and evaluate the results of a scientific study on a topic relevant to this chapter.
- Summarize and evaluate an online article that focuses on one of the topics considered here.

PART II

The Codes of Nonverbal Communication

This part of *The Nonverbal Communication Book* (consisting of eight chapters) explores the codes of nonverbal communication, the channels through which nonverbal messages are sent and received. Here we discuss eight main codes (each in its own chapter):

- Body Messages (Chapter 2)
- Facial Messages (Chapter 3)
- Eye Messages (Chapter 4)
- Artifactual Messages (Chapter 5)
- Space Messages (Chapter 6)
- Touch Messages (Chapter 7)
- Paralanguage and Silence Messages (Chapter 8)
- Time Messages (Chapter 9)

Messages, however, are rarely sent through only one channel and so our breaking down the discussion by code is really a matter of convenience and enables us to avoid a great deal of redundancy. Keep in mind, when reading these chapters, that messages work in packages, with signals from one code reinforcing (sometimes contradicting) signals from another code or, more often, other codes.

This part of the text also contains a variety of features to help you better understand and apply this material.

- **On the Job** boxes provide brief scenarios that encourage you to apply the insights of nonverbal communication to the world of work.
- **Politeness in Nonverbal Communication** items are intended to emphasize the importance of politeness in communication generally and in nonverbal communication in particular.
- **If you want to** items are designed to illustrate the practical nature of this material and also to illustrate that the codes all work together.

Chapter 2

Body Messages

CHAPTER TOPICS

- The Body General
  - Body Type
  - Body Height
  - Body Weight
  - Body Disabilities
- Body Movements
  - Emblems
  - Illustrators
  - Adaptors
  - Affect Displays
  - Regulators
- Body Posture
  - Inclusiveness/Noninclusiveness
  - Face-to-Face/Parallel
  - Congruence/Incongruence

Summary
Key Terms
And in Addition

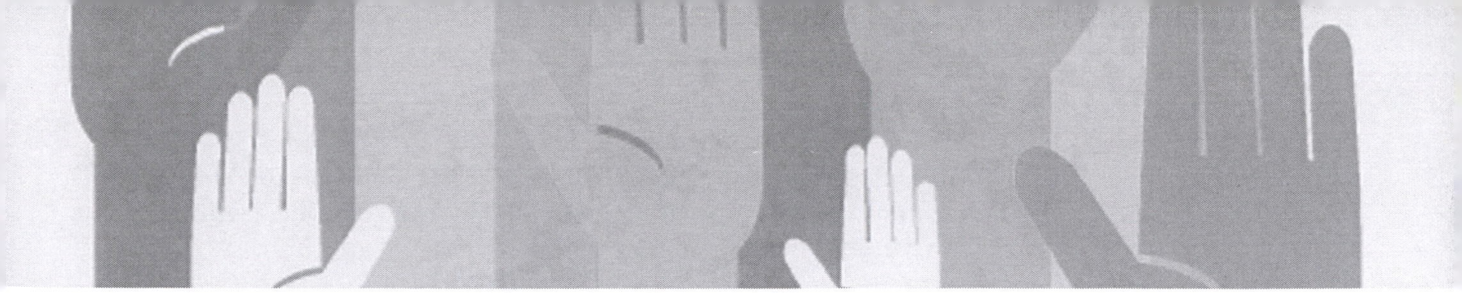

CHAPTER EXERCISES

[Exploring Body Types]
Identifying the Connection between Body Type and Personality
[Estimating Heights]
Explaining and Exemplifying the Five Body Gestures
Identifying the Meanings of the Three Postures

ON THE JOB

Smile, Smile, Smile
Leadership Material

POLITENESS IN NONVERBAL COMMUNICATION

Being polite with body messages

IF YOU WANT TO

Sell a car/refrigerator/house/your own talents
Signal interest/attraction/focus

CHAPTER OBJECTIVES

After completing this chapter, you should be able to:

1. Define the three body types and identity the common perceptions of each, explain the research findings on height and weight, and the suggestions for communication between people with and without disabilities.
2. Define and give examples of the five body movements.
3. Explain the three dimensions of body posture and the possible meanings each may communicate.

BEFORE reading about body messages, imagine that you're meeting a man for the first time. All you know about this man is that he can be described with the series of adjectives listed below.

Man 1. He's affectionate, content, cooperative, forgiving, generous, kind, relaxed, soft-hearted, sympathetic, and warm.
Man 2. He's active, adventurous, assertive, determined, dominant, energetic, hot-tempered, impetuous, outgoing, and reckless.
Man 3. He's anxious, cautious, cool, detached, introspective, precise, serious, shy, suspicious, and tense.

One of these men has a muscular body, one is tall and thin, and one is short and heavy. Who is who?

If you're like most people, you probably said that Man 1 was short and heavy, Man 2 was muscular, and Man 3 was tall and thin. Of course, there's no reason why a muscular person could not be affectionate, content, cooperative, etc., or a tall and thin person could not be active, adventurous, assertive, and determined. Yet some adjectives seem to be more apt descriptions than others for a particular body type. This is just one of the ways in which the body communicates messages. In this chapter we look at a wide variety of messages communicated by body type, height, weight, body movements, and posture.

THE BODY GENERAL

Perhaps the first nonverbal message you receive from someone is sent by their body. Here we look at body type, body height and weight, and some disabilities.

Body Type

These adjectives were taken from a study on body type (Cortes & Gatti, 1965) in which students were asked to describe themselves and how they think other people see them. Their responses were then compared to their body type. Generally, the results showed that people who were short and stout (called endomorphs) were more likely to use the adjectives noted above for Person 1. Muscular people (mesomorphs) used the adjectives noted for Person 2 while tall and thin people (ectomorphs) used the adjectives noted for Person 3.

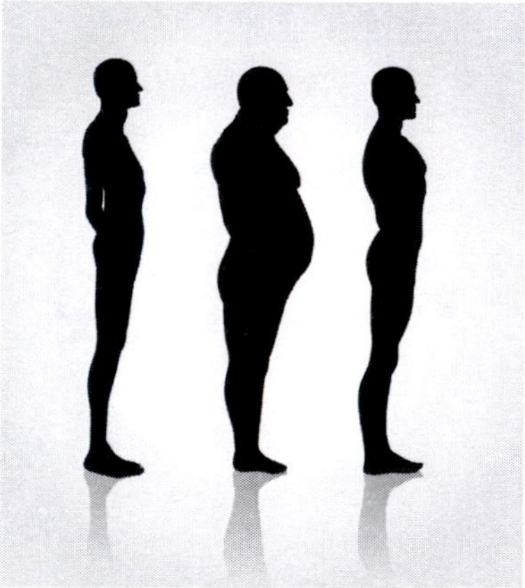

How would you describe the personalities of these three body types? Do your own observations confirm those cited here? If not, how do they differ? © 2013, rudall30, Shutterstock, Inc.

According to the early studies on body type, initiated largely by William Sheldon (1940, 1954) in a study he called **somatotyping**, each person actually has some of all three dimensions, which can be expressed with a three-digit number (each digit ranging from 1 to 7) signifying the degree to which each of these dimensions is present in a particular person. So, for example, the stereotypical fat man of the circus would be high on endomorphy and low on mesomorphy and ectomorphy; his body type number would be expressed as 7-1-1. A bodybuilder (a Mr. Universe contestant, say) would be high in mesomorphy and low in both endomorphy and ectomorphy; his body type number would be 1-7-1. And last, to go back to the circus, the thin man would be described as 1-1-7, indicating low endomorphy, low mesomorphy, and high ectomorphy.

This original research on body types was conducted on males (rather than both sexes) and attempted to correlate body type and personality.

The assumption made at the time was that body type influenced an individual's personality.

- *Viscerotonia* was characterized by slow reactions, a love of comfort, sociability, food, affection, and an easygoing temperament. This was thought to be the personality of the endomorphic (short and heavy) body type.
- *Somatotonia* was characterized by risk-taking, aggressiveness, courageousness, adventurousness, and dominance. This was the personality of the mesomorph (muscular).
- *Cerebrotonia* was characterized by secretiveness and self-consciousness and a preference for solitude. This was the personality of the ectomorph (tall and thin).

In a way similar to the way in which body type was classified with a three-digit number, it was thought that a person's personality could also be described with a three-digit number. And the assumption was made that the numbers for the body type and the personality would be very similar.

Much of this research has been discredited. Personality is formed from a wide variety of factors and not just one such as body type. However, there still remains the question of why we do attribute personality characteristics to people based on their body types. Do you, for example, assume that the heavier person is sociable and easygoing? Do you assume the muscular bodybuilder is aggressive and dominant? Do you assume the tall and thin person is self-conscious and anxious?

A related question is the preference we have for the various body types. Generally, men it seems would prefer to have a mesomorphic body type—tall, muscular, and well proportioned—at least if you judge from the male models and movie stars. Women, however, seem to prefer to have a more ectomorphic body—tall and thin. Women view the person with an ectomorphic body type as more attractive, as having the most dates, and as exercising the most (Spillman & Everington, 1989).

Body Height

Before reading about height, try your hand at estimating the heights of famous people whom you've probably read about or heard about (but probably not seen in person). Estimate their heights (in feet and inches) simply on the basis of the image you have of these people.

1. Baby Face Nelson (bank robber and murderer in the 1930s) __________
2. Ludwig Van Beethoven (influential German composer) __________
3. Bonnie Parker (gangster of the 1920s and 1930s, part of the Barrow Gang) __________
4. Buckminster Fuller (scientist, credited with inventing the geodesic dome) __________
5. Clyde Barrow (gangster of the 1920s and 1930s, leader of the Barrow Gang) __________
6. Mahatma Gandhi (Indian political leader whose civil disobedience led to India's independence from British rule) __________
7. James Madison (fourth President of the United States, largely credited with writing the Constitution) _______

EXERCISE

IDENTIFYING THE CONNECTION BETWEEN BODY TYPE AND PERSONALITY

To bring to consciousness at least one basis you use in forming impressions, examine the body types listed in Column 1. In Column 2 identify a character from the media or a celebrity (current or past) who exemplifies each of the three body types. In Column 3 describe the personality of the character with three, four, or five adjectives. Is your personality assessment similar to what we've described earlier or do you find major differences?

Body Type	Character in the media or celebrity	Personality Profile
Endomorph; short, heavy	*Mike (from* Mike and Molly*)*	*Humorous, playful, kind, well meaning*
Mesomorph: muscular		
Ectomorph: tall, thin		

8. Joan of Arc (15th-century French military leader, burned for heresy at 19, and declared a saint) __________
9. T. E. Lawrence [of Arabia] (adventurer and British Army officer) __________
10. Pablo Picasso (influential Spanish artist) __________

This exercise was designed to see if you would overestimate the heights of a good majority of these people. Fame seems to be associated with height and so most people would think these people were taller than they really were. The specific heights are: Baby Face Nelson, 5'5"; Ludwig Van Beethoven, 5'6"; Bonnie Parker, 4'10"; Buckminister Fuller, 5'2"; Clyde Barrow, 5'7"; Mahatma Gandhi, 5'3" James Madison, 5'4"; Joan of Arc, 4'11"; T. E. Lawrence, 5'5"; and Pablo Picasso, 5'4".

Ludwig van Beethoven.

Height is an especially important part of general body appearance and has been shown to be significant in a wide variety of situations (Keyes, 1980; Knapp & Hall, 2010). For example, when corporate recruiters were shown identical resumés for people some of whom were noted as being 5'5" and others as being 6'1"—everything else being the same—the taller individual was chosen significantly more often than were the shorter individuals.

In another study, it was found that the salaries of those between 6'2" and 6'4" were more than 12 percent higher than the salaries of those under

6 feet. Tall presidential candidates have a much better record of winning elections than do their shorter opponents.

In an investigation of height and satisfaction it was found that boys were less satisfied with their heights than were girls. Fifty percent of the boys surveyed indicated that they wanted to be taller, 2 percent said they wanted to be shorter, and 48 percent indicated satisfaction. Only 20 percent of the girls indicated that they wanted to be taller, 13 percent said they wanted to be shorter, and 67 percent indicated they were satisfied.

Preferences for different heights seem to be influenced greatly by culture. Today in the United States, tall seems to be preferred to short. For both men and women, being tall is an advantage, at least in the perceptions of other people.

Your body also reveals your race through skin color and tone and may even give clues as to your nationality. Your weight in proportion to your height will also communicate messages to others, as will the length, color, and style of your hair.

Body Weight

Weight is much in the news these days. Obesity is currently regarded as one of the major contributors to a variety of ailments—from diabetes and high blood pressure to high cholesterol. People who are heavy are therefore exhorted by the medical establishment to lose weight and reduce their likelihood of incurring these various problems or at least aggravating them.

Much of our thoughts and attitudes about weight come from the popular media—from television and film and from online and magazine advertising. The most popular television characters are usually extremely well proportioned or underweight. With the exception of *Mike & Molly*—in which the characters' obesity is the main comedic topic—most of the actors who play these characters and the characters themselves are thinner than the general population. And it's rare—extremely rare—to find an overweight model. Thin is definitely in. And it is likely that overweight people will consequently have their self-esteem attacked in various ways specifically because of their being overweight.

Some gender differences were suggested earlier in our discussion of the three body types. Another gender difference is found in self-perceptions. For example, in one study, females perceived themselves as being overweight even when they were not and conversely did not perceive themselves to be underweight even when they were. Even those who did not perceive themselves as being overweight thought they would like to lose a few pounds. Men, on the other hand, were more likely to want to gain weight (Connor-Greene, 1988).

Often people are prejudiced against overweight people, largely because they feel that the obesity is their fault—they simply eat too much. And that is true for the majority of overweight people. However, some do have physical problems that contribute to the obesity. Nevertheless, there is considerable prejudice.

Body Disabilities

While popular media routinely feature thin and unbelievably attractive female models and ripped, muscular, attractive male models, presumably for readers and viewers to emulate or at least identify with—they also hide people with disabilities, for example, people who have cerebral palsy or are in wheelchairs. Here, then,

What other suggestions might you offer for more effective communication between those who have and those who do not have a physical disability?

are just a few suggestions for more effective communication between those who have and those who don't have physical disabilities.

- Respect assistive devices such as wheelchairs, walkers, and crutches. Don't move these out of the way or lean on them; these are for the convenience of the person with the disability.
- Shake hands with the person with a disability if you also shake hands with others. Don't avoid shaking hands because the individual's hand has lost some normal function.
- Maintain similar eye level. For example, if the person is in a wheelchair, it might be helpful for you to sit down or kneel down to get to the same eye level.
- Don't assume that people who have a disability are intellectually impaired. Slurred speech—such as may occur with people who have cerebral palsy or cleft palate—should not be taken as indicating low-level intellect. Be careful not to talk down to such individuals as many people do.
- If you're the person with the disability and you want the person to make some adjustment—get on a lower level or talk louder, for example—say so. Similarly, if you detect discomfort in the other person, you might consider talking about it. However, do realize that you're under no obligation to educate the public, so don't feel this is something you have to do.

IF YOU WANT TO

Sell a car/refrigerator/house/your own talents

- ➤ Mirror the other's behavior to indicate a closeness and a position of agreement.
- ➤ Smile appropriately and genuinely.
- ➤ Express agreement with minimal response cues ("You're right about that feature," "I see you appreciate details").
- ➤ Maintain an open body posture; avoid postures that symbolize hiding something such as hands folded across the chest.
- ➤ Direct your eye contact and body posture toward the potential buyer.
- ➤ Avoid multitasking; show the buyer that he or she is your only concern.

BODY MOVEMENTS

Nonverbal researchers identify five major types of body movements: emblems, illustrators, affect displays, regulators, and adaptors (Ekman & Friesen, 1969; Knapp & Hall, 2010).

Emblems

Can you think of other examples of emblems meaning different things in different cultures? © 2013, mangostock, Shutterstock, Inc.

Emblems are body gestures that directly translate into words or phrases—for example, the OK sign, the thumbs-up for "good job," and the V for victory. You use these consciously and purposely to communicate the same meaning as the words. But emblems are culture specific, so be careful when using your culture's emblems in other cultures (see Figure 1.6 on page 00). For example, when President Richard Nixon visited Latin America and gestured with the OK sign, which he thought communicated something positive, he was quickly informed that this gesture was not universal. In Latin America the gesture has a far more negative meaning. Here are a few cultural differences in the emblems you may commonly use (Axtell, 1991):

- In the United States, you wave with your whole hand moving from side to side to say "hello"; but in a large part of Europe, that same signal means "no." In Greece such a signal would be considered insulting to the person to whom you were waving.
- The V for victory common throughout much of the world—if used with the palm toward your face—is as insulting in England as the raised middle finger is in the United States.
- In Texas the raised fist with raised little finger and index finger is a positive expression of support, because it represents the Texas longhorn steer. But in Italy it's an insult that means "cuckold," that your spouse is having a sexual relationship with someone else. In parts of South America, it is a gesture used to ward off evil. In parts of Africa, it is a curse: "May you experience bad times."
- In the United States and much of Asia, hugs are rarely exchanged among acquaintances; but among Latin Americans and southern Europeans, hugging is a common gesture of greeting, and failing to hug someone may communicate unfriendliness. In the United States, largely because of the Latin influence, hugging is becoming much more common.

Emblems are often referred to as coded gestures, meaning that each gesture has a specific meaning that would be recorded in a dictionary of nonverbal signs. American Sign Language, where finger and hand position signify the various letters of the alphabet, is a good example of a system of coded gestures. Another good example of a system of coded signs (though not gestural) is semaphore where different flag positions indicate different meanings. In both of these systems, you would have to learn specific meanings for specific gestures or flag positions. You can't look at the gestures or flag positions and figure out what they mean. Their meanings are arbitrary and the connections between the sign and the meaning have to be learned. This is exactly the same with verbal language. You cannot look at the form of a word and determine its meaning; you had to be taught the meaning for each word you now know.

Although emblems are, in fact, culture specific—much like words are culture specific—many emblems are becoming universally recognized, for example, the signs for come, go, yes, and no seem to be recognized throughout the world—no doubt from the media, which has homogenized much of what was once unique to a specific culture (Matsumoto & Hwang, 2013a).

Illustrators

Illustrators enhance (literally "illustrate") the verbal messages they accompany. For example, when referring to something to the left, you might gesture toward the left. Most often, you illustrate with your hands, but you can also illustrate with your head and general body movements. You might, for example, turn your head or your entire body toward the left. You might also use illustrators to communicate the shape or size of objects you're talking about. Research points to an interesting advantage of illustrators—namely, that they increase your ability to remember. In this research people who illustrated their verbal messages with gestures remembered some 20 percent more than those who didn't gesture (Goldin-Meadow, Nusbaum, Kelly, & Wagner, 2001).

Each nonverbal researcher has his or her own system for identifying the various types of illustrators (e.g., Andersen, 2009; Burgoon et al., 2010). Here we use the six-part system of Matsumoto and Hwang (2013), which seems to fit our needs best:

- **Batons.** Like a conductor's baton, illustrator batons emphasize a particular word or phrase with, say, a hand movement.
- **Ideographs**. These illustrators trace the path of an idea or thought. Interestingly enough, the use of these illustrators seem to increase a person's perceived influence (Maricchiolo, Livi, Bonaiuto, & Gnisci, 2011).
- **Deictic movements**. These illustrators point to a person or thing that you want someone else to focus on.
- **Spatial movements**. These illustrators help to indicate spatial relationships or size, for example.
- **Kinetographs**. These illustrators imitate or depict bodily movements.
- **Pictographs**. These illustrators draw a picture of the thing talked about.

Although illustrators are largely unconscious gestures that we use without awareness and are in large part universal, some vary from culture to culture. For example, in the United States you would point with your index finger and reserve your middle finger for an obscene gesture. In A Japanese person, however, might point with the middle finger—a simple situation that can easily create intercultural misunderstanding. Similarly, in some cultures, illustrators are relatively small movements of the hands, arms, and head; whereas, in other cultures—Latin cultures are good examples—the illustrators are large and extensive (Matsumoto & Hwang, 2013a).

Adaptors

Adaptors are gestures that help you adapt to the situation; they satisfy some personal need, such as scratching to relieve an itch or moving your hair out of your eyes, often without conscious awareness. Three kinds of adaptors are generally identified:

- **Self-adaptors** are self-touching movements—for example, rubbing your nose, scratching your head, cleaning your fingernails.
- **Alter-adaptors** are movements directed at the person with whom you're speaking—for example, removing lint from a person's jacket, straightening one's tie, or folding your arms in front of you to keep others a comfortable distance away.
- **Object-adaptors** are gestures focused on objects—for example, doodling or shredding a Styrofoam coffee cup.

Generally, adaptors are thought to signal a certain discomfort, an ill-at-ease feeling (e.g., if you tear the Styrofoam coffee cup to shreds), or an excessive self-focus (e.g., if you continually adjust your hair) and are best avoided when you want to appear confident and in control of a situation and focused on the other person.

What are some of the meanings that this gesture might communicate? In your own experiences, might you be likely to form impressions of this man on the basis of this gesture? What impressions would you form?

Affect Displays

Affect displays are movements of the face (smiling or frowning, for example) but also of the hands and general body (body tenseness or relaxed posture, for example) that communicate emotional meaning. You use affect displays to accompany and reinforce your verbal messages, but also as substitutes for words; for example, you might smile while saying how happy you are to see your friend, or you might simply smile. Affect displays, being primarily centered in the facial area, are covered in more detail in the next section.

ON THE JOB

Smile, Smile, Smile

The manager you just appointed to oversee about 20 workers smiles just about all the time. In fact, even when giving criticism, she smiles. As a result, workers don't take her seriously. Even when their work is negatively evaluated, they give it little thought—probably because the evaluation—even though negative—is accompanied by a smile. What are some of the things you can do to get this manager to change her nonverbals?

Regulators

Regulators monitor, control, coordinate, or maintain the speech of another individual. When you nod your head, for example, you tell the speaker to keep on speaking; when you lean forward and open your mouth, you tell the speaker that you would like to say something. These conversational turns are covered in more detail in Chapter 8 (pages 157–158).

ON THE JOB

Leadership Material

You've just entered a new job in a large firm and you want to be perceived as leadership material at regular department meetings. What are some of the things you can do with your body movements that will communicate this leadership potential? What are some of the body gestures you would want to avoid?

EXERCISE

EXPLAINING AND EXEMPLIFYING THE FIVE BODY GESTURES

Clarify your understanding of the five gestures listed in Column 1. In Column 2 explain in your own words the nature of the gesture and in Column 3 give an example and the meaning(s) that the gesture could communicate.

Body Gestures	Explanation of Gesture	Examples/Meanings
Emblems	*Translate, rather directly, words or phrases and vary from one culture to another*	*Making a circle with the thumb and index finger to mean: OK, zero, bad grade*
Illustrators		
Adaptors		
Regulators		
Affect displays		

BODY POSTURE

Nonverbal research from the 1960s and 1970s—which is still regarded as the best classification of body posture—has identified three dimensions of posture along which any given postural position may be analyzed: inclusiveness/noninclusiveness, face-to-face/parallel, and congruence/incongruence (Scheflen, 1964, 1974). These labels identify the extremes. Between these extremes there are a large number of body posture positions possible. What we describe here, then, are postural tendencies toward one end or the other of these three dimensions. These three dimensions are generally sufficient for analyzing and describing postural positioning in interpersonal interactions. In reading these descriptions, visualize two people on a couch.

IF YOU WANT TO

Signal **interest/attention/focus**

- Assume an inclusive posture that includes (rather than excludes) the person.
- Lean forward.
- Engage in direct eye contact.
- Give listening approval cues such as head nods and minimal responses such as "I see" or "yes."

Inclusiveness/Noninclusiveness

This dimension refers to the degree to which one person's body posture includes the other person. At the high inclusiveness end of the scale we would have one person's body posture being arranged so as to include the other person on the couch but to exclude all others from the interaction. At the noninclusive end, we would have body posture that does not include the other person on the couch and also does not exclude any other members.

High inclusiveness is generally found in situations where the individuals are involved in an intimate relationship or are engaged in some very private and personal conversation. Rarely would high inclusiveness be found with persons who dislike each other or who are unfriendly toward each other.

Face-to-Face/Parallel

This dimension refers to the degree to which the two people face each other directly (face-to-face) or position themselves so that their shoulders are in the same line, for example, both sitting on the couch facing forward. Face-to-face position is used when the individuals are mutually involved, as they would be in an intimate discussion. Parallel positioning might be seen if the two persons were watching television or reading.

POLITENESS IN NONVERBAL COMMUNICATION

Being polite with body messages

- Avoid gestures that might prove offensive or vulgar (no matter how funny you think they are).
- Adjust posture to communicate involvement; be careful that your body posture doesn't prove insulting to those you exclude.
- Avoid self-adaptors that signal your lack of involvement and concern for the other person or being overly self-absorbed.
- Before using emblems with persons from other cultures, check on their meanings.
- Be careful of your adaptors that may intrude on the comfort of others, for example, playing with your hair in a restaurant.

Congruence/Incongruence

This dimension refers to the degree to which one person mirrors or imitates the behavior of the other person. In high congruence, the two persons mirror each other's behavior. In low congruence (or incongruence) the behaviors of one person are not imitated by the other. In fact, in incongruent situations, one person may engage in behavior that is opposite to the behavior of the other person. For example, in an incongruent situation, if one person leans forward the other person may lean back.

Congruence, mirroring, or behavioral synchrony (the terms mean essentially the same thing) generally indicate a high degree of attraction and liking of one person for the other. Incongruence, on the other hand, generally indicates little attraction and little liking. But do be careful in applying this general principle to analyze interpersonal interactions. There are a great number of other factors that have to be taken into consideration. Remember the concept of packaging: we cannot (and should not) draw inferences from any one bit of nonverbal behavior without taking into consideration the entire package of signals (verbal as well as nonverbal).

Mirroring most often occurs without conscious awareness; but, in some cases, people may not feel a liking for the other person but will mirror the person's behavior simply as a persuasive strategy. So natural is mirroring that when it does not occur in an episode of *The Mentalist* ("Ring around the Rosie," October 13, 2011), Patrick Jane (the mentalist, "psychic") concludes that the person has no conscience, is not human. Surely this is an extreme, made-for-television observation, but it underscores the expectation people have for mirroring.

EXERCISE

IDENTIFYING THE MEANINGS OF THE THREE POSTURES

To illustrate how posture relates to the content of the message, consider the three body postures identified in Column 1. From television, movies, or personal observation, record, in Column 2, the activity taking place and the relationship between the individuals. Compare your findings with others and on the basis of the discussion try to come up with a general principle for each of the three configurations and record this in Column 3.

Postural Configuration	Activity and Relationship	General Principle
Inclusive/noninclusive	*A married couple sitting in a noninclusive configuration at a neighbor's party*	*Couples often assume a noninclusive posture when they're experiencing conflict, as a way of distancing themselves from the argument and the present unpleasant situation.*
Face-to-face/parallel		
Congruent/noncongruent		

Summary

1. Body types have been classified into three main types: (1) the endomorph is short and stout, (2) the mesomorph is muscular, and the (3) ectomorph is tall and thin. Generally taller people are perceived more positively than shorter people while heavy people are discriminated against, as are people with disabilities.
2. Body movements may be classified into emblems, illustrators, adaptors (self, alter, and object), affect displays, and regulators.
3. Three body postures are helpful in classifying the way people position their bodies in interactions: inclusiveness/noninclusiveness, face-to-face/parallel, and congruence/incongruence.

Key Terms

Supply a definition for each of the following terms. Once you've formulated these "standard" definitions, consider the following ideas for further defining and understanding. Not all will work for all key terms but some will work for some terms and some will work for others.

- Find a quotation that illustrates the term.
- Provide an example from personal interaction, television, film, novels, or plays.
- Create a short dialogue to illustrate the operation of the key term.
- Locate a research study investigating the key term and report its findings.
- Illustrate the concept nonverbally.
- Find a video that illustrates the key term.
- Find images—photos or graphics, abstract or specific, literal or metaphorical.
- Diagram the concept.
- Explain the negative, what the concept is not.
- State a skill that centers on the concept.

Key Concept	Definition
Body type	
Emblems	
Body height	
Body weight	

Key Concept	Definition
Illustrators	
Adaptors	
Affect displays	
Regulators	
Inclusiveness/noninclusiveness	
Face-to-face/parallel	
Congruence/incongruence	

AND IN ADDITION

Using your favorite search engine (in addition, use Google Scholar or the databases in your college library for the more scientific research articles), search for **body communication**, **body posture**, **sitting posture**, **body gestures**, **height**, or any of the other terms and topics considered in this chapter and add to the chapter contents. Depending on the structure of the course and the facilities available, you may want to post these additions to a course website; to a social media site such as Twitter, Facebook, or Google+; or to a listserv or through e-mail, for example. Here are a few ways in which you might make your addition:

- Write a paragraph that adds to the discussion of a particular concept.
- Provide a new, contradictory, or intercultural example of a concept.
- Create a figure or table to illustrate or organize a particular topic.
- Illustrate with an image or two or a 10- to 15-second video a particular concept of nonverbal behavior.
- Summarize and evaluate the results of a scientific study on a topic relevant to this chapter.
- Summarize and evaluate an online article that focuses on one of the topics considered here.

Chapter 3

Facial Messages

© 2013, Yuri Arcurs, Shutterstock, Inc.

CHAPTER TOPICS

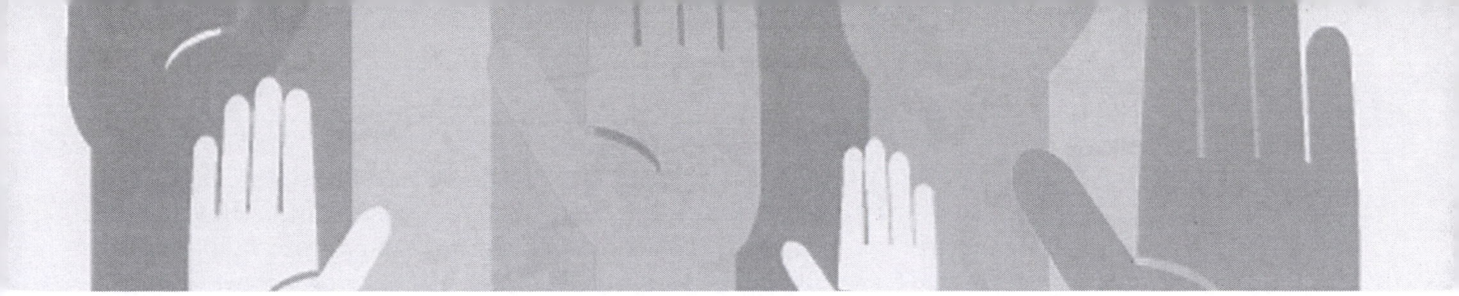

CHAPTER EXERCISES

[Describing Facial Movements]
Distinguishing Smiles
Identifying Facial Management Strategies
Recognizing First Impression Tendencies
[Testing the Facial Feedback Hypothesis]

ON THE JOB

Blanked Expressor
Displaying Authority

POLITENESS IN NONVERBAL COMMUNICATION

Being polite with facial messages

IF YOU WANT TO

Flirt/express romantic interest/initiate a relationship
Demonstrate credibility/competence/character/charisma

CHAPTER OBJECTIVES

After completing this chapter, you should be able to:

1. Define and distinguish between *primary affect displays* and *affect blends.*
2. Define the four main facial management techniques and explain the meanings each is designed to communicate.
3. Explain the concept of facial styles and identify three or four examples.
4. Define the facial feedback hypothesis.
5. Explain some of the cultural differences in facial expressions.

BEFORE reading about facial messages, try to describe your facial movements and expressions as you exhibit the following emotions. Describe these movements in as much detail as you can. For example, what's the shape of your mouth? Is your face relaxed for some emotions and tense for others? And, although we discuss eye messages in the next chapter, they too are part of the face so describe the shape of your eyes and eyebrows as well. This will not be easy to do but expressing these emotions while looking at yourself in a mirror will help a lot.

- **Happiness**
- **Anger**
- **Sadness**
- **Disgust**
- **Fear**
- **Surprise**
- **Contempt**

As this little experience should demonstrate, the face works as a whole to enable you communicate each of these emotions.

FACE COMMUNICATION

Throughout your interactions, your face communicates many things. Let's look at a few of the ways the face communicates.

Facial Shape and Size

One of the most interesting aspects of facial communication is the messages communicated by the shape and size of the face and particularly the WHR, or width-height ratio. Width is measured from the left upper cheekbone to the right upper cheekbone; height is measured from the upper lip to the lower part of the eyebrow. Most of these studies have focused on men; apparently there is less of a relationship between WHR and other characteristics with women.

Intuitively you would probably think that those with wide faces and those with narrow faces—essentially what the WHR focuses on—don't differ in any significant way. Yet research continues to uncover differences. For example, in two studies (one involving male varsity hockey players and one involving professional hockey players)

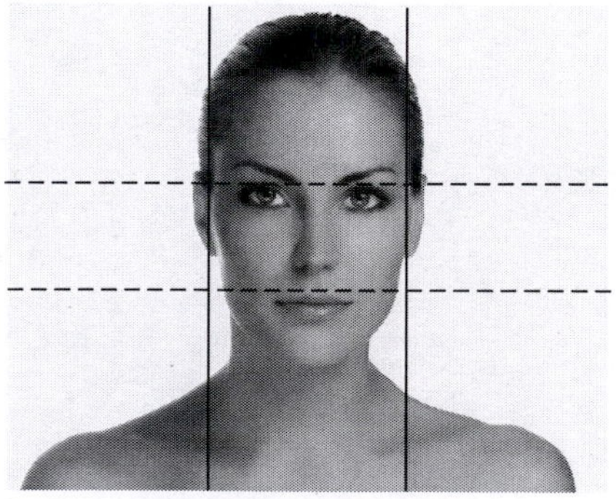

researchers found that players with wide faces were more aggressive (engaged in more slashing, high-sticking, boarding, and elbowing, for example) as measured in terms of the number of penalty minutes the players were given as well as their responses to psychological tests (Carré & McCormick, 2008).

Other evidence comes from studies showing that when people are shown facial photos of both criminals and noncriminals, they can reliably distinguish the criminal from the noncriminal—even when the researchers controlled for gender, attractiveness, race, and age (Valla, Ceci, & Williams, 2011). Still another study finds that men with wider faces are more willing to deceive others in a negotiation situation and are more willing to cheat to get money (Haselhuhn & Wong, 2011).

On the other side of the equation, some research has shown that those men with wider faces are more likely than their narrower-faced counterparts to engage in more self-sacrificing cooperative behavior when their group was in competition with another group (Stirrat & Perrett, 2012).

A word of caution needs to be interjected here: Avoid making judgments about people on the basis of the width-height ratio. Many factors influence a person's willingness to deceive or act aggressively or cooperatively and it's always dangerous to focus on only one factor or nonverbal cue. Furthermore, the findings from these studies are limited to specific situations and may not apply in different situations and with different people.

Facial Emotional Expression

Perhaps the most obvious type of facial communication is emotional. In fact, facial movements alone seem to communicate the degree of pleasantness, agreement, and sympathy felt; the rest of the body doesn't provide any additional information in those realms. But for other aspects—for example, the intensity with which an emotion is felt—both facial and bodily cues are used (Graham & Argyle, 1975; Graham, Bitti, & Argyle, 1975). These cues are so important in communicating your full meaning that graphic representations are now commonly used in Internet communication. In many computer programs, buttons are available to help you encode your emotions graphically with smileys. And, of course, you can use other symbols, font styles (bold, italic, etc.), and uppercase letters to help you communicate your feelings.

Although not all research is in agreement, most nonverbal research claims that facial movements may communicate at least the following seven emotions, known as

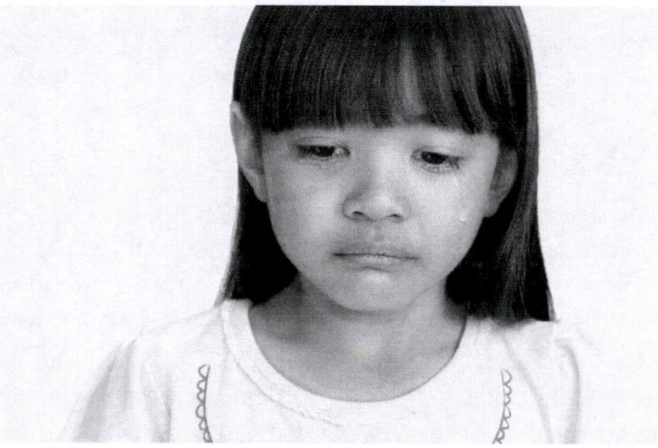

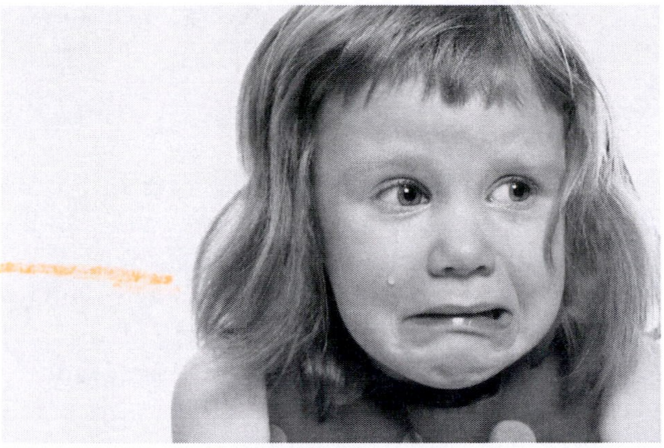

© 2013, Dmitry Kalinosky, Shutterstock, Inc.

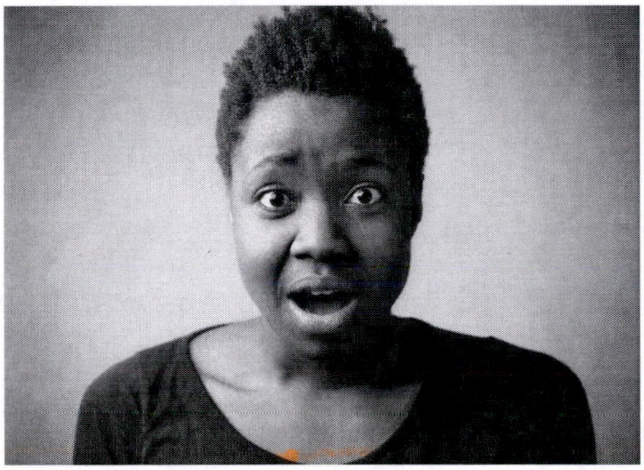

© 2013, ollyy, Shutterstock, Inc.

© 2013, ollyy, Shutterstock, Inc.

These photos illustrate the 7 basic emotions: happiness, anger, sadness, disgust, fear, surprise, and contempt. Do the descriptions offered here adequately represent the facial expressions? If not, what else might be said?

primary affect displays (Ekman, Friesen, & Ellsworth, 1972; explanations compliments of Matsumoto & Hwang, 2013c):

- **Happiness** or joy is experienced when you get something you wanted or achieve something you've worked to get, for example. In expressing happiness you raise the corners of your lips and cheeks and your eyes narrow, with crow's feet forming.
- **Anger** is experienced when your goal is obstructed and you can't achieve what you wanted and hoped to achieve. In expressing anger, the brows are brought together, the eyelids rise, and the lips tighten.
- **Sadness** is experienced when you experience a loss of something you considered especially important. A sad face is one in which the cheeks are raised, the upper eyelids droop, and the lip corners turn down.
- **Disgust** is experienced when you feel repulsion for something or someone. Disgust is expressed either with a wrinkled nose or with raised upper lips. In either case, the face appears scrunched.
- **Fear** is experienced when you feel threatened either psychologically or physically. Fear is generally expressed with raised and drawn together brows, raised eyelids, tension in the lower eyelids, and a horizontal stretch of the lips.
- **Surprise** is experienced when you're startled, when you're confronted with something unexpected. Surprise is expressed with raised brows and eyelids, a dropped jaw, and an open mouth.
- **Contempt** is experienced when you look down upon or deride something, considering it beneath your own level. Contempt is signaled with a tightening of one side of the lip or a slight smile.

There are also **affect blends**, facial displays that are combinations of these various primary emotions. For example, we may experience both happiness and sadness at the same time; the happiness may be signaled by the lower face while the sadness may be signaled by the upper face.

The ability to understand the varied emotions and their nonverbal expression may be aided by enlarging your emotional vocabulary. Table 3.1 identifies the seven primary emotions noted here and offers a variety of synonyms and antonyms.

Some emotions are easier to communicate and to decode than others. For example, in one study, participants judged happiness with accuracy ranging from 55 to 100 percent, surprise with 38-86 percent accuracy, and sadness with 19-88 percent accuracy (Ekman et al., 1972). Research finds that women and girls are more accurate judges of facial emotional expression than men and boys (Argyle, 1988; Hall, 1984).

Facial Recognition and Judgments

Another aspect of facial messages that is closely related to the ability to decode the meanings behind others' facial expressions is the general ability of facial recognition. Some people are known as prosopagnosics (the term comes from the Greek *prosopon*, meaning face, and *agnosia*, meaning ignorance) and have little ability to recognize and remember faces, sometimes even family members. Prosopagnosia is often the result of brain injury or some genetic defect. The 2011 film *Faces in the Crowd* is a crime thriller that centers on a woman who has survived an attack by a serial killer but cannot identify him or even her boyfriend or close friends.

TABLE 3.1 The Basic Emotions (Primary Affect Displays)

Basic Emotion	Synonyms	Antonyms
Joy 	Happiness, bliss, cheer, contentment, delight, ecstasy, enchantment, enjoyment, felicity, rapture, gratification, pleasure, satisfaction, well-being	Sadness, sorrow, unhappiness, woe, depression, gloom, misery, pain
Anger 	Acrimony, annoyance, bitterness, displeasure, exasperation, fury, ire, irritation, outrage, rage, resentment, tantrum, umbrage, wrath, hostility	Calmness, contentment, enjoyment, peace, joy, pleasantness
Sadness 	Dejected, depressed, dismal, distressed, grief, loneliness, melancholy, misery, sorrowful, unhappiness	Happiness, gladness, joy, cheer
Disgust 	Abhorrence, aversion, loathing, repugnance, repulsion, revulsion, sickness, nausea, offensiveness	Admiration, desire, esteem, fondness, liking, loving, reverence, respect
Fear 	Anxiety, apprehension, awe, concern, consternation, dread, fright, misgiving, phobia, trepidation, worry, qualm, terror	Courage, fearlessness, heroism, unconcern
Surprise 	Amazement, astonishment, awe, eye-opener, incredulity, jolt, revelation, shock, unexpectedness, wonder, startle, catch off-guard, unforeseen	Expectation, assurance, confidence, fear, intention, likelihood, possibility, prediction, surmise
Contempt 	Antipathy, aversion, defiance, derision, disregard, hatred, malice, repugnance, scorn	Admiration, approbation, approval, regard, respect, endorsement

Other people are "super-recognizers" who have an exceptional ability to identify and remember faces (Rabin, 2009). Most of us, clearly, are in between these extremes. This facial recognition ability exists on a continuum, some people are better at it than others. As you've probably experienced, some people (those closer to the super-recognizers' side of the continuum) have an amazing ability to identify, say, movie or television stars from minimal cues, from small photos and fast-moving film scenes. Others need a lot more cues and more time to identify the individual.

Not surprisingly computer programs for facial recognition are available and are becoming more and more proficient. For example, one study found that smiles of delight and smiles of aggravation were distinguished by the computer whereas human observation was unable to detect the difference (Massachusetts Institute of Technology, 2012).

Some of these emotions are communicated with broad and easily recognized facial movements. Much of our emotional expression is made by what are called **micromomentary expressions**, a concept explained briefly in Chapter 1. These extremely small movements are made very quickly and, therefore, are not easily recognized consciously. These emotional displays can be seen quite clearly, however, with the aid of slow-motion cameras. Micromomentary expressions are viewed by many as accurately revealing one's true emotions and are reliable cues to deception detection (a topic covered in Chapter 10).

You also make a variety of judgments based on the face—even when it is viewed at 100-millisecond speed. For example, one study finds that you make judgments not only of attractiveness (which is the obvious judgment) but also of likeability, competence, aggressiveness, and trustworthiness (Willis & Todorov, 2006).

THE SMILE

The smile is likely to be the first thing you think about when focusing on facial communication, probably because it's so important. The smile is, in fact, important in just about any relationship you can imagine.

One of the most interesting things about smiles is that they're more often displayed in social situations than in private ones (Andersen, 2004). Although you may smile when spotting a cute photo or joke you read even when alone, most smiling occurs in response to social situations; most often you smile at other people rather than at yourself.

Smiling is usually an expression of enjoyment and pleasure; it's a happy reaction and seems to be responded to positively in almost all situations. One study, for example, found that participants rated people who smile as more likeable and more approachable than people who don't smile or who only pretend to smile (Gladstone & Parker, 2002). In another study men and women signaled that they wanted to hitchhike (this study was done in France where it's legal and common to hitchhike) to some 800 motorists. Motorists stopped more often for the smiling women than for those who didn't smile. Smiling had no effect on whether motorists would stop for men (Guéguen & Fischer-Lokou, 2004).

Women, research finds, smile significantly more than men—regardless of whether women are talking with women or men (Hall, 1984; Helgeson, 2009). This is a difference that can be observed in very young girls and boys. The reasons for these differences are interesting to consider. For example, is there a biological reason for the differences? Do women simply have more positive feelings than do men and consequently smile more simply to reflect their feelings? Did our culture teach women to smile and men not to smile?

Nonverbal researchers distinguish two kinds of smiles: the real and the fake. The real smile, known as the Duchenne smile, is genuine; it's an unconscious movement that accurately reflects your feelings at the time. The fake smile, on the other hand, is conscious. Distinguishing between these two is crucial in a wide variety of situations. For example, you distinguish between these smiles when you make judgments as to whether someone is genuinely pleased at your good fortune or is really jealous. You distinguish between these smiles when you infer that the person really likes you or is just being polite. In each of these cases, we're making judgments as to whether or not someone is lying; we're engaging in deception detection, a topic we return to in Chapter 10. Not surprisingly, then, Duchenne smiles are responded to positively and fake smiles—especially if they are obvious—are responded to negatively.

Interestingly enough, computer programs for facial recognition are available and are becoming more and more proficient. For example, one recent study reported in *Science Digest.com* found that smiles of delight and smiles of aggravation were distinguished by the computer, whereas human observation was unable to detect the difference (Hogue, McDuff, & Picard, 2012).

The top photo is of the Duchenne smile and the bottom is of a fake smile. What specific facial and eye features can you point out that distinguish the two smiles?

IF YOU WANT TO

Flirt/express romantic interest/initiate a relationship

- Smile and perhaps wink.
- Maintain eye contact a bit longer than normal.
- Preen a bit but not too much.
- Lean toward the person—not enough to crowd him or her—but enough so that a desire for closeness can be appreciated.
- Reduce the space between you a bit.
- Maintain an open body posture; for example, avoid crossing your arms over your chest.
- Touch the other's hand.

EXERCISE

DISTINGUISHING SMILES

The ability to recognize and distinguish between real and fake smiles is a useful skill in both personal and business relationships. Enlist the help of a friend to pose for different smiles or take photos of yourself or search for a photo or, if possible, a video of someone smiling and paste it, clip it, or describe it in Column 1. In Column 2 indicate whether you think the smile is real or fake and in Column 3 describe the nonverbals that contribute to your evaluation of it as real or fake. If possible share your photos or videos and conclusions with others to see if they agree with your assessment. Continue reading after you've completed this exercise.

	Real or Fake	Nonverbals that reveal whether the person's smile is real or fake
Photo 1		
Photo 2		

After you've completed the above exercise, consider the following factors that researchers find distinguish real from fake smiles (Burgoon et al., 2010). How many of these cues did you use?

- Fake smiles come and go more quickly than real smiles.
- Fake smiles are often larger in scope and last longer than real smiles.
- Fake smiles are often asymmetrical; the two sides of the face are not the same.
- Fake smiles are less likely to use eye movements.
- Fake smiles are less likely to involve the muscles around the lips curling up.

FACIAL MANAGEMENT

As you grew up, you learned your culture's system of nonverbal communication. You also learned certain facial management techniques that enable you to express feelings so as to achieve certain desired effects—for example, to hide certain emotions and to emphasize others. Nonverbal researchers have identified four reasons why you might use facial management techniques (Ekman & Friesen, 1975/2003). People manage their facial expressions:

1. To conform to the culture's rules for the appropriate display of emotions. As we emphasize throughout this chapter, cultural differences in facial expressions are more often due to members following the rules of their culture for displaying emotions. All people seem remarkably similar in the feeling of emotions.
2. To conform to personal display rules. Each person develops his or her rules for emotional display, often based on the family examples seen while growing up.
3. To meet vocational requirements. Exasperated kindergarten teachers hide their emotions from their students and from the students' parents. More obviously, actors, lawyers, medical workers, and politicians display the emotions that are helpful in their fulfilling their jobs.
4. To meet a need of the moment. If you're talking with a person experiencing grief, you'll inhibit the expression of any humorous experiences that might come to your mind and in fact put on a sad expression, which may or may not be genuine. Another example is the case where you're caught with the wrong person or in the wrong place and with your facial expressions (as well as the rest of your body) you protest your innocence.

Facial management techniques serve a variety of purposes. According to the pioneering work *Unmasking the Face* (Ekman & Friesen, 1975/2003), you can manage your facial expressions (1) to qualify the emotion you're actually feeling, (2) to modulate the feeling's expression, and (3) to falsify your message. As you read about the following techniques, consider your own use of them and the communication situations in which you would use such techniques.

To Qualify

When you qualify your emotional expression you communicate an additional expression as a comment on the expression you just exhibited. Often smiles are used to qualify emotional expressions. For example, if you express sadness—and perhaps worry those around you that you may do something foolish—a smile will qualify your expression of sadness as if to say "I'm not going to jump off a bridge." Qualifying, note Ekman and Friesen (1975/2003), is the mildest type of facial management and usually involves very little distortion of the original expression. Consequently, this facial management technique is treated very briefly in the nonverbal research literature.

To Modulate

When you modulate your facial expression of emotion, you increase or decrease your expression of the emotion; you intensify or deintensify your expression.

You *intensify* facial expressions when you wish to exaggerate an expression of emotion that you're feeling. Let's say you get a a $100 gift certificate for your birthday. You're pleased but, in all honesty, you expected a lot more. However, you want to express your appreciation for the gift and so you exaggerate and intensify your expression of pleasure in getting the gift. Your eyes grow wider than they would normally and you smile more broadly than you would if the gift certificate had arrived in the mail where no one would have seen your expression.

Deintensifying is the logical opposite of intensifying and occurs when you feel an emotion strongly but you reduce the strength of it in your facial expressions.

Assume, for example, that you and a friend are looking over the posted final grades for chemistry. You got an A but your friend got a C–. You would probably feel very happy for yourself, a happiness that would normally be reflected in your facial expression. But, because you don't want to make matters worse for your friend, you might deintensify your expression of happiness and perhaps even say something like, "At least we both passed." "Sore winners"—people who gloat after winning a poker game, for example—are violating the display rule in our culture that tells us to deintensify/minimize our expression of pleasure in light of another's unhappiness.

To Falsify

You can falsify your facial expressions by simulating, neutralizing, or masking.

When you *simulate*, you show a feeling that you're not really feeling. For example, upon hearing the good news of someone you dislike, you might smile and show a pleased expression when you're not feeling pleased at all.

When you *neutralize* your facial expression, you hide any outward expression of the emotions you're feeling. In much of the United States, men are generally supposed to engage in greater neutralizing than women who, for example, are allowed freedom to cry, to express elation, and to register fear facially. In various card games, neutralizing (the "poker face") is an important skill carefully cultivated by serious players.

When you *mask*, you replace or substitute the expression of one emotion for the expression of another. For example, consider the following. You're teaching a second-grade class and it begins to thunder and lightning—something that you normally fear and that you would normally express facially. But, given the situation of supervising small children, you might want to mask the expression of fear and substitute a calm and relaxed expression.

As you can see from the above examples, facial management techniques help you display emotions in socially acceptable ways. They enable you to follow the

IF YOU WANT TO

Demonstrate **credibility/competence/character/charisma**

- Maintain eye contact; avoid shifting your eyes from side to side.
- Avoid self-touching movements.
- Avoid vocalized pauses; maintain conversational tone.
- Vary facial expressions and vocal rhythm.
- Use large rather than small gestures.
- Avoid closed gestures, for example, hands folded across abdomen.
- Avoid yelling or raising your vocal volume, which can signal a loss of control.

display rules of your culture. For example, if someone gets bad news in which you secretly take pleasure, the social display rule dictates that you frown and otherwise nonverbally signal sorrow. If you place first in a race and your best friend barely finishes, the display rule requires that you minimize your expression of happiness—and certainly avoid any signs of gloating. If you violate these display rules, you'll appear insensitive.

POLITENESS IN NONVERBAL COMMUNICATION

Being polite with facial messages

- Avoid negative evaluative thoughts; when thinking negatively, your real feelings may leak out in tiny movements around the eyes and mouth.
- Avoid evaluating others' expressions with psychological explanations.
- Manage your facial expressions as appropriate to the interaction; although facial management techniques may be deceptive, they're expected and even required by the rules for polite social interaction.

IDENTIFYING FACIAL MANAGEMENT STRATEGIES

EXERCISE

To appreciate the ways in which facial management strategies (listed in Column 1) work (as well as your own ability to manage them and to detect them in others), explain in your own words the nature of the technique in Column 2. In Column 3 supply an example of each of the facial management techniques that you've observed in the media or in your own interactions or that you make up out of your imagination and the specific meanings it communicated.

Facial Management Technique	Explanation of the Technique	Example and Meaning(s) Communicated
To qualify	*You add another emotional expression to comment on the original expression.*	*Sean was visually upset after getting a B- on his term paper but then shrugged with a look of displeasure on his face to say, in effect,* I shouldn't be so upset; it's not the end of the world.
To modulate Intensifying Deintensifying		
To falsify Simulating Neutralizing Maskings		

FACIAL STYLES

In their landmark book in nonverbal communication, *Unmasking the Face*, researchers Paul Ekman and Wallace Friesen (1975/2003) identify eight styles of facial expression. These styles are an integral part of an individual's personality. As a result, you will exhibit these styles in a wide variety of situations and over long periods of time. Recognizing these facial styles may enable you to avoid those that will give a negative impression. Eight styles are identified:

The withholder. This person displays little to no emotion. It has been argued that this withholding of emotional expression feeds back and itself becomes a cause of the withholding personality. And so, this withholding tendency becomes stronger over time.

The revealer. This person is the opposite of the withholder and readily and easily displays emotional feeling without any attempt to engage in any of the facial management techniques discussed earlier.

The unwitting expressor. This person displays feelings without realizing it. Often this person assumes that he or she is effective in hiding any expression of feelings and frequently wonders how others know what he or she is in fact feeling.

The blanked expressor. Whereas the unwitting expressor displays feelings without wishing to, the blanked expressor wishes to express feelings but doesn't. This person may think he or she is expressing the felt emotions but only a relatively blank expression is actually displayed.

The substitute expressor. This person thinks he or she is communicating one emotion but is actually communicating a very different emotion. When this person is really feeling both emotions at the same time, only the emotion he or she is consciously aware of gets displayed.

The frozen-affect expressor. This person always displays the same facial expressions. Regardless of what is being felt, the same basic "frozen" expression is displayed.

The ever-ready expressor. This person has the same expression ready for initial display at all times. Regardless of the circumstances or the appropriateness of the expression, this person responds first and always with the same emotion. This is then followed by a more appropriate expression.

The flooded-affect expressor. In all circumstances, this person displays one emotion (that is generally characteristic of the individual) mixed with another (usually more appropriate to the situation) emotion. For example, the person might display annoyance and, when feeling surprise, would display both annoyance and surprise.

ON THE JOB

Blanked Expressor

One of your colleagues confides in you that at company meetings you're a blanked expressor and that others are uncomfortable in not knowing what you really think about what they're saying. What are some of the things you might do to deal with this problem?

EXERCISE

RECOGNIZING FIRST IMPRESSION TENDENCIES

Although, as noted above, these facial styles are a part of a person's personality, many of these expressions may be used on occasion (rather than always or almost always) because of unique circumstances, not because of personality. Yet, often we draw initial impressions of someone from their facial expressions and assume that that expression is their facial style and hence a reflection of their personality, a conclusion that may not be entirely or even remotely accurate. In order to bring this tendency to consciousness, the eight facial expressions just discussed are presented in Column 1. In Column 2 list the first impression you would get from meeting a person with one, two, three, or all of these facial expressions. In Column 3 identify other possible reasons for the person's display of the particular facial style.

Facial Style	First Impression	Other Possible Reasons
The withholder	*Has something to hide*	*Is shy. Feels ill. Doesn't like the other people. Is worried about other things.*
The revealer		
The unwitting expressor		
The blanked expressor		
The substitute expressor		
The frozen-affect expressor		
The ever-ready expressor		
The flooded-affect expressor		

THE FACIAL FEEDBACK HYPOTHESIS

Before reading about the facial feedback hypothesis, put a pencil in your mouth so that your teeth grab the middle of the pencil and the point and the eraser extend on either side of your mouth. Hold the pose for a minute or so. Did this experience influence the way you feel? Next, simulate a sad expression—check with a mirror to make sure you really do look sad—hold the expression for a minute or so. Did this experience influence the way you feel? With these two experiences, you've tested what is called the facial feedback hypothesis.

According to the facial feedback hypothesis, your facial expression influences your level of physiological arousal. People who exaggerate their facial expressions show higher physiological arousal than those who suppress these expressions. In research studies, those who neither exaggerated nor suppressed their expressions had arousal levels between these two extremes (Lanzetta, Cartwright-Smith, & Kleck, 1976; Zuckerman, Klorman, Larrance, & Spiegel, 1981). In one interesting study, subjects held a pen in their teeth in such a way as to simulate a sad expression. They were then asked to rate photographs. Results showed that mimicking sad expressions actually increased the degree of sadness the subjects reported feeling when viewing the photographs (Larsen, Kasimatis, & Frey, 1992). So not only does your facial expression influence the judgments and impressions others have of you, it also influences your own level of emotional arousal (Cappella, 1993).

EMOTIONAL CONTAGION

Emotional messages are often contagious (Cappella & Schreiber, 2006). If you've ever watched an infant and mother interacting, you can readily see how quickly the infant mimics the emotional expressions of the mother. If the mother smiles, the infant smiles; if the mother frowns, the infant frowns. As children get older, they begin to pick up more subtle expressions of emotions. For example, children quickly identify and often mimic a parent's anxiety or fear. Even among college roommates, the depression of one roommate spread to the other over a period of just 3 weeks (Joiner, 1994). In short, in **emotional contagion** emotions pass from one person to another; women are especially prone to this process (Cappella & Schreiber, 2006; Doherty, Orimoto, Singelis, Hatfield, & Hebb, 1995). In conversation and in small groups, the strong emotions of one person can easily prove contagious to others present; this can be productive when the emotions are productive or unproductive when the emotions are unproductive.

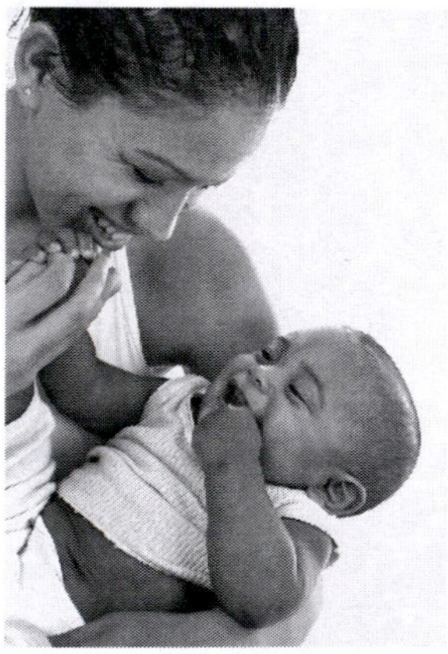

What practical applications to interpersonal or work relationships might you derive from this notion of emotional contagion?

One view of this process goes like this:

1. You perceive an emotional expression of another.
2. You mimic this emotional expression, perhaps unconsciously.
3. The feedback you get from expressing the emotion creates in you a replication of the other person's feelings.

You see another variant of intentional emotional contagion in attempts at persuasion that utilize **emotional appeals**. One popular appeal, which organizations use frequently in fundraising for needy children, is to the emotion of pity. By showing you images of hungry and destitute children, these fundraisers hope to get you to experience so much pity that you'll help finance their efforts. Similarly, people who beg for money often emphasize their difficulties in an effort to evoke pity and donations.

Emotional contagion also seems the goal of certain organizational display rules. For example, a company may require (or at least expect) that the sales force cheer enthusiastically as each new product is unveiled. This cheering is extremely useful and is likely to make the sales representatives more enthusiastic about and more emotionally committed to the product than if they didn't engage in this cheering.

CULTURE AND FACIAL EXPRESSION

The wide variations in facial communication that we observe in different cultures seem to have to do more with which reactions are publicly permissible than with differences in the ways people show their emotions. For example, in one study Japanese and American students watched a film of an operation (Ekman, 2009). The experimenters videotaped the students both in an interview about the film and alone while watching the film. When alone, the students showed very similar reactions. In the interview, however, the American students displayed facial expressions indicating displeasure, whereas the Japanese students did not show any great emotion. Similarly, it's considered "forward" or inappropriate for Japanese women to reveal broad smiles, so women in Japan will hide their smiles, sometimes with their hands (Ma, 1996). Women in the United States, on the other hand, have no such restrictions and are more likely to smile openly. Thus, many differences may reflect not the way different cultures express emotions but rather the display rules, the cultural rules for the appropriate display of emotions in public (Matsumoto, 1991; Matsumoto & Hwang, 2013b).

Cultural differences also exist in decoding the meaning of facial expressions. Visualize a person with a smiling face and a person with a neutral expression. Which person would you find more attractive? More intelligent? More sociable? The answer to this would depend on your culture. When researchers asked American and Japanese students to judge the meanings of smiling and neutral facial expressions, the Americans rated the smiling face as more attractive, more intelligent, and more sociable than the neutral face. The Japanese, however, rated the smiling face as more sociable but not as more attractive; and they rated the neutral face as more intelligent (Matsumoto & Kudoh, 1993).

ON THE JOB

Displaying Authority

Alice is having difficulties at work, centered primarily on her inability to supervise effectively five interns. "They just don't listen" is Alice's frequent explanation. What might Alice do to establish her authority more effectively with her facial expressions? Which should she avoid? Which should she display? But, don't limit yourself to a description of facial expressions—consider what other nonverbals Alice might use to establish her authority and get the interns to listen.

Summary

1. The face communicates messages in a variety of ways. Its shape and size communicates as does its expression of emotion.
2. Facial expressions may consist of primary affect displays (the basic emotions such as happiness and surprise) and affect blends (combinations of the basic emotions).
3. Smiles may be divided into real or Duchenne smiles, which are unconscious and genuinely reflect feelings, and fake smiles, which are conscious and often hide true feelings.
4. Three main purposes of facial management are to qualify, to modulate (intensify or deintensify), and to falsify (simulate, neutralize, or mask).
5. A variety of facial styles have been identified and are considered to be part of the person's personality, for example, the person who withholds expression or the or the person who expresses him- or herself facially without realizing it.
6. The facial feedback hypothesis says that your facial expressions can influence some emotions.
7. Emotional facial expressions and messages are often contagious; emotions pass easily from one person to another.
8. Facial expressions, like all aspects of nonverbal communication, will vary with the culture, largely because cultures teach their members different rules for the appropriate and inappropriate display of emotions.

Key Terms

Supply a definition for each of the following terms. Once you've formulated these "standard" definitions, consider the following ideas for further defining and understanding. Not all will work for all key terms but some will work for some terms and some will work for others.

- Find a quotation that illustrates the term.
- Provide an example from personal interaction, television, film, novels, or plays.
- Create a short dialogue to illustrate the operation of the key term.
- Locate a research study investigating the key term and report its findings.
- Illustrate the concept nonverbally.
- Find a video that illustrates the key term.
- Find images—photos or graphics, abstract or specific, literal or metaphorical.
- Diagram the concept.
- Explain the negative, what the concept is not.
- State a skill that centers on the concept.

Key Concept	Definition
Primary affect displays	
Affect blends	
Micromomentary expressions	
Duchenne smile	
Facial management	
Qualifying	
Modulating	
Intensifying	
Deintensifying	
Simulating	
Neutralizing	
Masking	
Facial styles	
Facial feedback	
Emotional contagion	

AND IN ADDITION

Using your favorite search engine (in addition, use Google Scholar or the databases in your college library for the more scientific research articles) search for **facial messages, smiling, facial management, facial feedback, facial styles, emotional contagion**, or any of the other terms and topics considered in this chapter and add to the chapter contents. Depending on the structure of the course and the facilities available, you may want to post these additions to a course website; to a social media site such as Twitter, Facebook, or Google+; or to a listserv or through e-mail, for example. Here are a few ways in which you might make your addition:

- Write a paragraph that adds to the discussion of a particular concept.
- Provide a new, contradictory, or intercultural example of a concept.
- Create a figure or table to illustrate or organize a particular topic.
- Illustrate with an image or two or a 10- to 15-second video a particular concept of nonverbal behavior.
- Summarize and evaluate the results of a scientific study on a topic relevant to this chapter.
- Summarize and evaluate an online article that focuses on one of the topics considered here.

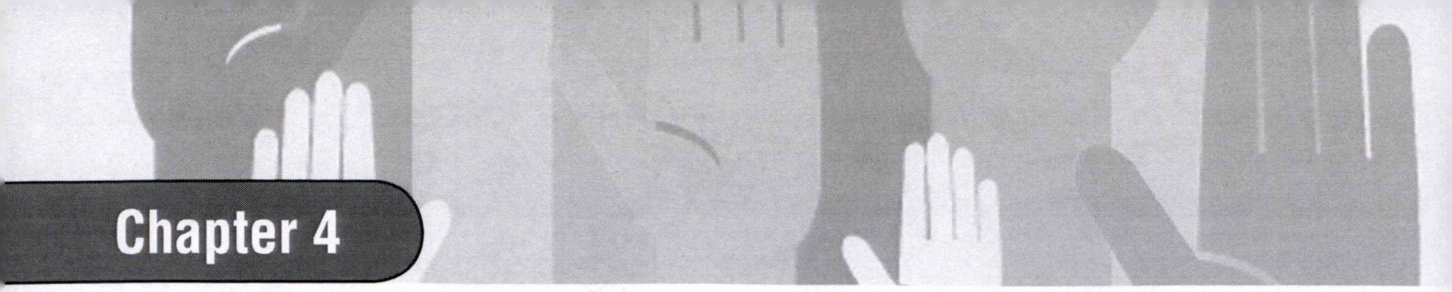

Chapter 4

Eye Messages

CHAPTER TOPICS

CHAPTER EXERCISES

[Expressing Meanings through Eye Communication]
Distinguishing Right and Left Movers
Identifying Eye Movement Functions
Explaining Eye Behavior Impressions
Identifying Pupil Dilation in Advertisements

ON THE JOB

Winking
Staring
Over Your Shoulder

POLITENESS IN NONVERBAL COMMUNICATION

Being polite with eye messages

IF YOU WANT TO

Show **supportiveness/empathy/concern**
Express **agreement/approval**

☛CHAPTER OBJECTIVES

After reading this chapter, you should be able to:

1. Identify the purposes and types of eye contact and eye avoidance.
2. Define *pupil dilation.*
3. Explain some of the cultural and gender differences in eye behavior.

BEFORE reading about eye messages think about your own eye communication. Specifically, how would you expresss the following messages through eye movements? Doing this in front of a mirror will help.

- **I'm genuinely interested.**
- **That's disgusting.**
- **I love you.**
- **I'm the boss and what I say goes.**
- **I respectfully disagree.**

As you can see, eye movements vary greatly depending on the message you want to communicate or the purpose you want your eye messages to serve, one of the topics to be considered in this chapter.

From Ben Jonson's poetic observation "Drink to me only with thine eyes, / And I will pledge with mine" to the scientific observations of contemporary researchers (Burgoon et al., 2010; Hess, 1975; Marshall, 1983), the eyes have long been regarded as one of the most important nonverbal message systems, an area known as **oculesis**—the study of eye movements.

So important are messages sent by the eyes that people routinely use eye enhancements without even thinking about it. Color contacts, designer eyeglasses and sunglasses, mascara, extended/false eyelashes and eyelash growth products, eyebrow shaping, eyebrow jewelry, and cream to remove crow's feet—those little lines around the eyes—are some of the ways we enhance our eyes. And we do this on the assumption that these enhancements will communicate more positive impressions than will eyes with no such enhancements.

PURPOSES OF EYE MOVEMENTS

Let's look first at some of the purposes eye messages serve (alternatively, the meanings they communicate or are used to communicate). There are actually a variety of systems used to identify the purposes of eye movements. Here we use a simple classification of five purposes: to help you think, to reveal and conceal emotions, to regulate conversation, to change psychological distance, and to include or to exclude others.

Before explaining these five purposes, complete the exercise on the next page.

To Help You Think

This purpose is unlike the purposes to be discussed next in that the movements involved in thinking are not normally conscious. However, we do use eye movements during cognitive processing—when thinking out a problem or choosing among alternatives, for example. These movements are referred to as CLEMs (conjugate lateral eye movements). Generally, these movements consist of looking upward and to the right or to the left. In fact, most people routinely look to the right or to the left, leading researchers to group people as right movers or left movers.

EXERCISE

DISTINGUISHING RIGHT AND LEFT MOVERS

To understand the connection between eye movements and thinking, try this exercise, based on the research conducted by nonverbal researchers (Galin & Ornstein, 1974). Form dyads. One person is designed A and the other B. For Round One, Person A will be the observer and Person B will be the observed. Person A should read the following questions to Person B and observe B's eye movements as closely as possible. Person B should respond to these questions by figuring out the answers in his or her head.

Round One. Questions for Person B as read by Person A:

1. How much is 8 × 21?
2. How many letters are in the word *tomorrow*?
3. What does it mean to say "Beauty is in the eye of the beholder"?

Round Two. Questions for Person A as read by Person B:

1. How much is 6 × 14?
2. How many letters are in the word *ambiguous*?
3. What does it mean to say "An eye for an eye, a tooth for a tooth"?

This experience was intended to illustrate the first purpose of eye movements discussed below: to help you think. It's been found that approximately 75 percent of a person's eye movements will be made in the same direction, either to the left or to the right. In what directions did each person's eyes move in answering the questions? Some researchers have suggested that right movers are using their left brain hemisphere to process information, whereas left movers are using their right brain hemisphere. Accord to nonverbal researchers (Knapp & Hall, 2010; Richmond et al., 2012), left movers are more susceptible to hypnosis, have more alpha brain waves, score higher on verbal SATs, have greater fluency in writing, have greater visual imagery, are more likely to major in the humanities, and are more sociable. Right movers, on the other hand, are more likely to show tension in large muscles, score higher on quantitative SATs, are more likely to major in the sciences, have more "tics" and "twitches," prefer "cool" colors, and make their career choices earlier.

To Reveal and to Conceal Emotions

This is probably the most obvious function. The important point to see, however, is that eyes are used to both reveal and to conceal emotions. At times, your eyes will express your inner meaning—you open them wide when interested or amazed and tighten them when appalled or disgusted, for example. To indicate your romantic interest in another person you might wink. Eye contact also reveals the degree to which you are involved in the relationship. With much and focused eye contact you reveal closeness; with little and scattered eye contact, you reveal distance.

You can also signal your power through "visual dominance behavior" (Exline, Ellyson, & Long, 1975). The average speaker, for example, maintains a high level of eye contact while listening and a lower level while speaking. When people want to signal dominance, they may reverse this pattern—maintaining a high level of eye contact while talking but a lower level while listening. You'll see this pattern if you

How would you describe the eye contact and the possible meanings communicated by these women? © 2013, Tyler Olson, Shutterstock, Inc.

visualize a manager criticizing a subordinate. You'll probably picture the manager maintaining direct eye contact with the subordinate while criticizing and with little eye contact when listening to excuses he or she considers inadequate.

IF YOU WANT TO

Show **supportiveness/empathy/concern**

- Maintain eye contact.
- Position yourself face-to-face.
- Give affirmative head nods that say "I understand."
- Use a soft, warm voice.
- Maintain a relatively close distance.

To Regulate Conversation

You often use eye movements to regulate the conversation. For example, you might open your eyes wide (and lean forward) to signal that you want to say something. Or you might avoid eye contact with the speaker who has the habit of asking you to comment when you don't want to. This purpose is often served when you're in conversation and you want feedback. You want to hear what others think and so you'll make eye contact with a questioning look on your face, as if to say, "Well, what do you think?" You can also inform the other person that the channel of communication is open and that he or she should now speak. You see this in college classrooms when the instructor asks a question and then locks eyes with a student. Without saying anything, the instructor conveys the expectation that the student will answer the question, and the student gets the message.

IF YOU WANT TO

Express **agreement/approval**

- Use the eyebrow flash (defined below).
- Lock eyes and nod.
- Tilt your head while maintaining a positive expression to indicate that you do in fact agree.

To Change Psychological Distance

This function is perhaps the most interesting because we don't think much about this. When you're in a crowded situation—say standing on a crowded bus or in an elevator—you probably avoid eye contact with the people around you in an effort to enlarge the psychological space between you. Similarly, say a dentist is examining your mouth. This distance is really too close for comfort, especially with someone you know only professionally. So, to increase the distance between you and the dentist, you might close your eyes. Alternatively, consider a situation in which you and your romantic partner are separated at a rally; you can see each other but only from a distance. Maintaining eye contact reduces the psychological distance between you and makes you feel closer to each other (at least psychologically).

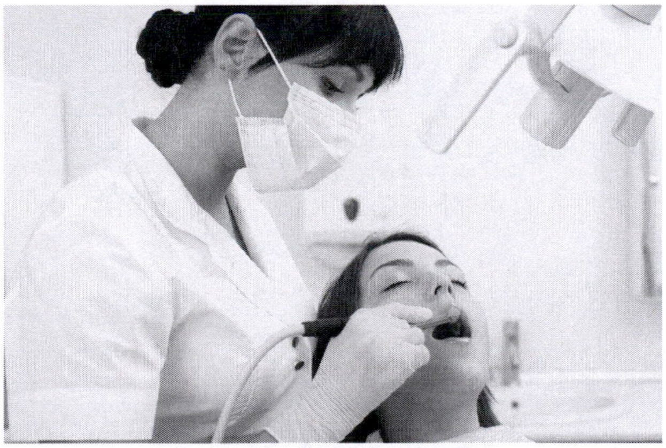

In what other instances might you close your eyes to increase psychological distance? Are there instances where you would close your eyes to increase psychological closeness? © 2013, konstantynov, Shutterstock, Inc.

ON THE JOB

Winking

A colleague at your company has been winking at you—sometimes at company meetings, sometimes in the hallway, sometimes in the cafeteria. You're just not sure what these winks mean. Is this colleague simply saying "hello" with the winking or is this an expression of romantic interest (which you would welcome)? What are some of the things you might do to disambiguate this situation and discover the meaning behind the winking?

To Include and to Exclude Others

Eye contact includes; eye avoidance excludes. In a group setting, for example, when you maintain eye contact (even intermittent eye contact) you are indicating that this other person is included. When you avoid making eye contact with one member of a group, say, you're in effect excluding this person from the interaction.

EXERCISE

IDENTIFYING EYE MOVEMENT FUNCTIONS

To understand better the functions that eye communication serves, consider the five functions just discussed and noted in Column 1. In Column 2 indicate a more specific function (e.g., to seek feedback on your last speech or to signal that you and this other person are a romantic couple). In Column 3 indicate the specific eye movements that would be used to signal these functions.

Functions	More Specifically	Specific Eye Movements
To help you think	*To recall what I did last Saturday.*	*Raised eyes to the left while trying to recall and then lowered eyes to normal position once I remembered*
To reveal and to conceal emotions		
To regulate conversation		
To change psychological distance		
To include and to exclude others		

TYPES OF EYE MOVEMENTS

There are a variety of eye movements that we use daily without even thinking about them. Here are some of the major types compiled from a wide variety of researchers (Andersen, 2004; Burgoon et al., 2010; Marsh, 1988).

- **Mutual gaze.** Mutual gaze refers to an interaction in which two people look at each other at the same time. It's often helpful to distinguish mutual gaze in which people are making eye to eye contact from those in which people are gazing at each other's faces.
- **One-sided looking.** This occurs when one person gazes at the face of another but the gaze is not returned.
- **Intermittent glancing.** This is the kind of eye movement that occurs in normal conversation. You establish eye-to-eye contact, glance at the person's face, then to the right or the left, up or down, then back to eye-to-eye contact, and so on.
- **Survey glance.** This type of eye movement might occur when you enter a classroom on the first day of the semester and you survey the people in the room without making direct eye contact with any of the other students.
- **Secretive glance.** Looking at someone without him or her seeing you do so is often a preliminary to flirting behavior. You're looking someone over to see, for example, if this person is available (is the person wearing a wedding ring or acting as if he or she is expecting to meet someone).
- **Public stare.** This type of eye movement is the kind you'd use listening to a public speaker or watching a performer on the street or on the stage. This type of staring would be totally out of place in a small group or interpersonal interaction.

ON THE JOB

Staring

One of the workers in your firm has the habit of staring at others for longer periods of time than is considered normal. Although this habit of staring is perfectly innocent, many feel it comes off as leering or ogling and are uncomfortable with it. How might you deal with this problem if you were friends with this person? If you were this person's supervisor? Would what you say to this person be different depending on whether this was a man or a woman?

How would you describe the eye movements seen in a typical college classroom? © 2013, Anton Gvozdikov, Shutterstock, Inc.

- **Gaze aversion.** This type of eye movement occurs when you want to avoid making contact with another person and so you avert your gaze hoping the person hasn't seen you. It's an intentional avoidance of eye contact. When you avoid eye contact or avert your glance, you help others maintain their privacy. You may engage in this **civil inattention** when you see a couple arguing in public or even

EXERCISE

EXPLAINING EYE BEHAVIOR IMPRESSIONS

In order to gain greater awareness for how you use eye behaviors to form impressions of others and that other use to form impressions of you, consider the eye behaviors noted in Column 1. In Column 2 indicate your first impressions, and then, in Column 3, indicate some other possible reason for the eye behavior, something ideally very different from your first impressions.

Eye Behaviors	Most Likely First Impressions	Alternative Explanation
Avoids eye contact almost completely	*Isn't interested in me or in having a conversation with me.*	*Is shy. Had a really bad day and needs some space. Is embarrassed at something. Is going to tell me bad news.*
Maintains abnormally long and focused eye contact		
Looks behind and around the other person, never at the person		
Blinks a great deal		
Closes eyes periodically while you're talking		

just engaged in conversation, for example (Goffman, 1967). You acknowledge the presence of the other person but do so without intruding, either as a friend or an opponent. You turn your eyes away (although your eyes may be wide open) as if to say, "I don't mean to intrude; I respect your privacy." Eye avoidance also can signal lack of interest—in a person, a conversation, or some visual stimulus. At times you may hide your eyes to block off unpleasant stimuli or close your eyes to block out visual stimuli and thus heighten other senses. For example, you may listen to music with your eyes closed. Lovers often close their eyes while kissing, and many prefer to make love in a dark or dimly lit room.

- **Gaze omission.** This is similar to gaze aversion except that it's not intentional; you didn't make eye contact because you didn't see the person or didn't recognize the person.
- **Eye roll.** This often occurs when you hear something that you simply find inane or perhaps you want to signal that you don't believe the person. You'd roll your eyes. This eye roll has been found to be an extremely hurtful form of nonverbal behavior. It disconfirms the person and what the person is saying.
- **Eyebrow flash.** This is a very quick, single up–down movement of both eyebrows. This type of eye movement signals recognition and acknowledgment. When passing a colleague in the hallway, you might respond with an eyebrow flash that says "hello." And, not surprisingly, it's important to return this eyebrow flash; if you don't, you'll likely be seen as unfriendly and as not wanting to interact.

POLITENESS IN NONVERBAL COMMUNICATION

Being polite with eye messages

- Avoid staring or ogling; you'll be perceived as a sleaze.
- Make eye contact when interacting.
- Avoid the eye roll; it's hurtful and unlikely to win you any friends.
- Engage in civil inattention when appropriate to show that you don't intend to intrude on someone's privacy.
- Return the eyebrow flash; if you don't you'll signal a lack of interest and respect.

PUPIL DILATION

In the 15th and 16th centuries, Italian women put drops of belladonna (which literally means "beautiful woman") into their eyes to enlarge the pupils so that they would look more attractive. Contemporary **pupillometrics** research supports the intuitive logic of these women; dilated pupils are judged more attractive than constricted ones (Hess, 1975; Marshall, 1983). In one study, researchers retouched photographs of women; in half they enlarged the pupils and in the other half they made them smaller (Hess, 1975). Men were then asked to judge the women's personalities from the photographs. The photos of women with small pupils drew responses such as "cold," "hard," and "selfish"; those with dilated pupils drew responses such as "feminine" and "soft." Interestingly, the male observers could not verbalize the reasons for their different perceptions. Pupil dilation and our reactions to changes in the pupil size of others may function below the level of conscious awareness.

Pupil size also reveals your interest and level of emotional arousal. Your pupils enlarge when you're interested in something or when you are emotionally aroused. When homosexuals and heterosexuals were shown pictures of nude bodies, the homosexuals' pupils dilated more when they viewed same-sex bodies, whereas the heterosexuals' pupils dilated more when they viewed opposite-sex bodies (Hess, Seltzer, & Schlien, 1965). These pupillary responses are also observed in persons with profound mental retardation (Chaney, Givens, Aoki, & Gombiner, 1989). Perhaps we judge dilated pupils as more attractive because we respond to them as indicative of a person's interest in us. And that may be the reason why both models and fuzzy beanbag toys have exceptionally large pupils.

EXERCISE

IDENTIFYING PUPIL DILATION IN ADVERTISEMENTS

To appreciate the way advertisers try to influence you through the eyes of the models, examine a print or online advertising image or video in which the model's eyes are shown and complete the following table. In Column 1 paste, clip, or describe the ad. In Column 2 describe the pupils of the model(s) and in Column 3 identify the meanings you think the advertiser intends the ad to communicate and your estimate of the effectiveness of the advertisement (use a 10-point scale with 10 = extremely effective and 1 = extremely ineffective).

Advertisement	Description of Pupils	Meaning the Ad Is Communicating Effectiveness
Model advertising eye products	*Pupils are larger than normal*	*I'm attractive and you can be too; just buy our product.* Effectiveness rating _*8*__
		Effectiveness rating _____
		Effectiveness rating _____

CULTURE AND GENDER DIFFERENCES

Cultural differences in eye communication are significant. For example, every culture has rather strict, though unstated, rules for the proper duration of eye contact. In one study conducted in England, the average length of gaze was found to be 2.95 seconds. The average length of mutual gaze (two persons gazing at each other) is 1.18 seconds (Argyle, 1988; Argyle & Ingham, 1972). When eye contact falls short of this amount, members of some cultures may think the person is uninterested, shy, or preoccupied. When the average amount of time is exceeded, they may perceive the person as showing unusually high interest or even hostility.

The direction of the gaze also communicates. In the United States it is considered appropriate to glance alternately at the other person's face, then away, then again at the face, and so on. The rule for public speakers is to scan the entire audience, not focusing for too long on or ignoring any one area of the audience. When you break these directional rules, you communicate different meanings, as illustrated in the accompanying exercise.

Americans, for example, consider direct eye contact an expression of honesty and forthrightness, but the Japanese often view this as a lack of respect. A Japanese person will glance at the other person's face rarely, and then only for very short periods (Axtell, 1990). Interpreting another's eye contact messages with your own cultural rules is a risky undertaking; eye movements that you may interpret as insulting may have **been** intended to show respect.

Women make eye contact more and maintain it longer (both in speaking and in listening) than men. This holds true whether women are interacting with other women or with men. This difference in eye behavior may result from women's greater tendency to display their emotions (Wood, 1994). When women interact with other women, they display affiliative and supportive eye contact, whereas when men interact with other men, they avert their gaze (Gamble & Gamble, 2003).

In reading about eye messages, it's helpful to remember that not all people have perfect vision. In fact, people vary greatly in their visual abilities; some are totally blind, some are partially sighted, and some have unimpaired vision. Ninety percent of people who are "legally blind" have some vision. All people, however, have the same need for communication and information. Here are some tips for making communication better between those who have visual impairments and those without such difficulties.

ON THE JOB

Over Your Shoulder

One of your colleagues frequently comes into your office and looks over your shoulder and tries to read everything that's on your desk. Usually, there's nothing that you'd want to hide, but there are at times things you don't want anyone to see. Aside from this, these visits are often intrusive and prevent you from doing your work. What are some of the things you might say to stop these visits and the looking over your desk?

- Identify yourself. Don't assume the visually impaired person will recognize your voice.
- Face your listener. You'll be easier to hear. But don't shout. Most people who are visually impaired are not hearing impaired. Speak at your normal volume.

What other suggestions would you offer the person with or the person without visual impairment? © 2013, Lisa S., Shutterstock, Inc.

- Encode into speech all the meanings you wish to communicate. Remember that your gestures, eye movements, and facial expressions cannot be seen by the visually impaired.
- Use audible turn-taking cues. When you pass the role of speaker to a person who is visually impaired, don't rely on nonverbal cues; instead, say something like "Do you agree with that, Joe?"

- Use normal vocabulary and discuss topics that you would discuss with sighted people. Don't avoid terms like "see" or "look" or even "blind." Don't avoid discussing a television show or the way your new car looks; these are normal topics for all people.
- Help each other in the process of communicating. If you want your surroundings described, ask. If you want the sighted person to read the road signs, ask.
- Be patient. Many people are nervous talking with people who are visually impaired for fear of offending. Put them at ease in a way that also makes you more comfortable.
- Demonstrate your comfort. When appropriate, let the other person know that you're comfortable with the interaction, verbally or nonverbally.

Summary

1. Eye behavior serves a variety of functions and enables you to reveal and to conceal emotions, to regulate conversation, to change psychological distance, to include and to exclude others, and to help you think.
2. A variety of eye movements have been identified: mutual gaze, one-sided looking, intermittent glancing, survey glance, secretive glance, public stare, gaze aversion, gaze omission, eye roll, and eyebrow flash.
3. Dilated pupils generally signal heightened interest and are frequently used in advertisements.
4. Different cultures teach their members different display rules, the rules that specify what is and what is not appropriate eye behavior.

Key Terms

Supply a definition for each of the following terms. Once you've formulated these "standard" definitions, consider the following ideas for further defining and understanding. Not all will work for all key terms, but some will work for some terms and some will work for others.

- Find a quotation that illustrates the term.
- Provide an example from personal interaction, television, film, novels, or plays.
- Create a short dialogue to illustrate the operation of the key term.
- Locate a research study investigating the key term and report its findings.
- Illustrate the concept nonverbally.
- Find a video that illustrates the key term.
- Find images—photos or graphics, abstract or specific, literal or metaphorical.
- Diagram the concept.
- Explain the negative, what the concept is not.
- State a skill that centers on the concept.

Key Concept	Definition
Oculesics	
Functions of eye movements	
Eye contact	
Eye avoidance	
Pupil dilation	
Civil inattention	
Gaze aversion and gaze omission	

AND IN ADDITION

Using your favorite search engine (in addition, use Google Scholar or the databases in your college library for the more scientific research articles), search for **eye movements**, **pupil dilation**, **eye contact**, **eye avoidance**, **gaze**, or any of the other terms and topics considered in this chapter and add to the chapter contents. Depending on the structure of the course and the facilities available, you may want to post these additions to a course website; to a social media site such as Twitter, Facebook, or Google+; or to a listserv or through e-mail, for example. Here are a few ways in which you might make your addition:

- Write a paragraph that adds to the discussion of a particular concept.
- Provide a new, contradictory, or intercultural example of a concept.
- Create a figure or table to illustrate or organize a particular topic.
- Illustrate with an image or two or a 10- to 15-second video a particular concept of nonverbal behavior.
- Summarize and evaluate the results of a scientific study on a topic relevant to this chapter.
- Summarize and evaluate an online article that focuses on one of the topics considered here.

Chapter 5

Artifactual Messages

CHAPTER TOPICS

- Color Communication
  - Colors and Personality
  - Colors and Culture
- Space Decoration
  - Space Decoration and Person Perceptions
  - Space Decoration and Product Perceptions
  - Space Decoration and Emotional Perceptions
- Clothing
  - Protection
  - Gender, Cultural, and Religious Identification
  - Status
  - Occupation and Group Identification
  - Social Awareness, Social Consciousness
  - Personality and Inner Feelings
  - Cosmetic Clothing
  - Influence
  - Message-Sending Clothing
- Body Adornment
  - Jewelry
  - Hair
  - Body Piercings and Tattoos
- Smell Messages
  - Functions of Smell
  - Smell Phenomena

Summary
Key Terms
And in Addition

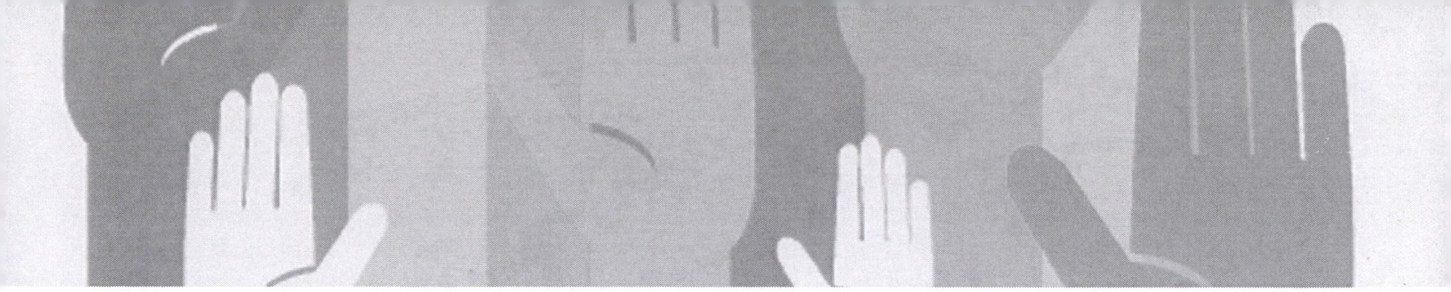

CHAPTER EXERCISES

[Identifying Clothing]
Explaining Color Meanings
Using Colors to Create a Product Image
Identifying Product Placement
Designing a Living Space
Clothing the Superhero
Illustrating the Functions of Clothing
Explaining the Holidays Nonverbally

ON THE JOB

The Power Desk
Clothing Appropriateness
Artifactual Code

POLITENESS IN NONVERBAL COMMUNICATION

Being polite with artifactual messages

IF YOU WANT TO

Dominate/control/lead the conversation
Ace the job interview/make a good impression/be viewed positively

CHAPTER OBJECTIVES

After reading this chapter, you should be able to:

1. Define *artifactual communication.*
2. Explain some of the meanings different colors communicate in different cultures.
3. Identify the several meanings that clothing may communicate.
4. Explain the possible messages that various types of jewelry, hairstyles, and body piercings and tattoos may communicate.
5. Define *olfactory communication* and identify the messages scent may communicate.

BEFORE reading about a variety of artifactual messages, consider the messages clothing might communicate. Assume you're a costume designer for a new movie set in the present time and you need to design clothing to distinguish a variety of characters. How might you use clothing to distinguish such characters as these?

- **Police detective and thief**
- **The president of a company and an intern**
- **Wealthy individual and one who is poverty stricken**

Costume and fashion designers and advertisers, for example, know that most people form impressions of others on the basis of clothing and so clothing becomes an essential element in communicating an image.

Artifactual messages (and clothing is just one of them) are messages conveyed through objects or arrangements of objects made by human hands. Color, the way you decorate your living and work spaces, the clothing or jewelry you wear, and even bodily scents communicate a wide variety of meanings.

COLOR COMMUNICATION

Throughout history, different colors have been symbolic of different meanings. Before reading about color communication, examine your own meanings for different colors with the exercise on the next page.

When you're in debt, you speak of being "in the red"; when you make a profit, you're "in the black." When you're sad, you're "blue"; when you're healthy, you're "in the pink"; when you're covetous, you're "green with envy." To be a coward is to be "yellow," and to be inexperienced is to be "green." When you talk a great deal, you talk "a blue streak"; when you are angry, you "see red." As these clichés reveal, color symbolism abounds in language. Color symbolism varies greatly in different cultures, however, as we'll see in the final section of this chapter.

There is some evidence that colors affect us physiologically. For example, respiration rates increase in the presence of red light and decrease in the presence of blue light. Similarly, eye blinks increase in frequency when eyes are exposed to red light and decrease when exposed to blue. These findings seem consistent with our intuitive feelings that blue is more soothing and red more provocative. At one school, in fact, after the administration changed the classroom walls from orange and white to blue, the students' blood pressure levels decreased and their academic performance improved (Ketcham, 1958; Malandro, Barker, & Barker, 1989).

Colors surely influence our perceptions and behaviors (Kanner, 1989). People's acceptance of a product, for example, is strongly influenced by its package. For example, in one experiment consumers in the United States described the very same coffee taken from a yellow can as weak, from a dark brown can as too strong, from a red can as rich, and from a blue can as mild. Even our acceptance of a person may depend on the colors that person wears. Consider, for example, the comments of one color expert (Kanner, 1989, p. 23): "If you have to pick the wardrobe for your defense lawyer heading into court and choose anything but blue, you deserve to lose the case. . . ." Black is so powerful that it can work against the lawyer with the jury. Brown lacks sufficient authority. Green will probably elicit a negative response.

EXERCISE

EXPLAINING COLOR MEANINGS

In Column 1 are listed seven popular colors. In Column 2 identity the first meanings that come to your mind as you think of the color. You may find it helpful to think of a specific item—say a jacket or smartphone or car. In Column 3 identify the meanings that would be considered opposite to the color, meanings that you would never get from that color. Sharing these meanings with others (especially those representing a variety of different cultures) will likely alert you to the wide variety of meanings color communicates and how different people have different meanings for the same color.

Colors	Color Meanings	Anti/Opposite Meanings
Red	*Cheerful, outgoing*	*Unfriendly, conservative*
Orange		
Green		
Black		
White		
Blue		
Yellow		
Purple		

Colors and Personality

Popular books on nonverbal communication often play up the relationship of color preferences and personality. The popularity of this topic seems, in part, to be based on the intuitive feelings we all have about the relationship between a person's color preferences—in, say, clothing—and their personality. Do outgoing people, for example, wear brighter colors than do introverts? Do conservative people prefer darker and more muted colors than do their more liberal counterparts? Some nonverbal watchers have gone much further and offer detailed personality diagnoses based solely on color preferences. In *The Lüscher Color Test*, for example, you're asked to indicate color likes and dislikes to a variety of colored squares and on the basis of these preferences, a personality profile is obtained.

In his *Color in Your World*, Faber Birren (1963) claims that if you like blue you are probably conservative, deliberate, and introspective. You have your own passions under control and are sensitive to the feelings of others. You're cautious in your communications, and your opinions and beliefs are generally resistant to change. You question everything you do not understand. If, on the other hand, you dislike blue then you are resentful of the success of others and may even take some joy in their failures. You feel unfulfilled in your emotional and intellectual lives. You are erratic and easily become irritated. These diagnoses seem a great deal to derive from a simple liking or disliking for blue.

Little research has confirmed the conclusions connecting color preferences and personality. One major reason seems to be that color preferences are influenced by a variety of factors—early exposure to color, past experiences with colors, occupation, associates, sense of style, personality, and, of course, culture. Another reason is that color preferences change with the times and with fashion trends. In the 1970s kitchen appliances in avocado and harvest gold were favorites; in the 1990s they were hated; and today, they're back.

Colors and Culture

Colors vary greatly in their meanings from one culture to another. To illustrate this cultural variation here are just some of the many meanings that popular colors communicate in a variety of different cultures (Dresser, 1996; Dreyfuss, 1971; Hoft, 1995; Singh & Pereira, 2005; see also www.globalization-group.com/edge/.../color-meanings-by-culture/). As you read this section, you may want to consider your own meanings for these colors and where your meanings came from.

- **Red.** In China red signifies prosperity and rebirth and is used for festive and joyous occasions. In France and the United Kingdom it indicates masculinity. In many African countries it signifies blasphemy or death. And in Japan it symbolizes anger and danger. Red ink, especially among Korean Buddhists, is used only to write a person's name at the time of death or on the anniversary of the person's death; this can create problems when American teachers use red ink to mark homework.
- **Orange.** In the Ukraine it signifies strength, in India it means sacred, in Japan it means courage and love, and in Egypt it's the color of mourning.
- **Green.** In the United States green signifies capitalism, go ahead, and envy; in Ireland patriotism; among some Native Americans femininity; to the Egyptians fertility and strength; and to the Japanese youth and energy.
- **Black.** In Thailand black signifies old age, in parts of Malaysia courage, and in much of Europe death.
- **White.** In Thailand white signifies purity, in many Muslim and Hindu cultures purity and peace, and in Japan and other Asian countries death and mourning.
- **Blue.** In Iran blue signifies something negative, in Ghana joy. Among the Cherokee it signifies defeat, for the Egyptian virtue and truth, and for the Greek national pride.
- **Yellow.** In China yellow signifies wealth and authority, in the United States caution and cowardice, in Egypt happiness and prosperity, and in many countries throughout the world femininity.
- **Purple.** In Latin America purple signifies death, in Europe royalty, in Egypt virtue and faith, in Japan grace and nobility, in China barbarism, and in the United States nobility and bravery.

Interestingly enough, there has been some research on the color red and its relationship to attraction. For example, men, viewing photos of women in different colors, consider the woman in red to be the most attractive (Elliot & Niesta, 2008). And, as reported on the MedGuru website, and for reasons not really clear, women seem to prefer to take red pills, while men prefer pink pills.

One of the often written-about areas of color is the meanings we attribute to different colors (as previewed in the above example). According to one marketing website (www.precisionintermedia.com/color.html), the colors would communicate the following meanings in the United States. You may want to match these up with the ones you selected in the Explaining Color Meanings exercise.

Red: energy, excitement, movement, life
Orange: fun, happiness, warmth, ambition
Green: nature, money, growth, calming
Black: stability, power, authority, somber
White: cleanliness, neutrality, purity, safety
Blue: calm, dependability, loyalty, wisdom
Yellow: happiness, optimism, creative, cowardice
Purple: wealth, sophistication, success

USING COLORS TO CREATE A PRODUCT IMAGE

EXERCISE

To increase your awareness of the ways in which colors are used in influencing your behavior, consider yourself a member of a team charged with the selection of colors for a variety of new products (listen in Column 1). In Column 2 indicate the predominant color (as well as any additional colors) you'd select to create and communicate the desired product image. In Column 3 indicate the specific meanings you'd hope to communicate about this product and perhaps the people who would use or buy this product.

Product	Color(s)	Intended Meanings/Product Image
Expensive/gourmet chocolate chip cookies	*Dark brown w/black and red accents*	*Rich, elegant, tasty*
A mild liquid laxative		
A powerful detergent		
A new line of smartphone covers		
A textbook in psychology		
Pasta sauce in a jar		
An inexpensive but high-style sports car		
Coffee-flavored chewing gum		
An energy drink for women and an energy drink for men		

Of course, it's not important how similar your responses were to those given here. What is important is that you probably felt that some colors are more logically associated with certain feelings than are others.

SPACE DECORATION

The way you decorate your private spaces also communicates. In a sense it's a part of artifactual communication—since it involves the manipulation of items—but it's also a part of space communication as considered here.

Space Decoration and Person Perceptions

The office with the mahogany desk and bookcase set and Oriental rugs communicates your importance and status within the organization, just as the metal desk and bare floors indicate an entry-level employee much farther down in the company hierarchy.

Similarly, people will make inferences about you based on the way you decorate your home. The expensiveness of the furnishings may communicate your status and wealth; their coordination, your sense of style. The magazines on your coffee table may reflect your interests, and the arrangement of chairs around a television set may reveal how important watching television is to you. The contents of bookcases lining the walls reveal the importance of reading in your life. In fact, there is probably little in your home that would not send messages from which others would make inferences about you. Computers, wide-screen televisions, well-equipped kitchens, and oil paintings of great grandparents, for example, all say something about the people who live in a home.

ON THE JOB

The Power Desk

You're joining the company and getting the job of your dreams. You want to be perceived as conscientious, reliable, and most of all, leadership material. You now need to "decorate" your cubicle and your desk. What are some of the artifacts you might use to communicate these messages? What artifacts would you be sure to avoid? (You may want to return to this exercise after reading the section on power in Chapter 10. Or, read it now.)

photo courtesy of Frank C. Tansey

What impressions do you have of the people who would live in such spaces? What specific nonverbal elements might you use in forming your impressions? photo courtesy of Frank C. Tansey

People also will make judgments about your personality on the basis of room decorations. For example, research finds that people will form opinions about your openness to new experiences (distinctive decorating usually communicates this, as would different types of books and magazines and travel souvenirs), conscientiousness, emotional stability, degree of extroversion, and agreeableness. And, not surprisingly, bedrooms prove more revealing than offices (Gosling, Ko, Mannarelli, & Morris, 2002).

And, it's important to realize that the lack of certain items will also communicate something about you. Consider what messages you would get from a home where no television, phone, or books could be seen.

Space Decoration and Product Perceptions

In much the same way that you make judgments about people on the basis of the products they use (jewelry, furs, and name brands from Prada to Old Navy), you also make judgments about products on the basis of the people who use them, a tendency that has spawned huge product placement efforts by major corporations. Product placement refers simply to the placement of a product—for a fee but without any explicit advertising statements—within a scene of a movie or television show to give the product a certain image. The advertiser's hope is that you'll identify with the actor using the product (i.e., you want to be like the character in some way) and that you too will then also buy the product. The actor and the movie give the product an image that the advertiser assumes will help sell the product.

In the 2012 James Bond movie *Skyfall*, for example, Heineken paid $45 million to have Bond drink its beer (*New York Daily News*, November 9, 2012). In addition, Bond wears a Tom Ford suit and an Omega watch while Q uses a Sony Vaio—all very clear to the viewer. Another Bond film, however, holds the record for product placements; the 1997 *Tomorrow Never Dies* earned $100 million for its product placements. The same is true on television; the Cheesecake Factory on *The Big Bang Theory* and McDonald's on *30 Rock* are good examples. Product placement is, of course, nothing new; recall James Bond's Aston Martin in the 1964 movie *Goldfinger* and E.T. eating Reese's Pieces in the 1982 movie *E. T. The Extra-Terrestrial*.

As you no doubt already know, product placement is occurring in television sitcoms and dramas and in feature films with ever increasing frequency. The fact that this type of advertising aims to influence you below the level of conscious awareness raises all sorts of serious ethical issues. Those who favor or defend product placement, such as the American Advertising Federation, argue:

> Product placement is a legitimate source of advertising revenue and is not deceptive. It benefits both content producers and consumers and adds verisimilitude to fictional programming. We oppose proposals that would require simultaneous "pop up" notices of every instance of product placement, believing this would make television unwatchable. We instead believe the current practice of disclosures at the end of the program works well.

Those who oppose product placement argue that it's deceptive because viewers are not aware that it's a paid advertisement. It is subliminal advertising—messages that somehow get communicated without mindfulness or awareness. And, despite the AAF's statement, no one can really read the disclosures at the end of a television program, nor would anyone want to. Furthermore, the enormous profits to be

EXERCISE

IDENTIFYING PRODUCT PLACEMENT

To sensitize you to the many ways in which advertisers try to influence you below the level of conscious awareness—and in effect counteract the influence of product placement— consider this exercise on product placement, another aspect of space decoration. During the next movie you watch—there are lots more in movies than in television shows—identify any product placements you notice and fill in the remaining columns of the accompanying table. The example provided will clarify the parts of this exercise.

Movie: ______________________________. **Year:** _______.

Product	How was the product used? What's the context?	Intended meaning
Burger King hamburger bag	Iron Man *Tony Stark wants an American hamburger before anything else*	*Burger King is the hamburger of choice, especially when you're dying for one*

What specific nonverbals tell you that the man standing is the leader of this group? © 2013, iofoto, Shutterstock, Inc.

IF YOU WANT TO

Dominate/control/lead the conversation (Burgoon & Dunbar, 2006)

- Display status cues, for example, the most expensive and the latest smartphone.
- Maintain direct eye contact with the other person and look at the person more when you're speaking and less when you're listening; this reverses the normal pattern.
- Avoid approval cues.
- Interrupt.
- Take a seat of prominence—at the head of the table, for example.
- Maintain a closer than normal interaction space.
- Ignore turn-requesting cues.
- Speak at a slightly faster rate than normal.
- Take the lead in initiating conversation, in selecting the topic to be discussed.

made from product placement will likely lead to its spread to news shows which will further erode fairness and objectivity.

Regardless of the possible ethical violations, product placement is likely to remain a part of movies and television; it is too lucrative a market for it to disappear anytime soon.

Space Decoration and Emotional Perceptions

In addition to space decoration in influencing the perceptions of a person or product, some would argue that space decoration also influences your emotional state. This assumption is at the heart of feng shui (pronounced *fung schway*, a term that combines the Chinese terms for *wind* and *water*), a principle of design gaining in popularity, which holds that living in a harmonious relationship with your surroundings will provide you with both psychological and physical benefits. When you arrange your surroundings (or even design a building or layout for a town) in accordance with feng shui, it produces energy and well-being, along with personal and professional success. When you don't, when you violate the principles, you're more likely to suffer both physical and psychological problems. Rodika Tchi provides a great tour of the feng shui bedroom at http://video.about.com/fengshui/Feng-Shui-Bedroom-Tips.htm and notes, among other things, that a bedroom in accordance with feng shui principles will have:

- The bed positioned so that you can see the door but not be aligned with it
- Nightstands (matching or not) on both sides of the bed
- No sharp angles pointing at you
- No electrical appliances
- A substantial headboard

EXERCISE

DESIGNING A LIVING SPACE

Increase your awareness of how space decoration figures into the impressions that you form of others on the basis of their space decoration and that others form of you on the basis of your space decoration. Your task here is to design two living rooms to emphasize the differences between the two occupants. In Column 1 are listed some elements you'd want to consider as you design your two rooms. In Column 2 indicate what items you'd use to decorate the living room of the Jones couple (who have everything and more) and in Column 3 indicate what items you'd use for the Nonjones (who have virtually nothing).

Living Room Element	The Jones Family/Rich as can be	The Nonjones Family/ Poor but not poverty stricken
The room itself	*Large space with high ceilings and large crown moldings*	*Small room with low ceilings, no moldings*
Colors		
Major furnishings		
Small furnishings		
Technology		
Ceiling, walls, and floor		

CLOTHING

You very likely make inferences about other people on the basis of their clothing and similarly, people make inferences about who you are partly on the basis of how you dress. Whether accurate or not, these inferences (yours and theirs) will affect what you think of others and what others think of you. And, of course, these inferences will influence the communication that takes place between you. Consider just one example: College students were found to perceive an instructor dressed informally as friendly, fair, enthusiastic, and flexible and the very same instructor dressed formally as prepared, knowledgeable, and organized (Malandro et al., 1989). However, we know from our own experience that clothing communicates a wide variety of messages. Below are just a few.

Protection

Perhaps the most obvious function of clothing to come to mind is that of protection. You wear a rain coat to protect you from the rain, heavy clothes to protect you from the cold, long sleeves to protect you from the sun's rays, and sneakers to protect your feet when jogging. You also use clothing for protection when you wear a helmet when riding a bike or motorcycle, a hair net or cap to protect your hair from getting caught in machinery, or rubber gloves to protect yourself from potential germs.

Gender, Cultural, and Religious Identification

When seeing someone from a distance you probably judge their sex on the basis of their clothing. Men and women generally—though clearly not always—wear different clothes and the clothes have become identified with one gender or another. The style and cut of the clothes, the colors, the design, and the fabrics are among the defining differences.

Similarly, some clothing identifies the individual's culture. In the United States most people dress similarly but there are notable exceptions. For example, Hasidic

What functions do the clothing of this motorcyclist serve? In what ways are they the same (or different) from the functions served by the clothing you're wearing now?

Jews dress in a way that identifies them as members of this cultural group. In most large cities you'll also see clothing that identifies, for example, the Indian or African culture of the wearer. The Amish likewise wear clothing that shows their cultural identification.

A somewhat similar type of identification is the clothing worn by many clergy and members of religious orders. Catholic priests, for example, wear Roman collars that identify them as priests. Many Jewish rabbis dress in ways that identify their religious affiliation.

Status

Throughout history, clothes have been used to signal social status. In ancient Egypt, for example, only those of high status were allowed to wear sandals. And in Elizabethan England the colors and fabrics that a woman was allowed to wear were determined by her social position. Only the queen, for example, was allowed to wear silk and purple. Today clothing still communicates status meanings, though perhaps in more subtle ways. Designer styling (and often visible labels just in case someone doesn't realize the clothes are Armani or Prada), expensive materials, up-to-date styles, and the "right clothes for the right occasion" all communicate high social status. The wearer clearly has money and probably a good job (and therefore a good education as well). Off-the-rack, all-purpose, and synthetics, on the other hand, communicate lower status. Similarly, low status is often (and there are probably lots of exceptions) communicated by trendiness whereas higher social status is signaled by a more conservative wardrobe.

IF YOU WANT TO

Ace the job interview/make a good impression/be viewed positively

- Hide any tattoos and body piercings you can.
- Sit upright; avoid slouching (slouching does not make you appear comfortable or at ease, as some think; it makes you appear disinterested).
- Avoid self-touching adaptors.
- Avoid touching items on the desk of the interviewer—it will make you appear uncomfortable.
- Give positive listening cues; nod your head, smile, respond with "minimal response cues" ("yes," "I see," "right").
- Dress conservatively—one step above the normal clothing of workers in that division of the company.
- Avoid purposeless movements, shifting, touching your hair.
- Avoid interrupting and overly long periods of silence.
- Maintain eye contact but avoid staring.

Along with status generally comes power. And so the higher-status person is likely to be accorded greater power than the low-status person. And along with this power generally comes certain privileges—the right to invade the space of another, the right to interrupt, the right to have the last word, and so on. Of course, there are many exceptions to this but generally status equals power. The general is not only of higher status than the captain but is also more powerful; the general can tell the captain what to do, but the captain can't tell the general what to do.

Occupation and Group Identification

Clothing often signals occupation. Obvious examples are uniforms worn by police offers, doctors and nurses, military personnel, the clergy, and sanitation workers. However, there are other kinds of uniforms, although we don't call them "uniforms," that serve much the same function, namely to identify the occupation of the individual. For example, in some colleges, male faculty members are the only ones to wear jackets and ties. The famous "IBM uniform" of dark suit and white shirt or blouse is another example. And even when the clothing does not indicate a specific occupation, it often signals a type of occupation. Thus, a woman in a dark suit with heels is likely an executive rather than a cashier. A man going to work in jeans and a sweatshirt is more likely a laborer than a banker.

Clothing also helps you to announce your group affiliation. Gang colors and style of dress are probably the clearest example. You might wear a sweatshirt with a baseball team's name on it to signify that you're a Yankees fan, for example, and a member of the group of sports enthusiasts who support this particular team.

Social Awareness, Social Consciousness

Clothing also communicates your social awareness of the unwritten (but often vigorously defended) rules of dress. So, for example, you most likely wouldn't show up at a formal dinner in sneakers and jeans; you wouldn't show up at a funeral wearing shorts. If you did, you'd be showing a lack of an awareness of the rules of society.

What impressions are you likely to form of this woman based solely on what you see in this photo?

EXERCISE

CLOTHING THE SUPERHERO

You know someone is a superhero, in large part, by the hero's clothing. Consider how clothing or some outward symbol helps define who the superhero is and what powers the hero has. As you complete this, reflect on your own clothing and the impressions that others derive from the way you dress.

Superhero and superhero's powers	What type of clothing does the superhero wear?	What meaning is communicated by the clothing?
The Flash	*Red suit with lightning bolt*	*Red signifies strength; the lightning bolt symbolizes both speed and power*

Consider, for example, the messages sent by a social worker in a poor neighborhood who wears expensive clothing and jewelry.

Personality and Inner Feelings

Because clothing is such a personal affair, it reflects your inner feelings probably more than most people realize. When you're happy, you probably wear clothes that are brighter than you'd select if you felt depressed or sad. Similarly, when you're in good spirits, you probably give much great attention to the way you dress than when you are depressed. Clothing also influences the way you feel. For example, if you dress in dark, poor fitting, and generally unattractive clothing, you would probably feel more negatively than if you had dressed in bright, well-fitting, and attractive clothes. One reason for this connection between clothing and feeling is that people react to you on the basis of the way you dress; when you look pleasant, others are more likely to respond positively toward you. And this positive feedback is likely to make you feel better.

This close connection between clothing and the way you feel is probably the motivating factors behind the frequently offered suggestion to dress professionally even when you're being interviewed on the phone (even without Skype). Dressing professionally, the assumptions goes, will help you to act more professionally and that professional demeanor will come through in your phone communication.

Cosmetic Clothing

One of the major functions of clothing is to make you look better, to enhance your good features and minimize your less attractive features. And so women may wear certain kinds of bras or girdles to give them a better shape. Or, someone may wear dark stockings to cover varicose veins. Some may wear long-sleeved shirts because they think their arms are too skinny or too flabby. Similarly, they may avoid wearing shorts even in the warm weather to cover up unattractive legs.

Influence

Closely related to the cosmetic function is that of influence. Many people, perhaps most if not all, want to have power, want to feel in control of the situation they are in. Part of that influence is achieved through clothing. And so you may dress very conservatively to influence the interviewer at a conservative law firm or you may dress to show off your best features in the hope of meeting a potential romantic partner. Perhaps the most obvious case of clothing serving an influencing function is the uniform. The same man or woman in casual dress and then in a police officer's uniform is going to have a great deal more influence in the uniform. Military organizations have uniforms that not only influence those who don't have such uniforms but also communicate who has influence over whom—the general's star communicates an influence over those with just stripes or bars, the sergeants and the captains, for example.

ON THE JOB

Clothing Appropriateness

A colleague you've become friendly with dresses totally inappropriately. And, you're convinced—as are other colleagues—is consistently overlooked for promotion. It's as if the clothing is locking your colleague into a low-level position. You want to say something but are afraid you'll offend your colleague. What are some of the things you can do to help your colleague and yet not be offensive?

Message-Sending Clothing

Another class of clothing that needs to be mentioned is the clothing that contains messages of various sorts, often called legible clothing. It's clothing that can be literally read. In some instances it communicates status as already noted; the Gucci or Louis Vuitton logos on your luggage communicate your financial status. Many designers and manufacturers have their names integrated into the design of the clothing: DKNY, Calvin Klein, L.L. Bean, Gap, and Old Navy are just a few examples. At the same time that you're paying extra to buy the brand names, you're also forced to advertise for them. Your Bulls or Pirates sweatshirt communicates your interest in sports and your favorite team.

T-shirts and sweatshirts are especially popular as message senders. One study surveyed 600 male and female students as to the type of T-shirt messages they preferred (Sayre, 1992). Four kinds of messages were cited most often:

Examine your own wardrobe for legible clothing. What meanings, in general, do you wish your clothing (legible and otherwise) to communicate? © 2013, Callahan, Shutterstock, Inc.

- **Affiliation messages**, such as a club or school name, communicate that you're part of a large group.
- **Trophy names**, such as those of a high-status concert or perhaps a ski lodge, say that you were in the right place at the right time.

- **Metaphorical expressions**, such as pictures of rock groups or famous athletes, reveal that you're a part of the current trend.
- **Personal messages**, such as states of beliefs or philosophies, tell others that you're willing to express your beliefs publically whether they be political (Vote Democrat) or social (Save the Whales, No Fracking) messages.

EXERCISE

ILLUSTRATING THE FUNCTIONS OF CLOTHING

To increase awareness of your own clothing and its many meanings, consider the clothing functions listed in Column 1 and just discussed. Examine the clothing you're wearing now or go through your wardrobe and identify at least one object of clothing that serves (primarily) the functions noted in Column 2 (most clothing will serve more than one function). In Column 3 indicate an article of clothing you would like to have (dream big!) and the meanings you'd like it to communicate.

Clothing Functions	Article of Clothing You Own/Meanings	Article of Clothing You'd Like to Own/Meanings
Protection	*Overcoat/practical, stylish*	*Air force jacket/youthful/ stylish*
Gender, cultural, and religious identification		
Status		
Occupation and group identification		
Social awareness, social consciousness		
Personality and inner feelings		
Cosmetic clothing		
Influence		
Message-sending clothing		

BODY ADORNMENT

The ways in which you adorn your body also communicates. Here we need only mention a few such ways: jewelry, hair, and body piercings and tattoos.

Jewelry

Your jewelry, of course, communicates messages about you. Wedding and engagement rings are obvious examples that communicate specific messages. And now divorce rings are becoming popular, signifying that the wearer is divorced and most likely looking for a romantic relationship. High school and college rings and political buttons likewise communicate messages. If you wear a Rolex watch or large precious stones, others are likely to infer that you are rich. Men who wear earrings will be judged differently from men who don't.

Another aspect of jewelry is that it often identifies one's religious affiliation: the cross for Christians, the star and crescent for Muslims, and the Star of David for Jews, for example. Similarly, label pins often identify one's religion but also one's social affiliation with say a fraternity or lodge.

At times eyeglasses and often sunglasses are used as jewelry—or at least as part jewelry. Some glasses, of course, are used to help people see better. However, the vast number of eyeglass styles available (along with their designer prices) is evidence of their importance in our culture as jewelry. Often people have several sets to match different outfits or occasions.

Another type of jewelry being widely promoted as I write this is the charm bracelet made up of charms that have meaning for the wearer and perhaps for the person giving the bracelet. This type of bracelet—as the advertisements make clear—is an excellent example of "free information"—information about yourself that you display and that enables others to initiate communication with you more easily. And so, for example, you might say, "I see you have a tennis racket on your bracelet. Do you play?"

Jewelry often serves tie signs, as noted in Chapter 1. The wedding band and engagement ring are perfect examples of tie signs; they indicate a very specific type of relationship. Similarly, the necklace with a religious symbol serves as a tie sign between the wearer and a particular religious belief.

Hair

The way you wear your hair says something about who you are—from a concern about being up to date, to a desire to shock, to perhaps a lack of interest in appearance. Not surprisingly, men with shoulder-length hair or mullets, to take just one example, will likely be judged as less conservative than those with shorter hair. And in a study of male baldness, participants rated a man with a full head of hair as younger and more dominant, masculine, and dynamic than the same man without hair (Butler, Pryor, & Grieder, 1998). This, of course, is exactly what the ads for hair replacement are promising—you'll look more dominant, more masculine, and more dynamic.

It's interesting to note that in years long past, head shaving was often imposed as a punishment for women for some transgression; it was a visual sign for all to see and it lasted a long time. Some women today shave their heads as a fashion statement or as a response to alopecia areata, a condition in which the body develops an allergic reaction against hair and rather than have just blotches of hair, the entire head is shaved.

Recent studies show that men with shaved heads may actually have an interpersonal advantage. For example, men with shaved heads—when compared with men with hair—were perceived as more dominant, more masculine, taller, and to have greater leadership potential (Mannes, 2012).

Body Piercings and Tattoos

Body piercings and tattoos communicate too. Nose and nipple rings and tongue and belly-button jewelry send a variety of messages. Although people wearing such jewelry may wish to communicate positive meanings, those interpreting the messages of body piercings seem to infer that wearers are communicating an unwillingness to conform to social norms and a willingness to take greater risks than those without such piercings (Forbes, 2001). It's worth noting that in a study of employers' perceptions, employers rated and ranked job applicants with eyebrow piercings significantly lower than those without such piercings (Acor, 2001). Furthermore, health care providers sometimes see tattoos and piercings as signs of such undesirable traits as impulsiveness, unpredictability, and a tendency toward being reckless or violent (Rapsa & Cusack, 1990; Smith, 2003).

Tattoos—whether temporary or permanent—likewise communicate a variety of messages, often the name of a loved one or some symbol of allegiance or affiliation. In this they serve the function of tie signs; they indicate permanently your relationship with another person. Tattoos also communicate to the wearers themselves. For example, tattooed students see themselves (and perhaps others do as well) as more adventurous, creative, individualistic, and risk prone than those without tattoos (Drews, Allison, & Probst, 2000).

Although body piercings and tattoos are becoming more accepted generally, business experts continue to note the negative effects in terms of getting a job and suggest hiding them during job interviews (Ingegneri, 2008; Varenik, 2010).

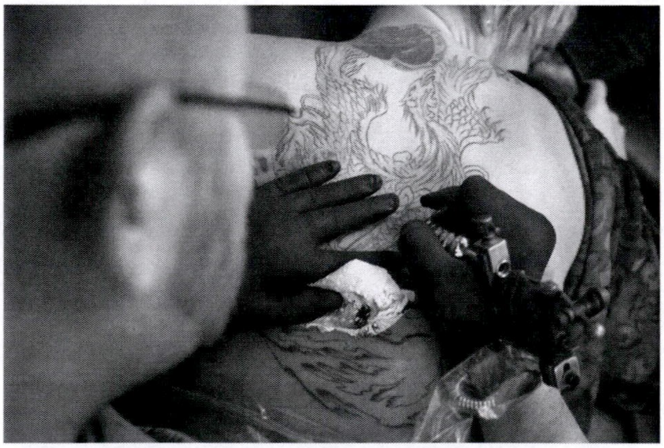

How do you feel about tattoos? Do you view them differently depending on the age and sex of the person?

POLITENESS IN NONVERBAL COMMUNICATION

Being polite with artifactual messages

- Avoid offensive, overly strong scents; test your scent strength on a friend.
- Avoid legible clothing that might prove offensive to some people.
- Use color with cultural awareness, especially at cultural rituals such as marriages, funerals, and business meetings.

SMELL MESSAGES

Smell is a peculiar aspect of nonverbal communication and is discussed in widely different ways by different writers. Here, because the emphasis is on using scents (e.g., perfume or cologne), it's grouped with artifactual communication. But recognize that body odor also communicates, and perhaps that part of smell is best thought of as a form of body communication.

Some smells may make you feel better. When the smells are pleasant, you feel better about yourself; when the smells are unpleasant, you feel less good about yourself. In fact, research finds that smells can influence your body's chemistry, which, in turn, influences your emotional state. For example, the smell of chocolate results in the reduction of theta brain waves, which produces a sense of relaxation and a reduced level of attention (Martin, 1998). In this connection take a look at the video at www.nlm.nih.gov/medicineplus/ency/article/003052.htm. It's a video on smell and smell impairment—a condition you may not have known existed. It may actually be a symptom of a nervous system disorder. And, of course, smell impairment deprives you of an important defensive sense—smelling the oven that you left on or the bread overtoasting, for example.

Olfactory communication, or olfactics, is extremely important in a wide variety of situations. Scientists estimate that you can smell some 10,000 different odors (Angier, 1995). There is some, though not conclusive, evidence showing that the smell of lemon contributes to a perception of health, the smells of lavender and eucalyptus seem to increase alertness, and the smell of rose oil seems to reduce blood pressure. Findings such as these have contributed to the growth of aromatherapy and to the profession of aromatherapist.

Functions of Smell

Some of the most important messages scent seems to communicate involve attraction, taste, memory, and identification.

- **To attract others.** In many animal species, the female gives off a scent that draws males, often from far distances, and thus ensures the continuation of the species. Humans, too, emit sexual attractants called sex pheromones, body secretions that arouse sexual desire (Kluger, 2008). Humans, of course, supplement pheromones with perfumes, colognes, after-shave lotions, powders, and the like to further enhance attractiveness and sexuality and, at the same time, to cover up any unpleasant body odor. And if we can judge from the advertisements and the space devoted to such products, men seem to be catching up with women in the number and diversity of such products. Women, research finds, prefer the scent of men who bear a close genetic similarity to themselves—a finding that may account in part for our attraction to people much like ourselves (Ober et al., 1997; Wade, 2002). And the Associated Press (June 23, 2012) reports that pheromone-sniffing parties, in which members submit a slept-in T-shirt to be smelled by others in an attempt to meet eligible singles, have been held in New York City and Los Angeles and are planned for other cities as well. The idea is that singles bring a slept-in T-shirt, coded for identification purposes, to a party. Others smell it and if they like the smell, they get together. It's seen by some as an alternative to online dating.

- **To aid taste.** Without smell, taste would be severely impaired. For example, it would be extremely difficult to taste the difference between a raw potato and an apple without the sense of smell. Street vendors selling hot dogs, sausages, and similar foods are aided greatly by the smells that stimulate the appetites of passersby.
- **To aid memory.** Smell is a powerful memory aid; you can often recall situations from months and even years ago when you happen upon a similar smell. One reason smell can so effectively recall a previous situation is that it's often associated with significant emotional experiences (Malandro et al., 1989; Rubin, Groth, & Goldsmith, 1984).
- **To create an image.** Smell is often used to create an image or an identity for a product. Advertisers and manufacturers spend millions of dollars each year creating scents for cleaning products and toothpastes, for example. These scents have nothing to do with the products' cleaning power. Instead, they function solely to help create product images or identities. There is also evidence that we can identify specific significant others by smell. For example, infants find their mothers' breasts through smell, mothers can identify their newborns solely through smell, and children are able to identify the T-shirts of their brothers and sisters solely on the basis of smell (Angier, 1995; Porter & Moore, 1981). One researcher goes so far as to advise: "If your man's odor reminds you of Dad or your brother, you may want genetic tests before trying to conceive a child" (Furlow, 1996, p. 41).

Smell Phenomena

As with most sensations, we can discuss smell in terms of a variety of psychophysiological concepts. Here we consider briefly smell blindness, smell adaption, and smell memory (Malandro et al., 1989) as well as smell overload, smell discrimination, and smell satiation.

Smell Blindness

People vary greatly in their ability to identify particular smells and to distinguish among smells. Those who are unable to detect smells that others detect readily suffer from what is called smell blindness. Actually, everyone suffers from smell blindness to some extent. There is no known remedy to correct this problem other than addressing physiological problems that may be at the cause of this type of blindness.

Smell Adaption

In much the same way that our eyes gradually adapt to the darkness of a movie house, we can also adapt to smells. Smell adaption, then, refers to the phenomena by which you gradually lose the distinctiveness of a particular smell through repeated association with it. This phenomenon has a positive and a negative side to it. Thus, for example, if placed in a situation in which there is an unpleasant odor, you will soon adapt to it and soon cease to be disturbed by its unpleasantness. The speed with which you adapt, of course, would depend in part on the strength of the smell; mild smells will be adapted to more quickly than stronger smells. On the other hand, we also quickly adapt to the pleasant smell of cologne (or pizza, if you prefer) and thus soon lose the pleasant sensation you feel upon the first encounter.

Smell Memory

Smell memory refers to your ability to recall previous situations from the particular smells with which it was associated. For example, you recall meeting the love of your life, when you smell a particular cologne, for example.

Smell Overload

On the analogy of information overload, smell overload refers to the phenomenon by which your sense of smell is bombarded by an exceptionally large number or extremely powerful odors. Sometimes you may actually lose (temporarily) your ability to discriminate among or even detect odors you would normally have no difficulty identifying. You have probably experienced smell overload when walking through a large cosmetics display.

Smell Discrimination

It's widely reported that people can smell hundreds, possibly thousands, of smells. For example, spouses can identify each other solely through the sense of smell. We learn this smell association for our mate—but also for our dog and for a variety of other people, animals, and things—through frequent association. However, you probably could not describe these smells in any way that would be meaningful to another person.

Smell Satiation

Smell satiation can be most easily appreciated by looking briefly at its analogue, semantic satiation. When you repeat a word over and over again, that word temporarily loses part of its

ON THE JOB

Artifactual Code

Your office manager has charged you with developing an Artifactual Code of Conduct for your office complex of approximately 40 people, both men and women, both new hires and people who have been with the firm for 20 or 30 years. Some of the problems your supervisor wants addressed are the desk clutter with "cutesy" items that look unprofessional, especially when clients come to the office; the strong perfume and cologne that some employees wear; and the unprofessional-looking clothing that a few employees wear, especially on casual Fridays. What are some of the things you might include in this code?

meaning. Try saying a word like "elephant" over and over again and it will seem to have lost some of its meaning, almost as if it were nonsense syllables or in a foreign language. Smell satiation, which occurs in a similar way, occurs when you lose your ability to smell or your ability to identify a smell because of your too-frequent exposure to it. This phenomenon is found easily in the heavy smoker who has lost the ability to smell the smoke on his or her clothing, though everyone else can smell it with no problem.

EXERCISE

EXPLAINING THE HOLIDAYS NONVERBALLY

To increase your understanding of the role of nonverbal communication in defining holidays (religious or secular), select a holiday (any one you'd like) and indicate how it is represented nonverbally. In Column 1 some likely categories are provided, but don't let these restrict your thinking. Use any others you feel may be revealing. In Column 2 indicate the specific colors, objects, audio, etc. that are used, how they are used, and where they are used. Not all holidays will be distinctive in terms of all these categories, so just fill in those parts of the table that are relevant to the holiday you select. In Column 3 indicate the meanings communicated by the use of these nonverbal elements. Because many holidays are cultural or religious celebrations, it would be an added bonus if you shared your responses with those who have affiliations (or holidays) very different from your own. In this way you'll see the really broad range of nonverbal communication and also learn more about holidays you might not have heard of previously.

Holiday: ____.

Nonverbal Element	Uses, How and Where	Meanings Communicated
Colors. Does the holiday have dominant colors? How are they used? What meanings are the colors intended to communicate?	*[Halloween] Orange and black*	*Pumpkins, jack o'lanterns, autumn;* *bats, cats, witches, vampires, night*
Objects. Are specific objects (e.g., statues, paintings, books) associated with the holiday? What meanings are they intended to communicate?		
Audio. Is music or speaking a part of the holiday?		
Clothing. Is special clothing required of those who officiate? Of those who attend the holiday rites?		
Smell. Are specific smells associated with the holiday? Time. Do the holidays have a fixed date(s) or time during which the holiday rite is held?		

Summary

1. Artifactual communication concerns the messages communicated through objects or arrangements of objects made by human hands.
2. Colors communicate a variety of meanings, which vary greatly from one culture to another.
3. The way a space is decorated communicates a variety of messages about the owner's style and interests.
4. Clothing serves several important functions and communicates messages of status, occupation, social awareness and social consciousness, inner feelings, and specific messages of identification.
5. Jewelry, hairstyle, and body piercings and tattoos likely communicate different meanings, which vary greatly with the social group and the culture as a whole.
6. Smell messages may attract others, aid taste, aid memory, and create an image and may be viewed in terms of such phenomena as smell blindness, adaption, memory, overload, discrimination, and satiation.

Key Terms

Supply a definition for each of the following terms. Once you've formulated these "standard" definitions, consider the following ideas for further defining and understanding. Not all will work for all key terms, but some will work for some terms and some will work for others.

- Find a quotation that illustrates the term.
- Provide an example from personal interaction, television, film, novels, or plays.
- Create a short dialogue to illustrate the operation of the key term.
- Locate a research study investigating the key term and report its findings.
- Illustrate the concept nonverbally.
- Find a video that illustrates the key term.
- Find images—photos or graphics, abstract or specific, literal or metaphorical.
- Diagram the concept.
- Explain the negative, what the concept is not.
- State a skill that centers on the concept.

Key Concept	Definition
Artifactual communication	
Color communication	
Space decoration	
Feng shui	
Clothing	
Status	
Occupation	
Social awareness, social consciousness	
Inner feelings	
Message clothing	
Body adornment	
Jewelry	
Hair	
Body piercings and tattoos	
Olfactory communication	
Olfactics	

AND IN ADDITION

Using your favorite search engine (in addition, use Google Scholar or the databases in your college library for the more scientific research articles), search for **color**, **space decoration**, **clothing**, **body adornmen**t, or any of the other terms and topics considered in this chapter and add to the chapter contents. Depending on the structure of the course and the facilities available, you may want to post these additions to a course website; to a social media site such as Twitter, Facebook, or Google+; or to a listserv or through e-mail, for example. Here are a few ways in which you might make your addition:

- Write a paragraph that adds to the discussion of a particular concept.
- Provide a new, contradictory, or intercultural example of a concept.
- Create a figure or table to illustrate or organize a particular topic.
- Illustrate with an image or two or a 10- to 15-second video a particular concept of nonverbal behavior.
- Summarize and evaluate the results of a scientific study on a topic relevant to this chapter.
- Summarize and evaluate an online article that focuses on one of the topics considered here.

Chapter 6

Space Messages

photo courtesy of Frank C. Tansey

CHAPTER TOPICS

- Proxemic Distances
- Theories of Space
  - Protection Theory
  - Equilibrium Theory
  - Expectancy Violations Theory
- Crowding and Privacy
  - Crowding
  - Privacy
- Territoriality
  - Types of Territories
  - Territorial Encroachment
  - Reactions to Encroachment
  - Territorial Markers

Summary

Key Terms

And in Addition

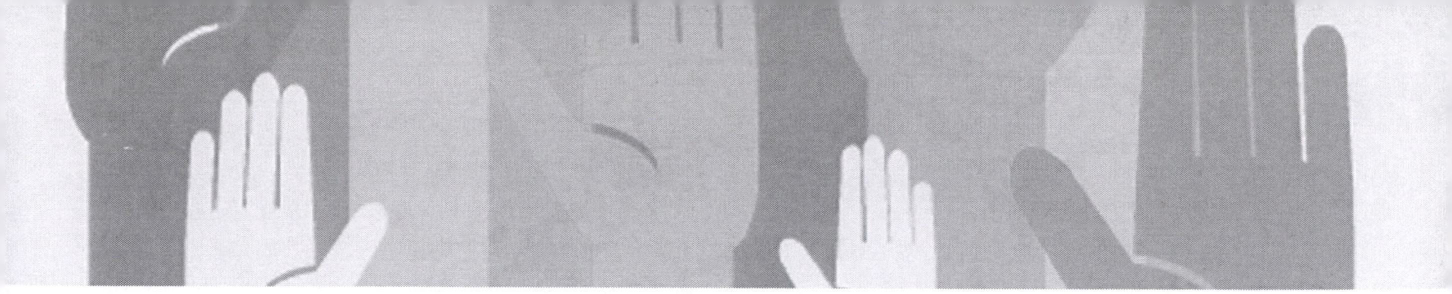

CHAPTER EXERCISES

[Identifying Your Own Use of Space]
Illustrating Proxemic Distances
Creating Seating Arrangements
Identifying the Factors Contributing to Crowding
Describing Your Privacy Settings
Selecting Seats at the Company Meeting
Examining Your Territories
Using Markers Effectively

ON THE JOB

Close Talking
Space Hog
Space Invasion

POLITENESS IN NONVERBAL COMMUNICATION

Being polite with spatial messages

IF YOU WANT TO

Appear approachable/friendly/open
Appear likeable/attractive/friendly

CHAPTER OBJECTIVES

After reading this chapter, you should be able to:

1. Define the four proxemic distances and give examples of the interactions that occur at each one.
2. Explain the assumptions and predictions of three theories of space.
3. Define *crowding* and *density* and the three factors that contribute to crowding discomfort.
4. Define *territoriality* and distinguish among primary, secondary, and public territories.
5. Explain territorial encroachment, its types, and the ways in which people react to it.
6. Define *markers* and distinguish among central, boundary, and earmarkers.

BEFORE reading about space communication, consider your own use of space. How far away would you stand (measure this in inches and feet) in each of the following situations?

- **Discussing secrets with a best friend.**
- **Asking a stranger for directions.**
- **Interviewing the president of your college.**
- **Presenting a public speech in a classroom.**

As you can see, you maintain different distances depending on the specific communication situation and the relationship between you and the other person, one of the topics we explore in this chapter.

Although we seldom think of it, space is an especially important factor in nonverbal communication. In this chapter we explore the wide variety of messages that space communicates, beginning with a consideration of proxemic distances.

PROXEMIC DISTANCES

Anthropologist Edward T. Hall (1959, 1963, 1966), who pioneered the study of spatial communication, called the study of space communication **proxemics**. We can sample this broad area by looking at proxemic distances, crowding and privacy, and territoriality.

Hall (1959, 1966) distinguishes four distances that define types of relationships between people; each distance communicates specific kinds of messages. As you read about these distances, realize that the specific distances that you maintain between yourself and other individuals depend on a wide variety of factors (Burgoon et al., 2010). Among the most significant factors are gender (women in same-sex dyads sit and stand closer to each other than do men, people approach women more closely than they approach men); age (people maintain closer distances with similarly aged others than they do with those much older or much younger); and personality (introverts and highly anxious people maintain greater distances than do extroverts). Not surprisingly, you'll tend to maintain shorter distances with people you're familiar with than with strangers, and with people you like than with those whom you don't like.

ON THE JOB

Close Talking

One of your colleagues maintains an abnormally short distance between you when talking. This annoys you and makes you uncomfortable. What are some of the things you might do to minimize (perhaps even solve) this problem?

At an **intimate distance**, ranging from actually touching to 18 inches, the presence of the other individual is unmistakable. Each person experiences the sound, smell, and feel of the other's breath. You use intimate distance for lovemaking and wrestling, for comforting and protecting. This distance is so short that most people do not consider it proper in public.

Personal distance constitutes the protective "bubble" that defines your personal space, which measures from 18 inches to 4 feet. This imaginary bubble keeps you protected and untouched by others. You can still hold or grasp another person at this distance—but only by extending your arms—allowing you to take certain individuals such as loved ones into your protective bubble. At the outer limit of personal distance, you can touch another person only if both of you extend your arms.

At **social distance**, ranging from 4 to 12 feet, you lose the visual detail you have at personal distance. You conduct impersonal business and interact at a social gathering at this social distance. The more distance you maintain in your interactions, the more formal they appear. Many people in executive and management positions place their desks so that they are assured of at least this distance from employees.

Public distance, measuring from 12 to 25 feet or more, protects you. At this distance you could take defensive action if threatened. On a public bus or train, for example, you might keep at least this distance from a drunk. Although you lose fine details of the face and eyes at this distance, you are still close enough to see what is happening. These four distances are summarized in Table 6.1.

On the basis of your own observations of conversations (which surely must number in the thousands), what gender and cultural differences have you seen?

TABLE 6.1 Relationships and Proxemic Distances

These four proxemic distances can be further divided into close and far phases. Note that the far phase of one level (say, personal) blends into the close phase of the next level (social). Do your relationships also blend into one another? Or are your personal relationships totally separate from your social relationships?

Relationship	Distance	
Intimate Relationship	Intimate Distance 0 ____________ Close phase	 18 inches Far phase
Personal Relationship	Personal Distance 1½ ____________ Close phase	 4 feet Far phase
Social Relationship	Social Distance 4 ____________ Close phase	 12 feet Far phase
Public Relationship	Public Distance 12 ____________ Close phase	 25+ feet Far phase

IF YOU WANT TO

Appear **approachable/friendly/open**

- Maintain a relatively close distance between you and the other person.
- Maintain an open posture; be careful of postures that tell people to stay away.
- Smile.
- Make eye contact and hold it for a bit longer than normal.
- Avoid adaptors that will focus attention on you rather than the other person.

EXERCISE

ILLUSTRATING PROXEMIC DISTANCES

Clarify and personalize the four proxemic distances listed in Column 1 by first providing a verbal definition for each of the proxemic distances (in Column 2) and in Column 3 provide a visual example—paste images of them, clip them, or describe them.

Proxemic Distance	Verbal Description	Visual Example
Intimate distance	*Touching to about a foot and a half.*	*A couple walking down the street with their arms around each other.*
Personal distance		
Social distance		
Public distance		

THEORIES OF SPACE

A number of researchers in nonverbal communication have offered explanations as to why people maintain the distances they do. Prominent among these theories are protection theory, equilibrium theory, and expectancy violations theory—rather complex names for rather simple and interesting explanations.

Protection Theory

Protection theory holds that you establish a body buffer zone around yourself as protection against unwanted touching or attack (Hall, 1966). When you feel that you may be attacked, your body buffer zone increases, you want (and need) more space around you. For example, if you found yourself in a dangerous neighborhood at night, your body buffer zone would probably expand well beyond what it could be if you were in familiar and safe surroundings. If someone entered this buffer zone, you would probably feel threatened and seek to expand that distance by walking faster or crossing the street.

On the other hand, when you are feeling secure and protected, your buffer zone becomes much smaller. For example, if you are with a group of close friends and feel secure, your buffer zone would shrink and you may welcome the close distances and mutual touching.

Equilibrium Theory

Equilibrium theory holds that intimacy and distance vary together. The greater the intimacy, the closer the distance; the lower the intimacy, the greater the distance. This theory says that you maintain close distances with those with whom you have close interpersonal relationships and that you maintain greater distances with those with whom you do not have close relationships (Argyle & Dean, 1965).

At times, of course, your interpersonal distance does not accurately reflect your level of intimacy. When this happens you make adjustments. For example, let us say that you have an intimate relationship with someone but for some reason you are separated—perhaps because you could not get concert or theater seats next to each other. When this happens you would probably try to preserve your psychological closeness by, for example, looking in each other's directions, maintaining frequent eye contact, and smiling at each other. More frequently, however, you are forced into close distances with someone with whom you are not intimate (or may even dislike), for example, on a crowded bus or perhaps in the dentist's chair. In these situations, you also compensate, but this time you seek to make the psychological distance greater. You therefore might avoid eye contact and turn in an opposite direction. In the dentist's chair you probably close your eyes to increase your psychological distance and separation. If you are seated to the right of a stranger, you might cross your legs and turn your torso to the left.

Expectancy Violations Theory

Expectancy violations theory explains what happens when you increase or decrease the distance between yourself and another person in an interpersonal interaction (Burgoon et al., 2010). Each culture has certain norms for the distance people are expected to maintain in their conversations. And, of course, each person has certain idiosyncrasies. Together, these determine expected distance. If you violate the expected distance to a great extent (small violations most often go unnoticed), the relationship itself comes into focus; the other person begins to turn attention away from the topic of conversation to you and to your relationship with him or her.

If this other person perceives you positively—for example, if you're a high-status person or you're particularly attractive—then you'll be perceived even more positively if you violate the expected distance. If, on the other hand, you're perceived negatively and you violate the norm, you'll be perceived even more negatively.

IF YOU WANT TO

Appear **likeable/attractive/friendly**

- Reduce the normal space between you and the other person.
- Give positive listening cues, smiles, and head nods to show your interest in the person.
- Give cues that you like the other person, for example, smile (and that person will likely reciprocate).
- Smile as an expression of concern for the other person.
- Mirror the other's behavior just a bit; accommodate to the style of the other.
- Avoid fidgeting.

EXERCISE

CREATING SEATING ARRANGEMENTS

In order to appreciate the influence that seating arrangements have on communication, visualize yourself charged with the task of creating seating arrangements for five different functions. You have four square (4 × 4) tables and 20 chairs (four of which are arm chairs) in a large empty room to work with. In Column 1 are listed five communication functions. In Column 2 draw a picture of how you would arrange the table and chairs for each of the functions. Also note where you'll position the extra chairs and tables. In Column 3 indicate the design or arrangement principle you followed in arranging the tables and chairs.

Communication Purposes	Tables and Chairs Arrangement	Principle Governing Your Arrangement Decision
To hold a brainstorming session—six people getting together to generate ideas	*Visual of two tables next to each other (creating a rectangle) with one chair at each end and two chairs on each side (all without arms); remaining tables chairs against the wall.*	*To make all participants equal; to make for easy face-to-face interaction.*
To teach a class of 12 students the events leading up to the Civil War		
To serve dinner to 16 people		
To encourage 20 people to get to know one another		
To arrange for a speaker to address an audience of 15		

CROWDING AND PRIVACY

One of the most important dimensions of space is the degree of crowding or privacy that we experience. We seem to have needs that extend in both directions: we need to be one of the crowd, to feel a part of the happenings around us, but at the same time, we also have a need for privacy, to be removed from the crowd.

Crowding is a psychological perception that there are too many people around and we become conscious of restrictions on our spatial freedom. Crowding is clearly subjective. Two people in the exact same situation may develop very different perceptions: one may feel crowded and restricted and the other may feel totally free.

Density, on the other hand, is a term used to refer objectively to the number of people in a particular area of space. Thus, when we speak of the density of different cities we are referring to the number of people within each of the cities per square mile, say. When we speak of the crowding of different cities we are referring to the sensation that people feel restricted by other people.

Density may be positive or negative. If you go to the latest "in"-club, you probably want it to be pretty dense; the more people the better. So here high density is positive. On the other hand, if you go to the library to study, you may want it to be relatively sparse on the theory that the fewer the people, the fewer the possible distractions. So here high density would be negative.

Crowding

The nature of crowding can be further clarified by explaining the factors that nonverbal researchers have identified as the major contributors to a person's discomfort, to a person's perception of being crowded: surveillance, behavioral constraint, and stimulus control (Scheflen, 1964, 1974).

- **Surveillance.** The television drama *Person of Interest* gives an especially clear picture of surveillance as it is and as it could be used to keep track of people. Today, one of the most hotly debated topics is online surveillance—programs

In what types of situations are you most likely to feel crowded? How do you deal with this feeling? © 2013, Christian Mueller, Shutterstock, Inc.

keeping track of your Internet activity—and how this compromises your right to privacy. The cards you carry from retail stores likewise keep track of your buying—what you buy, how much you spend, where and when you spend it, and a host of other information that can help them sell you more goods. When you feel you are being watched, particularly by strangers, you may feel crowded. Visualize yourself on a relatively empty subway car while someone from across the aisle keeps staring at you. Although you are not physically crowded, you're likely to feel crowded psychologically. Their eyes intrude on your personal space, you feel crowded and perhaps annoyed or frightened.

- **Behavioral constraint.** You're more likely to feel crowded when your movements are restricted. For example, you're not likely to feel overly crowded on a plane that takes off and lands on schedule. However, your feelings of being crowded are likely to increase considerably if your plane is delayed several hours and you're not allowed off the plane. Prisoners are likely to feel crowded not only because of density—there are clearly too many inmates per square foot of space—but because of restrictions on their movements.
- **Sensory overload.** When the stimuli around you (visual, auditory, olfactory) become greater than you're comfortable with, you might well develop a case of stimulus overload. We know that animals, when placed in high-density environments, will engage in bizarre behaviors. For example, they become aggressive, will attack those with whom they would normally live peacefully in less dense conditions, and will no longer care for and feed their young. Similarly, in prisons of high density, there is greater aggression and a greater number of deaths. The inmates in high-density conditions also have higher blood pressure than those living in less dense conditions.

EXERCISE

IDENTIFYING THE FACTORS CONTRIBUTING TO CROWDING

To appreciate your own sense of and reactions to crowding, three factors that contribute to a sense of being crowded, and discussed above, are listed in Column 1. In Column 2 explain in your own words the nature of the factors and in Column 3 indicate how each of the factors impacts on your life.

Factors that Contribute to Crowding Discomfort	Explanation of Factor	Impact on Your Life
Surveillance	*The sense or feeling that other people are watching you*	*Increases cautiousness, descreases any tendency to violate the law*
Behavioral constraint		
Stimulus overload		

Privacy

In one sense privacy may be seen as the other end of the spectrum. Privacy is perceived when you are free to move about as you wish, free from the eyes of others, and when your senses can easily deal with the stimuli around you. Put differently, privacy may be seen as freedom from surveillance, behavioral constraint, and stimulus overload.

Another way of looking at privacy is to examine the four dimensions of privacy (Burgoon, 1982; Burgoon et al., 2010). These dimensions will make clear how you maintain and regulate your own privacy.

- **Informational privacy** refers to the extent to which you give others access to your personal information. To some you give total access (or nearly so) and to others you don't. For example, you may give such information as your income or net worth to some people but not to others. As you can appreciate, this is a type of privacy that is becoming more and more difficult to maintain as our personal data get stored and shared.
- **Physical privacy** refers to the extent to which you make yourself accessible to others. For example, you probably allow certain people to touch you or to hold your hand or to kiss you and there are no doubt those to whom you do not allow such accessibility.
- **Social privacy** refers to the extent to which you make yourself available to others for social interaction. For example, you probably make your home phone number available to certain people but not to others. Similarly, you may allow certain people to drop by your apartment or house without calling but not allow others to do the same.

DESCRIBING YOUR PRIVACY SETTINGS

EXERCISE

To heighten your awareness of the ways in which primacy operates in your life, examine the four types of privacy discussed above and listed in Column 1. In Column 2 explain how this type of privacy operates in your own life. In Column 3 provide examples of people with whom you are likely to maintain little privacy (you give them full access to yourself) and people with whom you would likely maintain great privacy (you give them little access to yourself).

Privacy Type	Privacy in Life	Low- and High-Privacy People
Informational	*I'm generally a private person and so generally don't allow most people to know me as well as perhaps I should*	*Low: Spouse with whom I'm totally open in all things* *High: Strangers, largely because I'm shy and also somewhat self-conscious*
Physical		
Social		
Psychological		

- **Psychological privacy** refers to the extent to which you control the thoughts and emotions you reveal to others—without interference—and that others reveal to you. For example, it's likely that you can be totally (or nearly so) open with certain people but not with others. Similarly, you may make yourself available to listen to the thoughts and feelings of some but not others.

TERRITORIALITY

Another type of communication having to do with space is territoriality, a possessive reaction to an area or to particular objects.

Types of Territories

Various nonverbal researchers have identified different types of territories. Here we consider five types, combining these insights (Altman, 1975; Lyman & Scott, 1967).

Primary Territories

Primary territories are areas that you might call your own; these areas are your exclusive preserves. Primary territories might include your room, apartment, or house; your desk, office, or briefcase. It's interesting to note that when you operate in your own primary territory, you have an interpersonal advantage, often called the *home field advantage*. In their own home or office, people take on a kind of leadership role: They initiate conversations, fill in silences, assume relaxed and comfortable postures, and maintain their positions with greater conviction. Because the territorial owner is dominant, you stand a better chance of getting your raise approved, your point accepted, or a contract resolved in your favor if you're in your own territory (your office, your home) rather than in someone else's (your supervisor's office, for example) (Marsh, 1988).

Your primary territory communicates a great deal about your status, power, and dominance. Generally, the size and location of a person's territory communicates a person's status and power (Burgoon et al., 2010). A large apartment or office in midtown Manhattan or downtown Tokyo, for example, is extremely high-status territory; the cost of the territory restricts it to those who have lots of money (and are likely to be of high status and powerful).

How would you describe your ideal territory, say your house or apartment or your office? Try to identify at least five characteristics of the territory that contribute to its being "ideal." © 2013, ChameleonsEye, Shutterstock, Inc.

Secondary Territories

Secondary territories are areas that don't belong to you but which you have occupied and with which you're associated. They might include your usual table in the cafeteria, your regular seat in the classroom, or your neighborhood turf. You feel a definite ownership-like reaction to these territories and react negatively when "outsiders" attempt to occupy "your" territory.

EXERCISE

SELECTING SEATS AT THE COMPANY MEETING

To illustrate the importance of seating to achieving a variety of specific purposes, examine the graphics of a meeting table with 12 chairs, one of which is occupied by the boss (given in Column 2). In Column 1 are listed purposes you want your seating position to communicate or faciliate. In Column 2 indicate where you would sit and in Column 3 indicate your reason for selecting the seat you chose.

Communication Purposes	Seat Selection	Reasoning Behind Your Seat Selection
You want to ingratiate yourself with your boss.		*Physical proximity usually leads to increased liking.*
You aren't prepared and want to be ignored.		
You want to challenge a proposal by your boss that's scheduled to come up for a vote.		
You want to get to know better the person seated at number 7.		

The placement of towels on a public beach is a great example of claiming a private territory (at least temporarily) within a public one. Can you identify other examples?

Public Territories

Public territories are areas that are open to all people; they may be owned by some person or organization, but they are used by everyone. They are places such as movie houses, restaurants, and shopping malls. However, even though these areas are public, you might nevertheless stake out a specific area for your exclusive but temporary use. So, for example, you lay out your beach towel, radio, and cooler in a way that communicates your "ownership" of this space. Friends may enter but strangers may not.

At times, there are private territories within public ones. And so, for example, the company parking lot is in a way public, but certain spaces may be reserved for the president or CEO. Similarly, some spaces are reserved for the handicapped and are public only for those with handicaps.

ON THE JOB

SPACE HOG

At the company cafeteria one of your coworkers repeatedly surrounds himself with folders and papers, taking up two or three extra seats—ideal seats by the window, as it turns out. It's not that he uses these materials; he just brings them to prevent others from sitting next to him. What are some of the things you might do to resolve this issue?

Interactional Territories

These territories are areas where people congregate or simply where they're talking together. And so, **interactional territories** are often dinner tables where members interact. Or an interactional territory might be a fraternity or sorority house where members gather to interact. Or it might be a bar, lounge, arcade, water cooler, or college cafeteria. When such interactions are ongoing these areas are generally restricted in the sense that another person would probably not walk through the group. And, depending on the composition of the group, another person would not be free to join in the conversation. For example, if a group of managers were talking in the hallway, it would be considered inappropriate for an intern or associate to join in the interaction. On the other hand, if it were a group of peers with whom you often interact, then joining-in would definitely be an option.

Body Territories

Body territory refers to the area around you that you need to perform your functions. Sometimes that area is small—if you're using your laptop, making a call on your cell, or reading a book, your body territory extends not much beyond one or two feet from your actual physical self. On the other hand, if you were up at bat in baseball or ready to tee-off on a golf course, your body territory would be much larger. People who are upset or agitated often need a larger body territory than people who feel calm and friendly. Generally, research finds that women are regarded as having smaller body territories—people will approach women more closely than they'll approach men. Similarly, women will approach others more closely than will men.

EXERCISE

EXAMINING YOUR TERRITORIES

Increase your awareness of your own territories and your sense of territoriality by examining the five types of territories listed in Column 1 and discussed above. In Column 2 explain the nature of the territory and in Column 3 provide an example of each type of territory in your own life and its importance to you (use a 10-point scale with 10 = extremely important and 1 = extremely unimportant).

Territory Types	Explanation	Example and Importance
Primary	*My exclusive preserve; no one is allowed to use it but me.*	*My desk, largely because I don't want anything upset or moved; I know where everything is. And I don't want others to see what I'm working on.* *Importance rating __10___*
Secondary		Importance rating _____
Public		Importance rating _____
Interactional		Importance rating _____
Body		Importance rating _____

POLITENESS IN NONVERBAL COMMUNICATION

Being polite with spatial messages

- Give others space; everyone needs space.
- Compliment others' space; it's a part of the person's personality.
- Respect others' markers; they're there for a reason—to keep you out.
- Don't intrude into others' interactional space without an invitation, even your colleague's cubicle.

Territorial Encroachment

On occasion your territory may be encroached upon by others. Not surprisingly, researchers have identified the most important type of territorial encroachments (Lyman & Scott, 1967; Richmond et al., 2012).

- **Violation**. In violation there is unwarranted use of another's territory, as when you enter another's office or home without permission or go through your e-mail files. It may also refer to using someone's "regular chair" or seat on a couch—as often parodied on *The Big Bang Theory*.
- **Invasion**. In invasion you enter the territory of another and by your invasion actually change the meaning of that territory. For example, the parent who suddenly comes home during a teen party (invading the territory) will actually change the meaning of the current interaction, in this case the party. Similarly, if a supervisor enters a meeting of the office staff, this invasion would change the situation—perhaps what is talked about or how things are said. Often, as you can imagine, the invader is more powerful than the person whose territory is invaded.
- **Contamination**. In contamination you render the territory impure as when, for example, someone smokes a smelly cigar in a windowless room. The room is contaminated. In this case, we have a physical contamination. There is also psychological contamination, which is a person's perception of the territory being impure. For example, if someone dies in a bed, members of the family might not want to use the bed again.

Reactions to Encroachment

Generally, you'd resist encroachment. And you'd resist this on the basis of your answers to such questions as these (compliments of Knapp & Hall, 2010):

- **Who violated your territory?** You'd probably react very different depending on whether this is a friend or foe, whether this is someone you regularly allow to violate your territory (and don't even consider it a violation) or whether this is someone from whom you keep your distance. If you're an inmate in a prison, you'd likely tolerate (willingly or not) violation from the warden or the guards but not, say, from a fellow inmate.

- **What's the reason for the violation?** If there's a good reason, then, again, you'd not be offended and hence not react negatively. If there is not a good reason, then you'd likely resent it and perhaps plan a response.
- **What type of territory was violated?** If someone just sat in your normally occupied chair, then it probably would be no cause for alarm or reaction (unless you're Sheldon from *The Big Bang Theory*). If it were your private Google+ or Facebook profile, you might resent it and take steps to prevent this from happening again.

Have you used any of these four reactions to territorial invasion? Have others used any of these in response to your invasion of their territory? © 2013, romakoma, Shutterstock, Inc.

When someone does enter your territory, you'd likely react in a number of ways. Four ways are commonly identified (Lyman & Scott, 1967):

- **Withdrawal**. One option is to simply withdraw—for example, take another seat, leave the office, or move to another neighborhood or country.
- **Turf defense**. Another choice is to defend your space. You can say "this is my seat" or start a war. Here you attempt to eject the invader from your territory by verbal threat or physical force.
- **Insulation**. This reaction involves insulating yourself by, say, building a barrier between yourself and those who would encroach upon your space. For example, you might build a fence to separate your house from the annoying neighbors or you might place a jacket on the seat next to you to make it difficult for anyone to encroach on your territory.
- **Linguistic collusion**. Another reaction is to speak in a language or jargon that the invaders do not understand and so you exclude them from the interpersonal interaction.

Territorial Markers

Like animals, humans mark both their primary and secondary territories to signal ownership. Humans use three types of markers: central, boundary, and earmarkers (Goffman, 1971).

ON THE JOB

SPACE INVASION

One of your colleagues continually invades your cubicle space, moves the papers you had on a chair to your already crowded desk, sits down, and, day after day, tells you the most inane things that happened on the way to work. What are some of your options for stopping this behavior? What might you say? What might you do?

- **Central markers** are items you place in a territory to reserve it for you—for example, a drink at the bar, books on your desk, or a sweater over a library chair.
- **Boundary markers** serve to divide your territory from that of others. In the supermarket checkout line, the bar placed between your groceries and those of the person behind you is a boundary marker, as are fences, armrests that separate your chair from those on either side, and the contours of the molded plastic seats on a bus. Workplace cubicles are also boundary markers—dividing the territory between one worker and another. Office doors, in general, and office doors with signs (e.g., *Keep Out* or *Authorized Personnel Only*), in particular, would also be examples. Extreme examples are doors that require entrance codes, iris scans, and thumbprint identification.

- **Earmarkers**—a term taken from the practice of branding animals on their ears—are identifying marks that indicate your possession of a territory or object. Trademarks, nameplates, and initials on a shirt or attaché case are all examples of earmarkers.

Markers are also important in giving you a feeling of belonging. For example, one study found that students who marked their college dorm rooms by displaying personal items stayed in school longer than did those who didn't personalize their spaces (Marsh, 1988).

Like animals, humans use territory to signal their status. For example, the size and location of your territory (your home or office, say) indicates something about your status. Status is also signaled by the unwritten law governing the right of invasion. Higher-status individuals have a "right" to invade the territory of lower-status people, but the reverse is not true. The boss of a large company, for example, can barge into the office of a junior executive, but the reverse would be unthinkable. Similarly, a teacher may invade a student's personal space by looking over her or his shoulder as the student writes, but the student cannot do the same to the teacher.

EXERCISE

USING MARKERS EFFECTIVELY

Understanding the way markers work will contribute to your more effective use of them yourself and to your greater sensitivity in responding to the markers of others. In Column 1 are listed the three main kinds of markers just discussed. In Column 2 provide at least one specific example of each marker that you've encountered in the last day or so. In Column 3 indicate the purposes that each of these markers served.

Types of Markers	Specific Examples	Purposes Served
Central markers	*Customer put her pocketbook on the counter seat next to her at the diner*	*She probably didn't want anyone sitting next to her and wanted her pocketbook in plain sight*
Boundary markers		
Earmarkers		

Summary

1. Proxemics is the study of spatial communication.
2. Four major proxemic distances, which correspond to the types of relationships we have, are identified: intimate, personal, social, and public.
3. Protection, equilibrium, and expectancy violation theories explain how spatial communication works.
4. Crowding is a psychological perception that there are too many people around you; density is an objective measure of the number of people in a particular space.
5. Three factors contribute to a feeling of being crowded: surveillance, behavioral constraint, and stimulus control.
6. Privacy refers to a sense of being free to move about as you wish, free from the eyes of others, and when your senses can easily deal with the stimuli around you.
7. Four types of privacy may be distinguished: informational, physical, social, and psychological.
8. Territoriality is a possessive or ownership-like reaction to an area of space. Three types of territories are generally identified: primary, secondary, and public.
9. Territorial encroachment can occur through violation of another's territory, invasion of the space, or contamination of the space.
10. Withdrawal, turf defense, insulation, and linguistic collusion are the popular reactions to resist encroachment.
11. Markers reserve a territory for a particular person and may be central, boundary, or earmarkers.

Key Terms

Supply a definition for each of the following terms. Once you've formulated these "standard" definitions, consider the following ideas for further defining and understanding. Not all will work for all key terms, but some will work for some terms and some will work for others.

- Find a quotation that illustrates the term.
- Provide an example from personal interaction, television, film, novels, or plays.
- Create a short dialogue to illustrate the operation of the key term.
- Locate a research study investigating the key term and report its findings.
- Illustrate the concept nonverbally.
- Find a video that illustrates the key term.
- Find images—photos or graphics, abstract or specific, literal or metaphorical.
- Diagram the concept.
- Explain the negative, what the concept is not.
- State a skill that centers on the concept.

Key Concept	Definition
Proxemic distances	
Protection theory	
Equilibrium theory	
Expectancy violations theory	
Crowding	
Surveillance	
Behavioral constraint	
Stimulus overload	
Privacy	
Territoriality	
Primary territories	
Secondary territories	
Public territories	
Interactional territories	
Body territories	
Territorial encroachment	
Reactions to encroachment	
Markers	

AND IN ADDITION

Using your favorite search engine (in addition, use Google Scholar or the databases in your college library for the more scientific research articles), search for proxemics, crowding, privacy, territoriality, markers, surveillance, territorial encroachment, or any of the other terms and topics considered in this chapter and add to the chapter contents. Depending on the structure of the course and the facilities available, you may want to post these additions to a course website; to a social media site such as Twitter, Facebook, or Google+; or to a listserv or through e-mail, for example. Here are a few ways in which you might make your addition:

- Write a paragraph that adds to the discussion of a particular concept.
- Provide a new, contradictory, or intercultural example of a concept.
- Create a figure or table to illustrate or organize a particular topic.
- Illustrate with an image or two or a 10- to 15-second video a particular concept of nonverbal behavior.
- Summarize and evaluate the results of a scientific study on a topic relevant to this chapter.
- Summarize and evaluate an online article that focuses on one of the topics considered here.

Chapter 7

Touch Communication

CHAPTER TOPICS

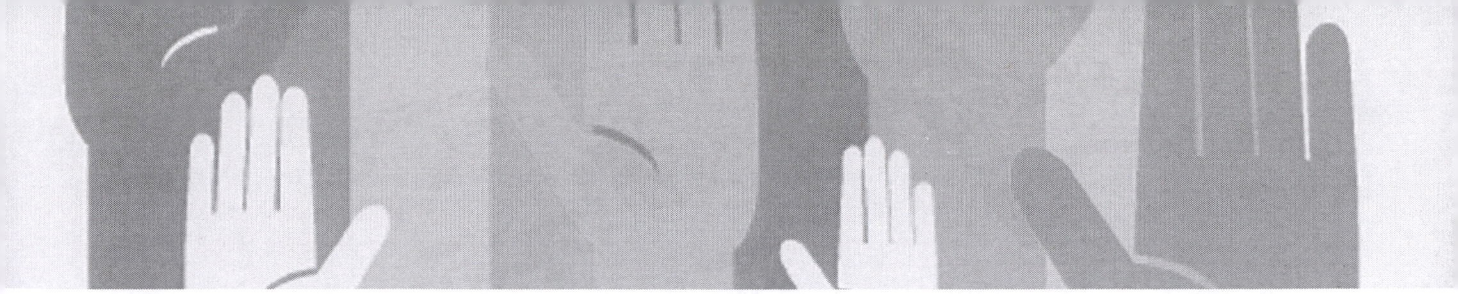

CHAPTER EXERCISES

[Explaining Who Touches Whom]
Shaking Hands
Identifying the Meanings of Touch
[Recognizing the 14 Touch Tie Signs]
Relationships and Touching

ON THE JOB

Shake or Hug
Too Much Touching

POLITENESS IN NONVERBAL COMMUNICATION

Being polite with touch messages

IF YOU WANT TO

Show **rapport/similarity/understanding**
Apologize/gain forgiveness/lessen a bad impression

CHAPTER OBJECTIVES

After reading this chapter, you should be able to:

1. Define five meanings that touch communicates.
2. Explain the nature of touch avoidance and touch deprivation.
3. Define *tie signs* and give examples of touch tie signs.
4. Explain the major influences on touching behavior.

BEFORE reading about touch messages, consider who would touch whom in the following dyads:

- **General and private**
- **Patient and therapist**
- **Nurse and doctor**
- **Manager and trainee**
- **Teacher and student**
- **Prisoner and warden**

Most likely you said that the person doing the touching would be the general, therapist, doctor, manager, teacher, and warden rather than the other way around. And your choices were likely based on the status differences between the individuals; the higher-status person initiates touch. Status, as we'll see, is one of the influences on our touching behavior.

Touch communication, or tactile communication, is perhaps the most primitive form of nonverbal communication (Montagu, 1971). Touch develops before the other senses; a child is stimulated by touch even in the womb. Soon after birth, the child is fondled, caressed, patted, and stroked. In turn, the child explores its world through touch and quickly learns to communicate a variety of meanings through touch.

THE MEANINGS OF TOUCH

Researchers in the field of **haptics**, or the study of touch communication, have identified the major meanings of touch (Jones & Yarbrough, 1985). Here are five of the most important:

- **Emotional communication.** Touch may communicate positive emotions such as support, appreciation, inclusion, sexual interest or intent, and affection (Matsumoto & Hwang, 2013a). When you hug someone in greeting or when you put your arm around someone's shoulder, you're likely touching to express positive emotions, to say you like them, to express warmth and supportiveness. Touch, however, can also communicate such emotions as anger, fear, sadness, and disgust (Hertenstein, Holmes, McCullough, & Keltner, 2009).

How would you describe the touching in this photo? What meanings do these touching communicate to you?

IF YOU WANT TO

Show **rapport/similarity/understanding**

- Touch the other person's hand if appropriate.
- Smile genuinely; people can tell the difference.
- Mirror the other's behavior a bit. Too much mirroring may appear as if you're making fun of the other person.
- Use direct body orientation.
- Avoid crossing your legs or arms.
- Maintain moderate eye contact.
- Lean forward.

- **Playfulness**. Touch often communicates playfulness. Sometimes this playful touching is affectionate, when, for example, you'd "punch" someone in the arm as if to say "good job." Playful touching may also be more aggressive, as when you push someone as if to say "you've got to be kidding."
- **Control**. Touch may also control or direct the behaviors, attitudes, or feelings of another person. To get attention, for example, you may touch a person as if to say "look at me" or "look over here." Or you may control an elderly person's movements to help him or her get on a bus or out of a car.
- **Task-related touching**. Task touching occurs while you are performing some function—for example, removing a speck of dust from another person's face or helping someone out of a car. You'd engage in task-related touching if, for example, you were showing someone how to grasp a football or how to swing a golf club.
- **Ritual touching.** Ritual touching centers on greetings and departures as in hugging, kissing, putting your arm around another's shoulder when greeting or saying farewell, or shaking hands to say hello or good-bye.

One of the most important forms of touching is the handshake—at least in the United States. This nonverbal ritual follows rather precise rules and can be explained in a series of six steps:

- Make eye contact at the beginning and maintain it throughout the handshake. Avoid looking away from the person or down at the floor or at your shaking hand.
- Smile and otherwise signal positiveness. Avoid appearing static or negative.
- Extend your entire right hand. Avoid extending just your fingers or your left hand.
- Grasp the other person's hand firmly but without so much pressure that it would be uncomfortable. Avoid giving the appearance that you really don't want to shake hands but you're making a gesture to be polite.

EXERCISE

SHAKING HANDS

Before reading about the handshake, get a clearer idea of your own handshaking behavior and especially of the impressions you form about people based on the way they shake hands. In Column 1 are listed a few types of handshakes. Assume you're meeting the handshaker for the first time and, in Column 2, record the first impression you would form of this person from the handshake. Of course, in reality you form impressions based on the total person—not just the handshake—but, for this exercise, try to focus attention on the handshake itself. In Column 3 state the theory or assumption you used in forming your first impression.

Handshakes	First Impressions	Theory you used to form your impression
The three-finger shake; person extends three fingers for you to grab	*Uninterested in meeting me*	*People who are interested in the other person make substantial contact; those who don't, don't*
Strong but not overwhelming, pumps three times, and releases		
The wet-fish shake; extends totally lifeless hand		
Shakes your hand and then covers the clasped hand with the other hand		
Extremely powerful handshake, squeezing your hand until it hurts and holding it for an overly long time		

- Pump three times; a handshake in the United States lasts about 3–4 seconds. In other cultures, it might be shorter or, more often, longer. Avoid giving the person a "dead fish." Be careful that the other person's pumping doesn't lead you to withdraw your own pumping. Don't pump much more than three times.
- Release grasp while still maintaining eye contact. Avoid holding the grasp for too long a time or releasing too early.

When someone deviates drastically from this "normal" ritual, you may form a variety of negative or positive impressions of them, as you probably did in the earlier exercise.

The handshake is not universal, of course. Ritual greetings (of which the handshake is one) vary from culture to culture. In Muslim cultures people hug same-sex people but not the opposite sex. In Latin America, South America, and the Mediterranean, people are more likely to hug (and perhaps kiss on the cheek) than are northern Europeans, Asians, and many from the United States. Asians are more

How would you distinguish the handshake from the fist bump or the high-five? In what situations might the fist bump or the high-five be more appropriate than the handshake? © 2013, Stephen Coburn, Shutterstock, Inc.

reluctant to extend their hands and more often bow, with lower bows required when people of lower status meet someone of higher status, for example, an intern meeting a company executive or a private meeting a general.

As you can imagine, such cultural differences may create intercultural difficulties and misunderstandings. For example, if you shake hands in a culture that hugs and kisses, you may appear standoffish and as unwilling to be close. In contrast, if you hug and kiss in a culture that is used to shaking hands, you may seem presumptuous and overly friendly. The best advice here seems to be to watch what the people of the culture you're in do and try to do likewise. And don't get upset if members of other cultures "violate" your own culture's rituals. After all, one ritual is no more logical or right than any other; they're all arbitrary.

IDENTIFYING THE MEANINGS OF TOUCH

EXERCISE

To increase your own awareness of touch, consider the five functions of touch discussed above and identified in Column 1. For each function, supply an example that you've observed in others (face-to-face or on television, in movies, etc.) in Column 2 and a personal example of touching in which you touched others or others touched you in Column 3.

Touch Meanings	Observed Example	Personal Example
To express positive feelings	*Neighbor hugged his son after he fell off the bike.*	*I slapped (gently) my friend's shoulder as if to say "well done" when he aced the final.*
To play		
To control		
To participate in some ritual		
To perform some task		

TOUCH AND COMPLIANCE

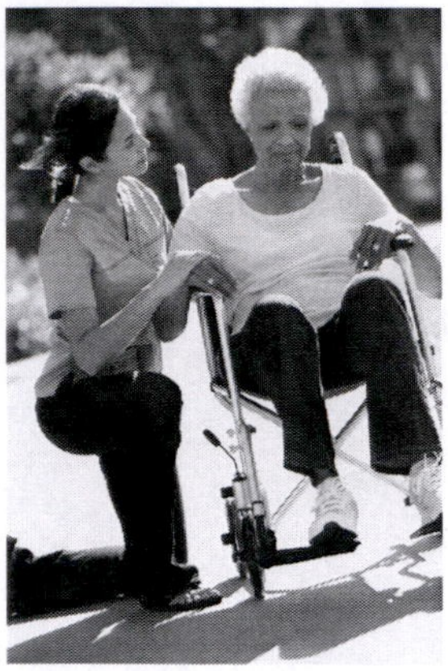

Can you identify other benefits of touching?

A great deal of research has been directed at the connection between touch and compliance, influence, or persuasion (Guéguen & Fischer-Lokou, 2003). For example, one nonverbal researcher found that when people were asked to fill out a questionnaire those who were touched for 1–2 seconds on the forearm complied with the researchers' request to complete the questionnaire significantly more often than those who had not been touched, regardless of whether they noticed being touched or not (Guéguen, 2002). In another study a woman asked 368 female smokers to give her a cigarette. Again, there was significantly higher compliance when the smoker was touched (Joule & Guéguen, 2007).

These are minor requests and you might ask would this work with requests that are more involved. It seems to. For example, in one study 53 men and 67 women were asked to look after a large and excited dog for 10 minutes while the owner went into a store that didn't allow dogs. Half the subjects were touched during the request while half were not touched. Fifty-five percent of those who were touched complied with this request but only 35 percent of those who weren't touched complied (Guéguen & Fischer-Lokou, 2002).

And, in a study with more practical implications, patients were either touched or not touched as the health care worker asked them to promise that they would take their medication as prescribed. Not surprisingly, those who were touched complied more closely with the prescription than those who were not touched (Guéguen & Vion, 2009). And, in a widely cited study, servers in a restaurant who touched the customers on the hand received larger tips than those who didn't touch (Crusco & Wetzel, 1984).

A related question here concerns the evaluation of the person who touches. In a clever experiment, the researchers had car salesmen touch or not touch potential buyers while they were discussing the car. Later the would-be buyers were asked to evaluate the salesmen. Those who touched were evaluated more positively than those who didn't touch (Erceau & Guéguen, 2007).

TIE SIGNS

In earlier chapters, tie signs were introduced. These are the nonverbal expressions that indicate you have a relationship with the other person. Because so many of these tie signs involve touching, this more complete discussion was reserved for this chapter on touch (Goffman, 1971; Morris, 1977).

Tie signs operate on at least three levels. On the *intrapersonal level* tie signs reinforce your perceptions of your relationship. On the *interpersonal level* tie signs communicate to each other your relationship; they reinforce your relationship status to both of you. On the *public level* tie signs communicate your relationship status to the outside world.

Nonverbal researchers have identified seven major functions tie signs serve (Afifi & Johnson, 2005):

- **Information management.** For example, you want to demonstrate your affection and its reciprocation and so you walk hand in hand or with one person's arms around the other.

- **Interaction regulation.** For example, you want to bring someone into your group conversation and so you hold eye contact and nod.
- **Intimacy expression.** For example, you want to show the other person that you like/love him or her and so you look longingly into each other eyes and perhaps kiss.
- **Social control.** For example, you want to persuade the other person or control that person's movements and so you might gently move the individual in the direction you want him or her to focus.
- **Relationship presentation**. For example, you want to publically announce that you're exclusive and so you display a variety of loving behaviors, such as hugging, holding hands, kissing.
- **Self presentation.** For example, you want to enhance your self-image with third parties and so you make sure you're seen "tied to" a prominent or A-list person.
- **Affect management.** For example, you want to express your feelings and moods to the other person and so you gently touch another's face or brush away another's tears.

At the same time, the particular tie sign you use will say something about the stage of your relationship. For example, if you shake hands in greeting someone, it's a pretty good sign that the relationship is a casual or business one. It would certainly not be an intimate relationship; you don't shake hands with a long-time lover. Also, the hug that would be expected if the relationship were an intimate one would be totally inappropriate between a supervisor and a first-year associate.

When you walk down the street holding hands, you communicate to anyone who sees you that you're a couple. Gay male and lesbian couples now hold hands in public, announcing their couplehood; but, in the not too distant past, such couples likely walked together without any visual tie signs.

Anthropologist and nonverbal theorist Desmond Morris (1977) identified 14 tie signs communicated by touch. You should be able to visualize each of these from the titles Morris gave them. As you read down the list, consider the meanings you might get from observing these touch tie signs in others.

1. The handshake
2. The body guide; you guide the other's body to focus his or her attention on something; a kind of pointing but with the other's body
3. The pat (on the shoulder, say)
4. The arm link
5. The shoulder embrace
6. The full embrace
7. The hand in hand
8. The waist embrace
9. The kiss
10. The hand to head
11. The head to head
12. The caress
13. The body support
14. The mock attack

© 2013, Blend Images, Shutterstock, Inc.

© AISPIX by Image Source

What meanings do the touching in these photos communicate to you as an observer? What meanings do you think are communicated to the people in the photos?

© 2013, R Ashrafov, Shutterstock, Inc.

ON THE JOB

Shake or Hug

At your company, which you just recently joined, you notice that when people greet each other some of them shake hands and some of them hug. You're not quite sure of the rule they follow—it almost seems random. What are some of the things you can do to make these greetings more comfortable and not shake hands when you're supposed to hug and not hug when you're supposed to shake hands?

There are also anti–tie signs, signs that communicate that you do not have a relationship. The best example seems to be the divorce ring, which announces that not only are you divorced but that you're in the market for a new relationship. Other prominent anti–tie signs would include eye contact avoidance and sitting apart from each other when closer seats are available. Interestingly enough, social network sites enable you to express both tie signs and anti–tie signs by simply changing your relationship status.

TOUCH AVOIDANCE AND TOUCH DEPRIVATION

Much as we have a tendency to touch and be touched, we also have a tendency to avoid touch from certain people or in certain circumstances. Researchers in nonverbal communication have found some interesting relationships between touch avoidance and touch deprivation and other significant communication variables (Andersen, 2005; Andersen & Leibowitz, 1978).

Touch Avoidance

Your tendency to avoid touching and being touched seems positively related to your level of communication apprehension: If you fear oral communication you're also more likely to avoid touching. Similarly, if you disclose little (you reveal little information about yourself to others), you are also more likely to avoid touch. Both touch and self-disclosure are intimate forms of communication. Both are means of getting close to another person and so it's not surprising that research finds these two forms of communication to be closely related; people who are reluctant to get close to another person by self-disclosing also seem reluctant to get close by touching.

Touch avoidance is also affected by age and gender (Crawford, 1994; Guérrero & Andersen, 1994). As we get older, we are touched less by members of the opposite sex, and this decreased frequency may lead us to further avoid touching. Females engage in more same-sex touching than do males; that is, men avoid touching other men, but women may and do touch other women.

Touch Deprivation

Touch deprivation refers to the abnormal absence of touching; it's extreme touch avoidance by others. Most people touch each other in the course of daily interactions. However, some people are not touched. For example, older people are touched a great deal less than are younger people. Similarly, those who have some physical deformity are touched less than those without such deformities. A variety of research studies (well summarized by Burgoon et al., 2010) point to the negative psychological and physiological effects of touch deprivation, ranging from increases in blood pressure and anxiety to lowered resistance to illness. And, of course, without touch much of your interpersonal relationship life would suffer from an absence of the closeness and affection that touching communicates.

POLITENESS IN NONVERBAL COMMUNICATION

Being polite with touch messages:

- Avoid touching that may be considered inappropriately intimate (when you're not at the intimacy stage of your relationship).
- Avoid self-touching movements that might prove offensive.
- Avoid touch that may appear unnecessarily controlling or that might hurt others, especially those who are infirm or very old.

TOUCH DIFFERENCES

In the introduction to this chapter you were asked to indicate who would touch whom, an exercise designed to highlight differences in touching, a topic we explore more fully here.

Status, Gender, and Touching

Nancy Henley, in her *Body Politics* (1977), argues that touching was a sign of status difference and particularly that, since males touched females more than the other way around, touching was also an expression of male dominance. So, in the last example of the exercise, Henley would argue, men initiate touch more often than would women as an expression of superior status, power, and dominance. In more recent research touching was investigated at professional meetings where no evidence was found to support the notion that higher-status people initial touching with lower status people. But the researcher found there was a difference in the type of touching (though not in who initiates the touch). When higher-status individuals initiated touch it was judged as more affectionate and the touch was on the arm or shoulder. When lower-status individuals initiated touch, it was judged as more formal, for example, in the form of handshakes. Here, males were found to initial touch more often than women, but not to any great extent (Hall, 1996).

When people are shown photographs of one person touching another and asked to judge who is the higher-status person, early research showed that the "toucher" was judged the higher-status person and the "touchee" was judged the lower-status person. Other research fails to find this difference (Storrs & Kleinke, 1990).

The reason for these differences may well be due to the changes in the way in which we look at touching. At one time, touch may well have been a sign of higher status, whereas today it has lost some (perhaps most) of that connotation.

Women are generally touched more than men; even baby girls are touched more than baby boys. Mothers do initiate more touching of their children than do fathers. Of course, attitudes and behaviors have changed a great deal since 1977 and it's likely that this gender difference has been reduced or perhaps even eliminated in many situations.

Touching provides an interesting example of the communication license, a type of privilege accorded those in power. It's much like the license that those in power have, say in an organization, to enter your space.

Relationship Stage and Touching

Not surprisingly, touch also varies with your relationship stage. In the early stages of a relationship there is relatively little touching and what touching does occur is relatively impersonal. As your relationship moves to greater involvement and intimacy, touching becomes more frequent and more intimate. Once a relationship becomes stable, the touching decreases. During relationship deterioration, as you might expect, there is little touching and what touching does occur is impersonal (Burgoon et al., 2010; Guérrero & Andersen, 1991).

Another way of looking at this is in terms of societal versus individually established rules. In the early stages of a relationship (or in temporary relationships such as that between a customer and a server), people operate within the rules established by the culture or the society. You don't, for example, pat the server on the rear or hug the server; that would involve breaking a societal (and unspoken) rule. However, in close relationships, the rules of society are put aside (especially in private though also in public) and you and the other person develop individual rules—you may (depending on the individual rules) pat the other's rear or hug.

The following exercise, Relationships and Touching, focuses on societal rules.

Culture and Touching

Touching varies greatly from one culture to another. In fact, some cultures are referred to as contact cultures (the cultures of Latin America and southern Europe, for example) and some are noncontact cultures (the cultures of Japan and Korea, for example). African Americans touch each other more than European Americans, and touching declines from kindergarten to the sixth grade for European American but not for African American children (Burgoon et al., 2010). Japanese people touch each other much less than Anglo-Saxons, who in turn touch much less than southern Europeans (Burgoon et al., 2010; Morris, 1977).

EXERCISE

RELATIONSHIPS AND TOUCHING

In Column 1 are presented several relationships with the first named person initiating touching with the second named person. In Column 2 indicate what touching would be appropriate and what touching would be inappropriate. In Column 3 explain any changes you would make in your Column 2 responses if the second named person were initiating touch with the first named person.

Relationship	Appropriate and Inappropriate Touching	Reversal
Doctor to patient	*Depending on the purpose of the examination, most touching would be appropriate; inappropriate touching would involve sexually suggestive touching.*	*Probably the patient would not touch the doctor other than, possibly, shaking hands.*
Interviewer to interviewee		
Teacher to student		
College president to first-time instructor		
Restaurant customer to server		
Coach to college player		

ON THE JOB

Too Much Touching

One of your supervisors touches you (and others) more than you (and others) would like. The touching is not obviously sexual and yet you get the feeling that there is a sexual component to it. Regardless of the intention, you want it stopped. What are some of the things you might say or do to stop this behavior?

The functions and examples of touching discussed earlier were based on studies in North America; in other cultures these functions are not served in the same way. In some cultures, for example, some task-related touching is viewed negatively and is to be avoided. Among Koreans it is considered disrespectful for a store owner to touch a customer in, say, handing back change; doing so is considered too intimate a gesture. Members of other cultures who are used to such touching may consider the Koreans' behavior cold and aloof. Muslim children are socialized to refrain from touching members of the opposite sex, a practice that can easily be interpreted as unfriendly by American children who are used to touching one another (Dresser, 1996). Hand-holding among same-sex partners may indicate a romantic attachment in some cultures but a friendship attachment in others.

IF YOU WANT TO

Apologize/gain forgiveness/lessen a bad impression

- Maintain eye contact.
- Assume a contrite posture, for example, eyes down and a sad facial expression.
- Use a direct body posture.

Students from the United States reported being touched twice as much as did Japanese students (Barnlund, 1975). In Japan there is a strong taboo against strangers touching, and the Japanese are therefore especially careful to maintain sufficient distance.

Some cultures, such as those of southern Europe and the Middle East, are contact cultures. Others, such as those of northern Europe and Japan, are noncontact cultures. Members of contact cultures maintain close distances, touch each other in conversation, face each other more directly, and maintain longer and more focused eye contact. Members of noncontact cultures maintain greater distance in their interactions, touch each other rarely if at all, avoid facing each other directly, and maintain much less direct eye contact. As a result, northern Europeans and Japanese may be perceived as cold, distant, and uninvolved by southern Europeans—who may in turn be perceived as pushy, aggressive, and inappropriately intimate.

Summary

1. Among the meanings that touch may communicate are positive emotions, playfulness, control, task relationship, and ritualistic.
2. Touch avoidance is positively correlated with communication apprehension and the unwillingness to self-disclose.
3. Tie signs are the nonverbal expressions that indicate you have a relationship with the other person, many of which involve touch. Tie signs operate on the intrapersonal, interpersonal, and public levels.
4. Touch varies on the basis of a variety of factors: status, gender, relationship stage, and culture.

Key Terms

Supply a definition for each of the following terms. Once you've formulated these "standard" definitions, consider the following ideas for further defining and understanding. Not all will work for all key terms, but some will work for some terms and some will work for others.

- Find a quotation that illustrates the term.
- Provide an example from personal interaction, television, film, novels, or plays.
- Create a short dialogue to illustrate the operation of the key term.
- Locate a research study investigating the key term and report its findings.
- Illustrate the concept nonverbally.
- Find a video that illustrates the key term.
- Find images—photos or graphics, abstract or specific, literal or metaphorical.
- Diagram the concept.
- Explain the negative, what the concept is not.
- State a skill that centers on the concept.

Key Concept	Definition
Tactile communication	
Touch avoidance	
Touch deprivation	
Tie signs	
Meanings of touch	
Touch differences	

AND IN ADDITION

Using your favorite search engine (in addition, use Google Scholar or the databases in your college library for the more scientific research articles), search for **tactile communication**, **touch avoidance**, **touch deprivation**, **tie signs**, **hugging**, **kissing**, **shaking hands**, or any of the other terms and topics considered in this chapter and add to the chapter contents. Depending on the structure of the course and the facilities available, you may want to post these additions to a course website; to a social media site such as Twitter, Facebook, or Google+; or to a listserv or through e-mail, for example. Here are a few ways in which you might make your addition:

- Write a paragraph that adds to the discussion of a particular concept.
- Provide a new, contradictory, or intercultural example of a concept.
- Create a figure or table to illustrate or organize a particular topic.
- Illustrate with an image or two or a 10- to 15-second video a particular concept of nonverbal behavior.
- Summarize and evaluate the results of a scientific study on a topic relevant to this chapter.
- Summarize and evaluate an online article that focuses on one of the topics considered here.

Chapter 8

Paralanguage and Silence

☛ CHAPTER TOPICS

Paralanguage
- Paralanguage and People
- Paralanguage and Communication Effectiveness
- Paralanguage and Conversational Regulation

Silence
- Culture and Silence
- The Spiral of Silence
- The Ethics of Silence

Summary

Key Terms

And in Addition

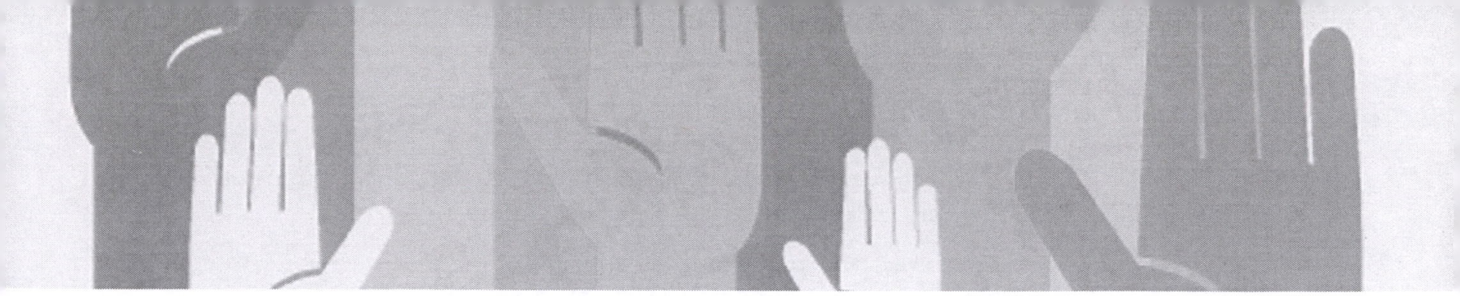

CHAPTER EXERCISES

[Regulating Paralanguage]
Expressing Praise and Criticism
Distinguishing between Literal and Opposite Meanings
Identifying and Illustrating the Functions of Silence
Making Silence Decisions

ON THE JOB

The Monotone
Unwanted Interruptions
Voicing Disagreement

POLITENESS IN NONVERBAL COMMUNICATION

Being polite with paralanguage messages
Being polite with silence messages

IF YOU WANT TO

Be especially **clear/unambiguous/understandable**
Appear **confident/in control/at ease/without apprehension**

CHAPTER OBJECTIVES

After reading this chapter, you should be able to:

1. Define *paralanguage* and the major paralanguage cues.
2. Explain the research findings on speech rate and effectiveness and credibility.
3. Define and distinguish between the varied speaker and listener turn-taking cues.
4. Define *silence* and identify at least four functions it may serve.
5. Explain some of the ways in which culture influences the silence that its members observe.
6. Paraphrase the spiral of silence theory.

BEFORE you read about paralanguage, describe your voice (in terms of rate, pitch, volume, and rhythm) in each of these situations:

- **You're very sad and are telling a friend of the unexpected death of a mutual friend.**
- **You're elated and are telling someone of your recent lottery win.**
- **You're arguing about a topic (about which you feel especially strongly) with someone with totally opposite beliefs and opinions.**
- **You're in love and are telling your beloved how you feel.**

You probably rarely consider your own speaking rate, pitch, volume, and rhythm. These features simply echo the way you're feeling. It happens automatically—usually. At other times, as say in public speaking or interviewing, you probably focus on your speech and wonder how you can make it more effective in persuading an audience or getting a job, for example.

These features of speech rate, pitch, volume, and rhythm are *vocal but nonverbal* aspects of communication and are grouped under the general title of **paralanguage**, the first topic we explore in this chapter. The second part of the chapter covers the closely related nonverbal dimension: silence.

PARALANGUAGE

An old exercise teachers used to increase students' ability to express different emotions, feelings, and attitudes was to have the students repeat a sentence while accenting or stressing different words each time. Increasing the volume on different words easily communicates significant differences in meaning. Consider the following variations of the sentence "Is this the face that launched a thousand ships?" (The reference is to Helen of Troy who, in Greek mythology, was abducted by Paris [from her husband Menelaus, the King of Sparta] and who brought about the famed Trojan War between Troy and Sparta.)

1. *Is* this the face that launched a thousand ships?
2. Is *this* the face that launched a thousand ships?
3. Is this *the face* that launched a thousand ships?
4. Is this the face that *launched* a thousand ships?
5. Is this the face that launched a *thousand ships*?

Each sentence communicates something different—in fact, each asks a different question, even though the words are the same. All that varies among the sentences is where the increase in volume is placed, one of the important dimensions of paralanguage. Paralanguage also includes vocalizations you make in crying, whispering, moaning, belching, yawning, and yelling (Argyle, 1988; Trager, 1958, 1961). A variation in any of these vocal features communicates some meaning. When you speak quickly, for example, you communicate something different from when you speak slowly. Even though the words are the same, if the speed (or volume, rhythm, or pitch) differs, the meanings people receive will also differ.

In this first section we look at three areas of paralanguage: paralanguage and people perception, paralanguage and communication effectiveness, and the ways in which conversations are regulated (a process that is largely, though not exclusively, paralinguistic).

EXERCISE

EXPRESSING PRAISE AND CRITICISM

To consider how nonverbal messages can communicate praise and criticism—and in general the cues that send positive and negative feedback—read aloud each of the statements in Column 1 to, first, communicate praise and, second, to express criticism. In Columns 2 and 3, record the nonverbal signals you used to help you communicate praise and criticism. Pay particular attention to paralinguistic cues, but don't ignore facial expressions and body movements.

Message	Nonverbal Cues that Communicate Praise	Nonverbal Cues that Communicate Criticism
You lost weight.	*Saying it in a matter-of-fact tone (with falling intonation at end of sentence) without emphasizing you or weight particularly; raised eyebrows; favorable facial expression with smile; slight head nod.*	*Saying it in a sneering tone as if to say "You did not lose weight" or "You lost so little it doesn't really matter"; questioning facial expression; rising intonation at end of sentence to make it seem more like a question; emphasis on the word lost.*
You look happy.		
You're an expert.		
Your parents are something else.		
Your home looks fabulous.		

Paralanguage and People

Do you make judgments about people's personalities on the basis of their paralinguistic cues? For example, do you conclude that your colleague who speaks softly when presenting ideas at a meeting isn't sure of the ideas' usefulness and believes

Review your own assumptions about the connection between personality and the way in which people speak. Write them down and then search for evidence and research findings that bear upon your assumptions. Does the research support or contradict your assumptions? © 2013, Yuri Arcurs, Shutterstock, Inc.

that no one really wants to listen to them? Do you assume that people who speak loudly have overinflated egos? Do those who speak with no variation, in a complete monotone, seem uninterested in what they are saying? Might you then assume that they have a lack of interest in life in general? All such judgments are based on little evidence, yet they persist in much popular talk.

Research has found that people can accurately judge the socioeconomic status (whether high, middle, or low) of speakers from 60-second voice samples (Davitz, 1964). Many listeners in this study made their judgments in less than 15 seconds. Participants also rated people whom they judged to be of high status as more credible than speakers judged middle and low.

Listeners also can accurately judge the emotional states of speakers from vocal expression alone. In these studies speakers recite the alphabet or numbers while expressing emotions. Some emotions are easier to identify than others; it is easy to distinguish between hate and sympathy but more difficult to distinguish between fear and anxiety. And, of course, listeners vary in their ability to decode, and speakers in their ability to encode, emotions (Scherer, 1986).

Paralanguage and Communication Effectiveness

One of the most important components of paralanguage is speech rate. In one-way communication (when one person is doing all or most of the speaking and the other person is doing all or most of the listening), those who talk fast (about 50 percent faster than normal) are more persuasive. That is, people agree more with a fast speaker than with a slow speaker and find the fast speaker more intelligent and objective (MacLachlan, 1979).

There are cultural differences in this persuasiveness effect, however. For example, among Koreans, researchers found the opposite effect: Male speakers who spoke

DISTINGUISHING BETWEEN LITERAL AND OPPOSITE MEANINGS

EXERCISE

To appreciate further the role of paralanguage in changing the meanings of what we say, try reading each of the statements in Column 1 aloud in two ways—first to communicate the statement's literal meaning, then to communicate a meaning opposite to the literal one. As you go along, try to identify the nonverbal differences between the literal and the opposite-meaning renditions. Look specifically at the paralinguistic features of rate, pauses, and volume as you read the statements—but don't neglect observing your facial expressions, eye movements, gestures, and body posture. If possible, record your two versions of each sentence (on your smartphone, tablet, or other device) and ask others to identify the meanings you're trying to communicate.

Statements	Nonverbals in Literal Meaning	Nonverbals in Opposite Meaning
I sure hate this place.	Meaning to convey: I really do hate this horrible place. *Matter-of-fact style with a falling intonation at end of sentence; relatively slow speaking rate; emphasis on hate; facial expression of disgust; shaking of the head from side to side.*	*Meaning to convey: I can't believe how great this place is.* *Lilting tone with pleasant facial expressions and a smile; relatively fast speaking rate.*
I can't wait for the grades to be posted.	Meaning to convey: I'm anxious to see my grades; I know I aced the exam.	Meaning to convey: I fear I'm going to fail.
My job is the greatest.	Meaning to convey: I can't imagine having a better job.	Meaning to convey: I hate this job.
Isn't this course wonderful?	Meaning to convey: This is the best course I've ever taken.	Meaning to convey: This has got to be the worst course imaginable.
I sure have the relationship of a lifetime.	Meaning to convey: I'm so lucky.	Meaning to convey: This relationship is horrible and is doomed to failure.

rapidly received unfavorable credibility ratings (Lee & Boster, 1992). Researchers have suggested that people in individualistic societies tend to see a rapid-rate speaker as more competent than a slow-rate speaker, whereas people in collectivist cultures judge a speaker who uses a slower rate to be more competent.

When we look at comprehension, rapid speech shows an interesting effect. When the speaking rate increases by 50 percent, the comprehension level drops by only 5 percent. When the rate doubles, the comprehension level drops only 10 percent. In terms of efficiency, then, these 5 and 10 percent comprehension losses are more than offset by the increased speed; faster speech rates are thus much more efficient in communicating information. If the speeds are more than twice that of normal speech, however, the comprehension level begins to fall dramatically. More recent research confirms these general findings (Swanbrow, 2011).

Exercise caution in applying this research to all forms of communication (MacLachlan, 1979). While the speaker is speaking, the listener is generating, or framing, a reply. If the speaker talks too rapidly, the listener may not have enough time to compose a reply and may become resentful. Furthermore, the increased rate may seem so unnatural that the listener may focus on the speed rather than on the message being communicated.

Pitch is another aspect of paralanguage and refers to the relative highness or lowness of tone. Each person has a range of pitches; the range for men is relatively low and the range for women relatively high. Vocal training, for singers, for example, can increase your range somewhat but most of your range is predetermined by your biology. Generally, variety rather than a monotone is considered more effective. However, in at least one study, men who used pitch variety were judged as more effeminate, dynamic, and creative than those who spoke with little pitch variation (Addington, 1968).

IF YOU WANT TO

Be especially **clear/unambiguous/understandable**

- Use vocal variety and avoid vocalized pauses.
- Use appropriate facial expressions that echo what you're saying.
- Move a bit or gesture to show transitions or a move from one point to another.
- Maintain a face-to-face posture.

ON THE JOB

The Monotone

Your work team has just completed 2 months of work on a new advertising campaign to pitch to a client. The problem is that the team leader, who is also the manager of the department, speaks with a monotone that drives people right to sleep. You're afraid that the pitch will fail if he delivers it in his customary monotone. What are some of the things you can do to avert what you see as sure disaster?

Perhaps the most obvious paralinguistic feature is that of volume, which ranges from extremely loud to extremely low. Volume varies naturally with the distance between the people talking (next to each other, across the room, or down the block), the general context (a quiet dinner, a football stadium, or a classroom), the surrounding noise level (loud music in the background, jackhammers in the street, or competing voices), and the type of message (a secret between the two of you, something you want others to overhear, something said in love or in anger), for example.

People who have hearing difficulties, however, may speak at a louder volume than normal because they hear themselves as speaking at normal volume while those with no hearing difficulties hear the person as louder than normally expected. If you speak too softly or too loudly, you'll likely be considered inappropriate.

This is an ideal place to note some of the suggestions for improving communication between those with and those without hearing difficulties. People with hearing loss differ greatly in their hearing ability: Some are totally deaf and can hear nothing, others have some hearing loss and can hear some sounds, and still others have impaired hearing but can hear most speech. Although people with profound hearing loss can speak, their speech may appear labored and may be less clear than the speech of those with unimpaired hearing. Here are some suggestions for more effective communication between people who hear well and those who have hearing problems.

- Set up a comfortable context. Reduce the distance between yourself and the other person. Reduce background noise. Make sure the lighting is adequate.
- If you're speaking to someone with a hearing impairment, make sure the visual cues from your speech are clearly observable; face the person squarely and avoid smoking, chewing gum, or holding your hand over your mouth.
- Phrase ideas in different ways. Because some words are easier to lip-read than others, it often helps if you can rephrase your ideas in different words.
- Avoid overlapping speech. In group situations only one person should speak at a time. Similarly, direct your comments to the person with hearing loss him- or herself; don't talk to the person through a third party.
- Don't avoid common terms. Feel free to use terms like *hear*, *listen*, *music*, or *deaf* when they're relevant to the conversation. Trying to avoid these common terms will make your speech sound artificial.
- Use nonverbal cues. Nonverbals can help communicate your meaning; gestures indicating size or location and facial expressions indicating feelings are often helpful to a person with a hearing impairment.

POLITENESS IN NONVERBAL COMMUNICATION

Being polite with paralanguage messages:

- Avoid parodying others' paralanguage.
- Repeat messages that may not be clear (e.g., when leaving a phone number on a recorder).
- Give clear turn-taking cues and respond to the turn-taking cues of others.

Paralanguage and Conversational Regulation

Throughout the speaking–listening process, both speaker and listener exchange what are called **conversational turn cues** (Burgoon et al., 2010; Duncan, 1972; Knapp & Hall, 2010; Pearson & Spitzberg, 1990). These cues enable the speaker and listener

Before reading about these cues, reflect on your own recent conversations. What kinds of cues were used to signal a desire to speak? © 2013, Monkey Business Images, Shutterstock, Inc.

to communicate about the communication in which they're currently engaged; it is a form of metacommunication that takes place through the exchange of these often subtle cues. The use of these cues—like just about every other aspect of human communication—will naturally vary from one culture to another. What follows here is largely true in the United States and in many Western cultures (Grossin, 1987; Iizuka, 1993; Lee, 1984; Ng, Loong, He, Liu, & Weatherall, 2000). As you'll see, many—but not all—of these cues are paralinguistic in nature.

Speaker Cues

Speakers regulate the conversation through two major types of cues: turn-maintaining cues and turn-yielding cues. Using these cues effectively not only ensures communication efficiency but also increases the user's likability (Heap, 1992; Knapp & Hall, 2010; Place & Becker, 1991).

Turn-Maintaining Cues. Turn-maintaining cues are designed to enable a person to maintain the role of speaker and can take a variety of forms:

- Audibly inhaling breath to show that the speaker has more to say.
- Continuing a gesture or series of gestures to show that the thought is not yet complete.
- Avoiding eye contact with the listener so as not to indicate that the speaking turn is being passed along.
- Sustaining the intonation pattern to indicate that more will be said.
- Vocalizing pauses ("er," "umm") to prevent the listener from speaking and to show that the speaker is still talking.

In most cases, we expect the speaker to maintain relatively brief speaking turns and to turn over the speaking role to the listener willingly (when so signaled by the listener). People who don't follow those unwritten rules are likely to be evaluated negatively.

Turn-Yielding Cues. Turn-yielding cues tell the listener that the speaker is finished and wishes to exchange the role of speaker for the role of listener. They tell the listener (and sometimes they're addressed to a specific listener rather than to just any listener) to take over the role of speaker. For example, at the end of a statement you may add some cue such as "okay?" or "right?", which asks one of the listeners to assume the role of speaker. You can also indicate that you've finished speaking by dropping your intonation or by pausing at length (Wennerstrom & Siegel, 2003), by making direct eye contact with a listener, by asking some question, or by nodding in the direction of a particular listener.

In much the same way that you expect a speaker to yield the role of speaker, you also expect the listener to assume the speaking role willingly. Those who don't may be regarded as reticent or as unwilling to involve themselves and take equal responsibility for the conversation. Perhaps the most important violation is interruption. Much research has addressed this issue, especially the question of whether men or women interrupt more. The research that has found a difference indicates that men interrupt more often than women, though much research finds no differences (Crown & Cummins, 1998; Donaldson, 1992; Smith-Lovin & Brody, 1989; Stratford, 1998).

Listener Cues

As a listener, you can regulate the conversation by using three types of cues: turn-requesting cues, turn-denying cues, and back-channeling cues.

Turn-Requesting Cues. Turn-requesting cues let the speaker know that you would like to say something and take a turn as speaker. Sometimes you can do this simply by saying, "I'd like to say something," but often it's done more subtly through some vocalized *er* or *um* that tells the speaker that you would now like to speak. The request to speak is also often made with facial and mouth gestures. Frequently a listener will indicate a desire to speak by opening his or her eyes and mouth wide as if to say something, by beginning to gesture with a hand, or by leaning forward.

> **ON THE JOB**
>
> **Unwanted Interruptions**
>
> One of your supervisors repeatedly interrupts you. Whenever you start to explain something, your supervisor interrupts you to change the topic or to finish your thought—sometimes accurately but most often inaccurately. You need to do something about this and are wondering if you're actually encouraging interruptions by your paralanguage—perhaps pausing too long. What are some of the things you might do in your own nonverbal communication to discourage another's interruptions? What might you say to one who interrupts repeatedly?

Turn-Denying Cues. You can use **turn-denying cues** to indicate your reluctance to assume the role of speaker; for example, by intoning a slurred "I don't know," or by giving some brief grunt that signals you have nothing to say. Often people accomplish turn-denying by avoiding eye contact with the speaker (who wishes them now to take on the role of speaker) or by engaging in some behavior that is incompatible with speaking—for example, coughing or blowing his or her nose.

Backchanneling Cues. People use **backchanneling cues** to communicate various types of information back to the speaker without assuming the role of the speaker. You can send a variety of messages with backchanneling cues (Burgoon et al., 2010; Pearson & Spitzberg, 1990). You can indicate your agreement or disagreement with the speaker through smiles or frowns, gestures of approval or disapproval, brief comments such as "right" or "never," or a vocalization such as *uh-huh.*

You can also indicate your degree of involvement or boredom with the speaker. Attentive posture, forward leaning, and focused eye contact will tell the speaker that you're involved in the conversation—and an inattentive posture, backward leaning, and avoidance of eye contact will communicate your lack of involvement.

What other nonverbal cues are likely to signal involvement or boredom?

You can also help regulate the speed of speech by giving the speaker pacing cues. You can, for example, ask the speaker to slow down by raising your hand near your ear and leaning forward and to speed up by continuously nodding your head. You can also do this verbally by simply asking the speaker to slow down ("Slow down, I want to make sure I'm getting all this"). Similarly, you can tell the speaker to speed up by saying something like "And—?" or "Go on, go on."

A request for clarification is still another function of backchanneling cues. A puzzled facial expression, perhaps coupled with a forward lean, will probably tell most speakers that you want some clarification. Similarly, you can ask for clarification by interjecting some interrogative: "Who?" "When?" "Where?"

Some of these backchanneling cues are actually interruptions. These interruptions, however, are generally confirming rather than disconfirming. They tell the speaker that you are listening and are involved, that you're interested and supportive (Kennedy & Camden, 1988).

Interruptions. Some interruptions, of course, are not confirming or supportive. Some interruptions are attempts to take over the role of the speaker. Some are attempts to change the topic to a subject that the interrupter knows more about or perhaps to emphasize the person's authority. Some interruptions are attempts to assert power and to maintain control. Not surprisingly, research finds that superiors (bosses and supervisors) and those in positions of authority (police officers and interviewers) interrupt those in inferior positions more than the other way around (Ashcraft, 1998; Carroll, 1994). In fact, it would probably strike you as strange to see a worker repeatedly interrupting a supervisor.

Another and even more often studied aspect of interruption is that of gender difference. The popular belief is that men interrupt more than women. This belief, research finds, is basically accurate. Men interrupt both women and other men more than women do. For example, one analysis of 43 published studies showed that men interrupted significantly more than women (Anderson & Leaper, 1998). In addition, the more male-like the person's gender identity—regardless of the person's biological sex—the more likely it is that the person will interrupt (Drass, 1986). Fathers, one research study shows, interrupt their children more than mothers do (Greif, 1980). These gender differences, however, are small. More important than gender in determining who interrupts is the specific type of situation; some contexts (e.g., task-oriented situations) may call for more interruptions, whereas others (e.g., relationship discussions) may call for more backchanneling cues (Anderson & Leaper, 1998).

IF YOU WANT TO

Appear **confident/in control/at ease/without apprehension**

- Don't interrupt.
- Avoid vocalized pauses and filler words.
- Listen attentively and give positive listening cues.
- Maintain an open posture; avoid postures that make you look uncomfortable or frightened.
- Smile but don't overdo it.
- Use gestures that might be considered a bit larger than normal.
- Avoid fidgeting, especially moving your feet when sitting down.
- Avoid self-touching movements.
- Use a bit more eye contact than usual.
- Stand up straight; avoid minimizing your stature by slouching.
- Speak with an adequate volume; especially, avoid decreasing volume at the ends of your sentences.

Figure 8.1 diagrams the various turn-taking cues and shows how they correspond to the conversational wants of speaker and listener.

Each quadrant represents a different type of turn-taking:

- Quadrant 1 represents the speaker who wishes to speak (or to continue speaking) and uses turn-*maintaining* cues.
- Quadrant 2 represents the speaker who wishes to listen and uses turn-*yielding* cues.
- Quadrant 3 represents the listener who wishes to speak and uses turn-*requesting* cues.
- Quadrant 4 represents the listener who wishes to listen (or to continue listening) and uses turn-*denying* cues.

Backchanneling cues would also appear in quadrant 4, as they are cues that listeners use while they continue to listen. Interruptions would appear in quadrant 3, although they're not so much cues that request a turn as takeovers of the speaker's position.

	Conversational Wants	
	To Speak	**To Listen**
Speaker	(1) Turn-maintaining cues	(2) Turn-yielding cues
Listener	(3) Turn-requesting cues	(4) Turn-denying cues

Figure 8.1 Turn-Taking

Reflect back on your recent interactions. In what ways was silence used? What purposes did it serve? © 2013, CREATISTA, Shutterstock, Inc.

SILENCE

"Speech," wrote Thomas Mann, "is civilization itself. The word, even the most contradictory word, preserves contact; it is silence which isolates." Philosopher Karl Jaspers, on the other hand, observed that "the ultimate in thinking as in communication is silence," and philosopher Max Picard noted that "silence is nothing merely negative; it is not the mere absence of speech. It is a positive, a complete world in itself." The one thing on which these contradictory observations agree is that silence communicates.

Silence is also seen in online communication. For example, when a close friend posts a message that asks for support or help and you remain silent, you're communicating a message—perhaps you simply didn't know what to say or you weren't interested or you didn't have online access (an excuse that is becoming increasingly difficult to advance convincingly). Or when someone sends you a lengthy e-mail and you fail to respond to its main theme (indicating you haven't really read the e-mail), you're communicating some message.

Your silence, whether face to face or online, can communicate a variety of meanings; below are a few (Jaworski, 1993).

Silence allows the speaker time to think, time to formulate and organize his or her verbal communications. Before messages of intense conflict, as well as before those confessing undying love, there is often silence. Silence seems to prepare the receiver for the importance of these messages.

Some people use silence as a weapon to hurt others. We often speak of giving someone "the silent treatment." After a conflict, for example, one or both individuals may remain silent as a kind of punishment. Silence used to hurt others may also take the form of refusal to acknowledge the presence of another person, as in disconfirmation; here silence is a dramatic demonstration of the total indifference one person feels toward the other.

Sometimes silence is used as a response to personal anxiety, shyness, or threats. You may feel anxious or shy among new people and prefer to remain silent. By remaining silent, you preclude the chance of rejection. Only when you break your silence, and make an attempt to communicate with another person, do you risk rejection.

Silence may be used to prevent communication of certain messages. In conflict situations, silence is sometimes used to prevent certain topics from surfacing and to prevent one or both parties from saying things they may later regret. In such situations, silence often allows us time to cool off before expressing hatred, severe criticism, or personal attacks—which, as we know, are irreversible.

Like the eyes, face, or hands, silence can also be used to communicate emotional responses (Ehrenhaus, 1988). Sometimes silence communicates a determination to be uncooperative or defiant; by refusing to engage in verbal communication, you defy the authority or the legitimacy of the other person's position. Silence is often used to communicate annoyance, particularly when accompanied by a pouting expression, arms crossed in front of the chest, and nostrils flared. Silence may express affection or love, especially when coupled with long and longing gazes into each other's eyes.

Silence also may be used strategically, to achieve specific effects. You may, for example, strategically position a pause before what you feel is an important comment to make your idea stand out. Interestingly enough, interviewers who paused about every 20 seconds were more successful in gaining compliance than were those who spoke without a pause (Swanbrow, 2011). A prolonged silence after someone voices disagreement may give the appearance of control and superiority. It's a way of saying, "I can respond in my own time." Generally, research finds that people use silence strategically more with strangers than they do with close friends (Hesegawa & Gudykunst, 1998). Or you may use silence to avoid responsibility for wrongdoing (Beach, 1990–91).

Silence may also signal respect. You may, for example, be especially quiet in houses of religious worship. And when in interaction with especially important people, you're likely to remain silent more than normal.

Of course, you may use silence when you simply have nothing to say—when nothing occurs to you or when you do not want to say anything. James Russell Lowell expressed this well: "Blessed are they who have nothing to say and who cannot be persuaded to say it."

Culture and Silence

Not all cultures view silence as functioning in the same way. In the United States, for example, silence often is interpreted negatively. At a business meeting or even in informal social groups, people may see a silent member as not listening, having nothing interesting to add, not understanding the issues, being insensitive, or being too self-absorbed to focus on the messages of others. Other cultures, however, view silence more positively. In many situations in Japan, for example, silence is considered a more appropriate response than speech (Haga, 1988).

ON THE JOB

Voicing Disagreement

You're leading an eight-person team charged with the responsibility of redesigning the company website. Your problem is that disagreements are never voiced. No idea—even ideas that are clearly worthless—is ever questioned. You need to encourage disagreement to give these ideas a fair hearing. What are some of the things you might do to encourage members to voice their feelings?

EXERCISE

IDENTIFYING AND ILLUSTRATING THE FUNCTIONS OF SILENCE

To illustrate the role of silence in your own life, consider the functions of silence just discussed and listed in Column 1. In Column 2 provide an illustration of one, two, three, or all of the functions from face-to-face interactions—whether you participated in them or observed them in others or in the media—and any background that would help explain your use of silence. In Column 3 identify examples from online interaction.

Function of Silence	Examples in Face-to-Face Interaction	Examples in Online Interaction
To provide time to think	*When Sally asked me out, I was so surprised I just remained silent and probably gave the impression that I didn't want to go out (but I did).*	*I remained silent after Harry wrote that critical e-mail; I needed time to think of how I should respond.*
To hurt another person		
To avoid communication (as a response to personal anxiety or shyness, say)		
To prevent communication		
To communicate feelings		
To achieve specific effects (strategically)		
To avoid responsibility		
To show respect		
To say nothing		

The traditional Apache regard silence very differently than European Americans (Basso, 1972). Among the Apache, mutual friends do not feel the need to introduce strangers who may be working in the same area or on the same project. The strangers may remain silent for several days. This period enables the individuals to observe and evaluate one another. After this assessment period, the individuals talk. When courting, especially during the initial stages, the Apache remain silent for hours; if they do talk, they generally talk very little. Only after a couple has been dating for several months will they have lengthy conversations. The use of silence is explicitly taught to Apache women, who are especially discouraged from engaging in long discussions with their dates. Silence during courtship is a sign of modesty to many Apache.

In the Iranian culture there's an expression, *qahr*, which means not being on speaking terms with someone, giving someone the silent treatment. For example, when children disobey their parents, they are given this silent treatment. With adults *qahr* may be instituted when one person insults or injures another (Behzadi, 1994).

POLITENESS IN NONVERBAL COMMUNICATION

Being polite with silence messages:

- Respond.
- Avoid silence that is designed to hurt, as in giving someone the silent treatment.
- Be silent when you have nothing to say.

The Spiral of Silence

The spiral of silence theory argues that you're more likely to voice agreement than disagreement (Noelle-Neumann, 1973, 1980, 1991; Windahl, Signitzer, & Olson, 1992). The theory claims that when a controversial issue arises, you try to estimate public opinion on the issue and figure out which views are popular and which are not, largely by attending to the media (Gonzenbach, King, & Jablonski, 1999; Jeffres, Neuendorf, & Atkin, 1999). At the same time, you also judge the likelihood and the severity of punishment for expressing minority opinions. You then use these estimates to regulate your expression of opinions.

The theory continues: When you agree with the majority, you're more likely to voice your opinions than when you disagree. You may avoid expressing minority opinions because you don't want to be isolated from the majority or confront the unpleasant possibility of being proven wrong. Or, you may assume that the majority, because they're a majority, are right..

Not all people seem affected equally by this spiral (Noelle-Neumann, 1991). For example, younger people and men are more likely to express minority opinions than are older people and women. Educated people are more likely to express minority opinions than are those who are less educated. Similarly, the tendency to voice minority opinions varies from one culture to another (Scheufele & Moy, 2000).

In any case, the "spiral" effect occurs when, as people with minority views remain silent, the media position gets stronger (because those who agree with it are the only ones speaking). As the media's position grows stronger, the voice of the opposition also gets weaker. Thus, the situation becomes an ever-widening spiral of silence.

As you think about the spiral of silence, consider the ways the process of silence operates in your own media life. For example, do you contribute to this spiral of silence? Under what conditions are you most likely to conform to the predictions of this theory? What are its effects on your self-image and on your popularity with peers?

The Ethics of Silence

In the U.S. legal system, you have the right to remain silent and to refuse to incriminate yourself. But in general you don't have the right to refuse to reveal information about, for example, the criminal activities of others that you may have witnessed. Rightly or wrongly (and this itself is an ethical issue), psychiatrists and lawyers are often exempt from this general rule. Similarly, a wife can't be forced to testify against her husband or a husband against his wife.

In most communication situations, however, there aren't any written rules—so it's not always clear if or when silence is ethical or unethical. For example, most people (though not all) would agree that you have the right to withhold information that has no bearing on the matter at hand. Thus, in job-related contexts your previous relationship history, sexual orientation, or religion is usually irrelevant to your ability to function and so may be kept private in most work settings.

EXERCISE

MAKING SILENCE DECISIONS

Bring your own ethical principles to greater consciousness by considering your own ethical position in these three situations. For each of the three scenarios listed in Column 1 indicate what you should do in Column 2 and what you would most likely do in Column 3. Are the responses in Columns 2 and 3 similar? If different, why? (Examples are purposely omitted here so as not to influence your responses.)

Ethical Situation	What do you think you should do?	What are you most likely to do?
Mother and Child. You witness a mother verbally abusing her 3-year-old child. Your first impulse is to tell this woman that verbal abuse can have lasting effects on the child and often leads to physical abuse. At the same time, you don't want to interfere with a mother's rights. Nor do you want to aggravate a mother who may later take out her frustration on the child. What is your ethical obligation in this case? What would you do in this situation?		
Witness to Crime. You witness a crime—three men robbed a pharmacy. No one was injured but a significant amount of drugs was stolen. Meanwhile, a police officer approaches you and asks if you've seen anything. You realize that you have a legal obligation to reveal what you've seen and yet you really don't want to get involved. It would be incredibly time-consuming and potentially dangerous and, very likely, the robbers won't get caught anyway. What do you do?		
Coming Clean. It's been assumed by your romantic partner that you both have come clean about your romantic past. The truth is, however, that your partner has revealed all but you have not. You're concerned about it; it doesn't seem right that your partner has been honest and you have not. And yet, you don't feel any real purpose would be served by your partner knowing of your previous relationship life. It's not something you're especially proud of. What should you do?		

Summary

1. Paralanguage refers to the vocal but nonverbal dimension of speech and consists of such elements as volume, rhythm, pitch, and rate of speech.
2. Through your paralanguage others can identify a variety of your characteristics.
3. Research on rate of speech shows that speech that is somewhat faster than normal will be more effective and the speaker will be thought more credible.
4. Silence is the absence of vocalization.
5. Silence serves a variety of functions, for example, allowing time to think, to hurt others, and to communicate emotional responses.
6. Different cultures regard silence differently.
7. The spiral of silence theory argues that you're more likely to voice agreement than disagreement.

Key Terms

Supply a definition for each of the following terms. Once you've formulated these "standard" definitions, consider the following ideas for further defining and understanding. Not all will work for all key terms, but some will work for some terms and some will work for others.

- Find a quotation that illustrates the term.
- Provide an example from personal interaction, television, film, novels, or plays.
- Create a short dialogue to illustrate the operation of the key term.
- Locate a research study investigating the key term and report its findings.
- Illustrate the concept nonverbally.
- Find a video that illustrates the key term.
- Find images—photos or graphics, abstract or specific, literal or metaphorical.
- Diagram the concept.
- Explain the negative, what the concept is not.
- State a skill that centers on the concept.

Key Concept	Definition
Paralanguage	
Speaker cues	
Listener cues	
Silence	
Functions of silence	
Spiral of silence	
Interruptions	

AND IN ADDITION

Using your favorite search engine (in addition, use Google Scholar or the databases in your college library for the more scientific research articles), search for **paralanguage, conversation management, turn-taking, interruptions, silence,** or any of the other terms and topics considered in this chapter and add to the chapter contents. Depending on the structure of the course and the facilities available, you may want to post these additions to a course website; to a social media site such as Twitter, Facebook, or Google+; or to a listserv or through e-mail, for example. Here are a few ways in which you might make your addition:

- Write a paragraph that adds to the discussion of a particular concept.
- Provide a new, contradictory, or intercultural example of a concept.
- Create a figure or table to illustrate or organize a particular topic.
- Illustrate with an image or two or a 10- to 15-second video a particular concept of nonverbal behavior.
- Summarize and evaluate the results of a scientific study on a topic relevant to this chapter.
- Summarize and evaluate an online article that focuses on one of the topics considered here.

Chapter 9

Time Messages

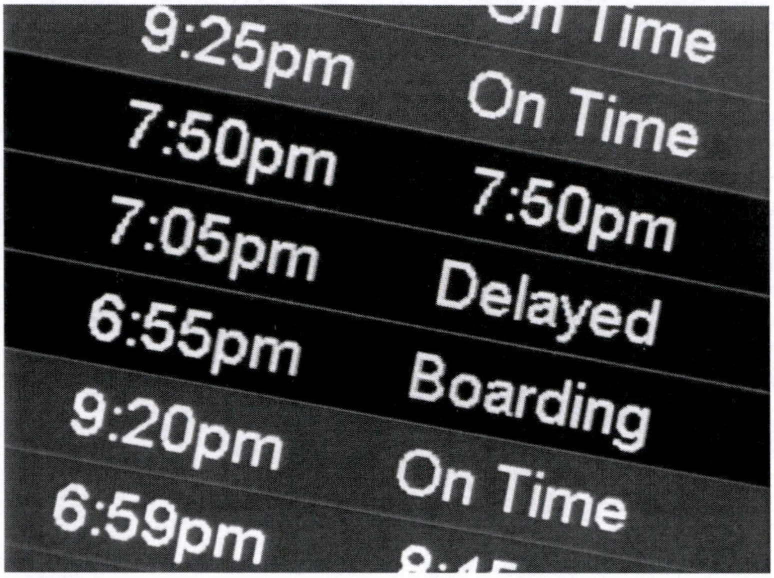

CHAPTER TOPICS

- Psychological Time
  - Past Orientation
  - Present Orientation
  - Future Orientation
- Interpersonal Time
  - Punctuality
  - Wait Time
  - Lead Time
  - Duration
  - Simultaneity
  - Talk Time
  - Work Time
  - Relationship Time
  - Synchronicity and Asynchronicity
  - Response Time
- Cultural Time
  - Formal and Informal Time
  - Monochronism and Polychronism
  - Displaced and Diffused Orientation
  - The Social Clock
- Biological Time
  - Biorhythms
  - Daytime Preferences
- Time Management

Summary
Key Terms
And in Addition

CHAPTER EXERCISES

[Identifying Your Psychological Time Orientation]
Distinguishing between Appropriate and Inappropriate Time Responses
Explaining Interpersonal Time
Analyzing Time Expressions
Making Self-Disclosure Decisions
Charting Your Biorhythms
[Identifying Your Daytime Orientation]
Analyzing Your Own Time Management

ON THE JOB

Workplace Promptness
Multitasking

POLITENESS IN NONVERBAL COMMUNICATION

Being polite with time messages

IF YOU WANT TO

Appear a professional **leader/in control of the situation,** especially at meetings
Express **intimacy/connection/liking for/warmth/affection**

CHAPTER OBJECTIVES

After reading this chapter, you should be able to:

1. Define *psychological time* and explain the different psychological time orientations.
2. Define *interpersonal time* and explain its essential dimensions.
3. Define and distinguish between formal and informal time and between monochronism and polychronism.
4. Define *social clock* and apply its implications to your own thinking about time.
5. Explain the nature of biological time and the nature of biorhythms.

BEFORE reading about time messages, consider your own time orientation. For each of the following statements, indicate which is TRUE and which is FALSE in terms of your general attitude and behavior.

_______ 1. I often turn to the past for guidance in the present.
_______ 2. Old people have wisdom that I can learn from.
_______ 3. I enjoy learning about and from the past.
_______ 4. Knowing about the past helps me in the present.
_______ 5. I enjoy life as it comes.
_______ 6. I avoid looking too far ahead.
_______ 7. I frequently put off work to enjoy the moment.
_______ 8. I look for immediate payoffs/rewards.
_______ 9. I work hard today basically because of tomorrow's expected rewards.
_______ 10. I enjoy planning for tomorrow and the future generally.
_______ 11. I'm willing to endure difficulties if there's a payoff/reward at the end.
_______ 12. I prepare "to do" lists fairly regularly.

These questions were designed to raise the issue of time orientation, whether you focus more on the past, the present, or the future. The idea for this test and the insights on psychological time owe their formulation to Gonzales and Zimbardo (1985). Past-oriented individuals would (as you can tell from the questions) respond with TRUE to Questions 1–4 and with either TRUE or FALSE for the remaining statements. Present-oriented individuals would response with TRUE to Questions 5–8, FALSE to Questions 9–12, and either TRUE or FALSE for Questions 1–4. Future-oriented individuals would respond with TRUE to Questions 9–12, FALSE for Questions 5–8, and either TRUE or FALSE for Questions 1–4. As you'll see, your time orientation has important implications for both your college and your professional career.

The study of temporal communication, known technically as **chronemics**, concerns the use of time—how you organize it, react to it, and communicate messages through it (Bruneau, 1990, 2009/2010). We identify four types of time: psychological time, interpersonal time, cultural time, and biological time. In addition, we offer some suggestions on effective time management.

PSYCHOLOGICAL TIME

Psychological time is concerned with a person's orientation to the past, present, or future. Let's look at each.

Past Orientation

With a **past orientation**—which is relatively rare in much of the United States but quite prevalent in other parts of the world—individuals look to the past for guidance. They believe that what was done in the past is good enough for the present. In these cultures, there is particular reverence for older people who are seen as having the wisdom necessary to guide us in the present and in the future. In some cases, present ways of doing things are looked upon with suspicion and they often resist innovations. They fight against embracing technology, for example.

Present Orientation

With a **present orientation**, you live in the present—for now—without planning for tomorrow or think back to the past. Present orientation is strongest among lowest-income males and also among those with high emotional distress and hopelessness (Zaleski, Cycon, & Kurc, 2001). One of the problems with present orientation is that you're left with an unprepared-for future. This is the person who spends his or her money early and is left with no retirement funds. This is the person who parties rather than studies and fails to develop the skills and competencies needed for profitable employment. The problems with present orientation, not surprisingly, are taught to us early. Consider, for example, the story of the Three Little Pigs. The pigs that didn't plan for the future and didn't protect themselves against the wolf had their houses blown away.

Future Orientation

With a **future orientation**, you look toward and live for the future. You follow the model of the little pig who spent his time building his house to withstand the wolf rather than play. You save today, work hard in college, and deny yourself luxuries because you're preparing for the future. In fact, college itself is a future-oriented activity. The fact that you are in college means that you are future oriented, at least to some major extent. This is not to deny that there aren't immediate rewards in college; there certainly are, probably every day. And yet, the activity itself—the investment of 4 years time and considerable money and forfeiture of earnings—is clearly future oriented. Not surprisingly, future income is positively related to future orientation; the more future oriented you are, the greater your income is likely to be (Gonzalez & Zimbardo, 1985).

The time orientation you develop depends on your culture, your socioeconomic class, and your personal experiences (Gonzalez & Zimbardo, 1985). Children with parents who work in unskilled occupations are brought up in a way that promotes a present orientation. Children whose parents are professionals (e.g., teachers, doctors, lawyers, accountants) are brought up with a future orientation. They're taught the value of preparing for tomorrow. For example, children of professionals are expected to go to college; it's almost an unwritten, unspoken assumption. Children of unskilled workers may or may not go to college.

What were you taught about time from your parents? Your teachers? Your peers? © 2013, iofoto, Shutterstock, Inc.

As you might expect, communication problems can easily occur between future and present-oriented people. For example, the future-oriented person who works for tomorrow's goals will frequently look down on the present-oriented person as lazy and poorly motivated for enjoying today and not planning for tomorrow. (In fact, much of the current financial debate over social security and health insurance and austerity in Europe centers on the belief that people must be future oriented and must plan for their future.) In turn, the present-oriented person may see those with strong future orientations as obsessed with amassing wealth or rising in status and failing to "smell the roses." Present-oriented people may criticize future-oriented parents who pursue careers while their children are young for their failure to enjoy the present and to make the present the time that really counts.

INTERPERSONAL TIME

Interpersonal time refers to a wide variety of time-related elements that figure into interpersonal interaction. Burgoon et al. (2010) discuss punctuality, wait time, lead time, duration, and simultaneity and Andersen and Bowman (1999) discuss waiting-time, talk-time, and work-time in their discussion of time and its relationship to power. To these we add relationship time, synchronicity–asynchronicity, and response time, the last two of which have taken on added importance due to the frequency with which you communicate via some kind of computer connection, and group them under the heading of *Interpersonal Time.*

Punctuality

Punctuality refers to being on time for a variety of occasions—for company meetings, for class, for teacher–student appointments, for a ball game, for a movie or television show, and for completing assignments, to take just a few examples. Some people are always on time or early and others are consistently late, likely a personality difference. However, much of it is learned. If you were taught the values and appropriateness (by example as well as by explicit instruction) then it's likely that you act in accordance with these "instructions." One way you learn this is by observing any hierarchy such as those in most organizations. Generally, those of higher status have greater leeway when it comes to punctuality; the boss may be late but the workers need to be on time. The professor may be late for a conference but the student needs to be on time. The dean or president may be late for a conference but the professor needs to be on time. As a patient you're expected to be on time though the doctor rarely is.

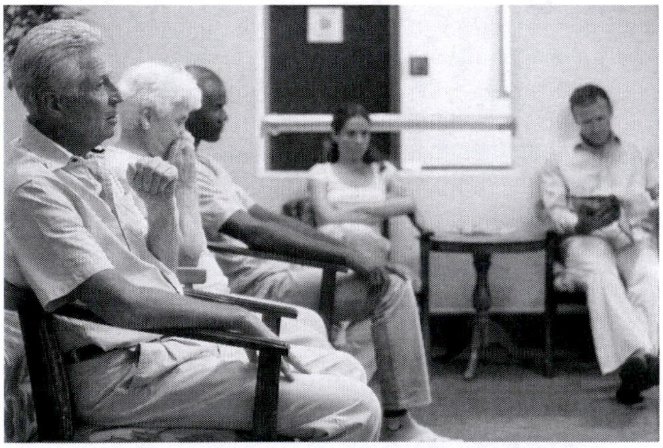

What other situations might you mention as having different rules depending on your status?

Different cultures view punctuality differently, which can on occasion create difficulties. For example, members of some Latin cultures would rather be late for an appointment than end a conversation abruptly. The Latin person sees this behavior as politeness toward the person with whom he or she is conversing—but others, especially future-oriented people, may see this as impolite to the person with whom he or she had the appointment (Hall & Hall, 1987).

IF YOU WANT TO

Appear a professional **leader/in control of the situation,** especially at meetings

- Arrive a bit early (not too early).
- Be totally prepared.
- End on time.
- Dress appropriately (perhaps one step up from the usual).

Wait Time

Wait time refers to the amount of time it's considered appropriate to wait for something or someone. Burgoon et al. (2010) relate the practice of college students being required to wait for a late instructor a certain length of time depending on the instructor's rank, a situation I recall from my own college days. Then, we had to wait a full 30 minutes for a full professor but only 10 minutes for an assistant professor. This, by the way, was taught to all incoming students during orientation classes and it may still be a practice in some colleges today. Actually, this isn't uncommon. Police officers, firefighters, and military personnel all follow similar rules—though many are unwritten.

Consider some of the messages this type of rule might communicate, for example:

- The time of high-ranking people is more important than the time of low-ranking people.
- The value of a student's time is related to the rank of the instructor.
- Rank is crucial to all of life's relationships.

There are of course factors other than status that figure into this equation. For example, if this was the first time you were meeting face to face with someone you've communicated with for 2 years via a social network and the person was late, you'd probably wait a lot longer than if this were someone you didn't care about or if you were not looking forward to the meeting.

Wait time can also be used strategically to signal power differences and to dominate the interaction. Just being late and having someone wait for you communicates that you're more important—or at least that's the message many would get from this situation. And since it's usually the superior who makes the other person wait, the power difference already exists and the wait time just emphasizes it.

Lead Time

Lead time refers to the time needed for making decisions. For example, you'd expect to ask for a date sometime in advance of the actual date (and this will vary greatly from one culture to another), especially if it's something like a prom or a major event. You'd expect an invitation for a wedding, for example, to arrive with considerable lead time and you'd expect more lead time if the wedding were in another state or country. Similarly, you're expected to give an employer a certain amount of time if you quit (and it may well be written in your contract). Employers seem to vary; some will give terminated employees notice and others will usher the fired individual out the door with virtually no lead time.

Duration

Duration refers to the length of time that a particular interaction will take. When you go to the doctor or dentist you're likely given a specific amount of time. If you use a consultant, lawyer, or accountant you may be charged for the length of time you interact and the length of time he or she works on your project. Appropriately enough, the practice is referred to as being "on the clock." The more important the topic is, generally, the longer the duration. And, not surprisingly, higher-status people will ration their time more rigidly than will a lower-status person. For example, you'd normally talk for a longer duration with your immediate supervisor than with the president of the company.

Simultaneity

Simultaneity refers to whether one thing or many things are done at the same time. Again, status differences emerge here as well. The physician, for example, may take a call during your examination but it would be considered highly unusual if you interrupted the examination with a call. The boss may talk about irrelevant issues during a meeting but a trainee may not. The United States is generally considered a monochronic culture where one thing is done per unit of time as opposed to say some Arab countries in which several things may be done at one meeting. Yet, from just looking around at home, at school, or on the job, we are fast becoming (if we haven't arrived already) a polychronic culture or, in popular terms, a multitasking culture. We watch television while we text and talk on the phone; we jog while listening to music or an audio book; we eat, text, and watch television all at the same time.

Talk Time

Talk time refers to, for example, who initiates and who terminates a conversation, who talks more, and who selects and directs the topics for discussion. As with so many such factors, status plays an important role here. It's the higher-status person who makes the decisions. Perhaps the best example of high status and talk time is the privilege to interrupt. The person higher up in the hierarchy interrupts lower hierarchical members and not the other way around. It's a way of saying and meaning:

"What I have to say is more important than what you have to say. And since I'm the boss, that's the way it's going to be."

Work Time

Work time refers to the time schedule of your working life. If you're a low-level employee, you may have to punch a clock. And you're probably paid per unit of time, per hour or per day. You need to arrive on time and not leave before the workday is finished. And you need to wait for your lunch break to eat even if you were hungry for the last 2 hours. If you're a high-level employee or the boss, you may actually spend more time at work but it will be of your own choosing; you won't have to punch a time clock, get permission to arrive late or leave early, and of course you don't have to wait for your lunch break to eat.

Relationship Time

Relationship time is similar to work time but refers to the time one gives or should give to the various people with whom one has a relationship. In our culture, committed romantic couples normally spend a considerable amount of time together and when that time is abbreviated (and considered too little by one of the partners), the relationship may be headed for trouble. Even long-distance relationships normally have relationship time—whether on the phone, through periodic visits, or via Skype. Even at social gatherings you're expected to devote your time on the basis of the relationships you have with the other members. So, you're expected to spend more time with close friends (especially if you've not seen them for a long time) than with acquaintances. Parents are expected to devote a great deal of time to their children (especially when the children are young) and those who don't are often criticized by those who do. And adult children are expected to spend less and less time with their parents and more and more time with their romantic partner or friends.

In addition to simple amount of time, relationship time demands some measure of "quality time." Watching television together is probably not as high in quality as having a romantic dinner at the neighborhood bistro where you had your first date.

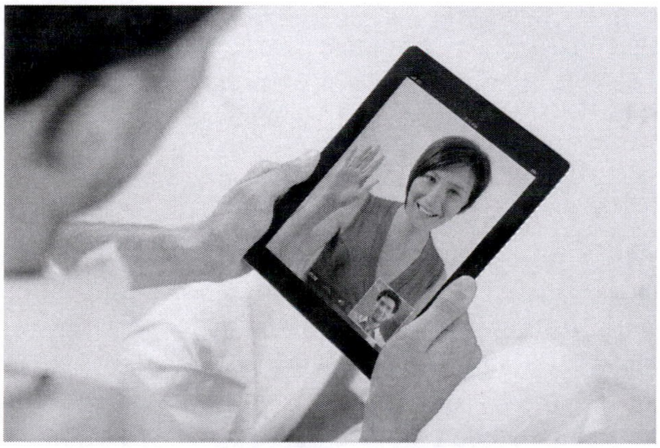

What are some of the things you might do to increase the feeling that you are spending more time together than you really are? © 2013, bloomua, Shutterstock, Inc.

Similarly, conversation with one eye on the television or your smartphone is not as high in quality as conversation with none of these distractions, with direct eye contact and an inclusive, face-to-face, and congruent posture.

IF YOU WANT TO

Express **intimacy/connection/liking for/warmth/affection**

- Lean forward.
- Smile.
- Gaze at other's eyes.
- Nod head in affirmation.
- Reciprocate the other's behaviors.
- Maintain shorter distance between you.
- Use a direct, face-to-face body orientation.

Synchronicity and Asynchronicity

Synchronicity and **asynchronicity** refer to whether the communication takes place in real time—simultaneously, as in face-to-face communication (this would be synchronous)—or whether messages are sent at one time and received at another, as in e-mail communication (this would be asynchronous). If you want to reduce or lessen the chance for misunderstanding, brainstorm, or get a quick response, then synchronous communication will probably work better. If you wanted to communicate extremely complex messages (e.g., reports) that need to be thought about at length or messages that need to be stated with great explicitness (e.g., contracts), then asynchronous communication might work better. Table 9.1 identifies some of the differences between synchronous and asynchronous communication.

Response Time

Response time refers to the time it takes a person to respond. Response time is observed in both synchronous and asynchronous communication. For example, in face-to-face communication, the response time to some statements and questions must be immediate. There should be very little response lag between one's person's "Will you marry me?" and the other's "Yes." When the response time is inappropriately long, you may sense some kind of disagreement or lack of certainty. A recent article in *The Week* (June 1, 2012, p. 12) gives a perfect example of inappropriate response time. An Indian woman filed a motion for divorce from her husband of 2 months because he took too long to change his relationship status on Facebook to

TABLE 9.1 Synchronous and Asynchronous Communication

Here is an overview of synchronous and asynchronous communication, highlighting some of their major differences.

	Synchronous Communication	Asynchronous Communication
Definition	Communication in which messages are sent and received at essentially the same time	Communication in which messages are sent at one time and received at another time
Examples	Face to face Telephone Chat Instant messaging Often through Skype, Ms Live, or similar programs	Mail (e-mail, voice mail, snail mail)
Especially useful for	Reduce ambiguity Brainstorming Getting quick action	Complex messages (e.g., reports) that need to be thought about at length Messages that may need to be stated with great explicitness (e.g., contracts)
Advantages	Provides opportunity for two-way communication Takes a relatively short time to accomplish a task or reach a decision	Each person can deal with the message when convenient Takes a relatively long time
Disadvantages	Special time is needed; often difficult to get the relevant people together at the same time	Does not allow for two-way communication

"married." Her reasoning was that this was an indication that he was probably cheating; the judge didn't agree and ordered them to undergo counseling.

You also expect people to respond immediately when you're in need of support or comfort; if not, you may perceive any eventual support as forced or not genuine. Response time is also extremely important in asynchronous communication—for example, the time it takes someone to respond to your e-mail or poke or invitation to connect on some social media site will communicate some message. From different response times, you send different messages—messages of interest and concern and immediacy and messages of indicating the opposite. Sometimes our impressions are correct and sometimes not.

EXERCISE

DISTINGUISHING BETWEEN APPROPRIATE AND INAPPROPRIATE TIME RESPONSES

Understanding your own time responses, and the expectations that others have, will likely help you avoid a variety of interpersonal conflicts. In Column 1 are listed several situations calling for a response. Add situations you've experienced in the two blank spaces. In Column 2 indicate what you feel would be an appropriate time range for responding. In Column 3 indicate the rule that you feel identifies appropriate time responding such as might appear in a manual on appropriate time responses.

Situations	Appropriate time range for responding	Rule identifying time appropriateness for responding
Patient emails MD to renew prescription	*Immediately to 48 hours*	*MDs should respond to patient's e-mail within 48 hours, earlier if it's an emergency*
E-mail invitation to dinner (sent 2 weeks before the scheduled dinner)		
Instructor responding to student e-mail		
Leaving a phone message asking a friend to call you back		
Asking friends to "like" a cause on Facebook		
Asking a friend for a loan of $300 via e-mail		

All of these types of interpersonal time will be influenced by a variety of factors involved in the interpersonal communication process. Status differences, as already illustrated, will influence significantly the way in which interpersonal time is treated. Other factors also come into play. For example, your personality will likely influence your punctuality, how long you wait for someone, whether or not you interrupt others, and your response time to invitations. Similarly, the context and purpose of the communication will influence how you'll treat interpersonal time. For example, if you're interviewing for the job of a lifetime and the interviewer is late, you'll no doubt wait. In contrast, if you're simply meeting someone to walk to classes with and the person is late, you'd be more likely to move on. Also, the relationship between you and the other person or persons will influence your interpersonal time. For example, if the relationship is an important one to you personally, you'll likely excuse the lack of punctuality. In contrast, if the relationship is only a casual one or perhaps one of hostility, you might become annoyed, increase your dislike for this person who has no consideration for your time, and resolve not to wait any longer.

EXERCISE

EXPLAINING INTERPERSONAL TIME

To get a better idea of how you use time and how you might improve your use of time, examine the types of interpersonal time listed in Column 1 and identified above. In Column 2 describe your general behavior in regard to your use of one, two, three, or all of the dimensions of interpersonal time. If you're unhappy or dissatisfied with the way you treat any of these dimensions of time, record in Column 3 the behavior you'd like to develop, exhibit, and make a regular part of your communication life and how you might go about achieving this.

Interpersonal time dimensions	You as you are (your normal, everyday behavior)	You as you'd like to be and what you might do
Punctuality	*Too often late for appointments.*	*Be always on time or even a bit early; set phone/computer to give me a 30-minute reminder before any appointment.*
Wait time		
Lead time		
Duration		
Simultaneity		
Talk time		
Work time		
Relationship time		
Synchronicity and asynchronicity		
Response time		

POLITENESS IN NONVERBAL COMMUNICATION

Being polite with time messages:

- Be respectful of others' time. Many see time as their most important possession.
- Ask if this is a good time to talk. And make it clear that a "no" answer is perfectly fine.
- Be sensitive to cultural differences. Don't assume that all cultures treat time similarly.
- Respond to others' messages within a reasonable time frame.

CULTURAL TIME

Culture influences time communication in a variety of ways. Before reading about the types of cultural time, try the following exercise.

Here we look at four aspects of cultural time: formal and informal time, monochronism and polychronism, displaced and diffused orientation, and the social clock.

EXERCISE

ANALYZING TIME EXPRESSIONS

Before reading about the cultural dimension of time, consider the time expressions listed in Column 1. In Column 2 indicate the meaning of these expressions (which are all cultural views of time) and in Column 3 indicate exceptions to these general cultural prescriptions.

Time Expressions	Meaning	Exceptions
Haste makes waste.	*Doing something too quickly often results in errors.*	*If an angry pit bull is chasing you, close the door as quickly as you can.*
Time is money.		
Time heals all wounds.		
A stitch in time saves nine.		
Every dog has its day.		
Time waits for no one.		
One who hesitates is lost.		

Formal and Informal Time

In the United States and in most of the world, **formal time** divisions consist of units such as seconds, minutes, hours, days, weeks, months, and years. Some cultures, however, may use phases of the moon or changing seasons to delineate time periods. In the United States, if your college is on the semester system, your courses are divided into 50- or 75-minute periods that meet two or three times a week for 14-week periods. Eight semesters of 15 or 16 periods per week equal a college education. As these examples illustrate, formal time units are arbitrary. The culture establishes them for convenience.

Informal time terms denote approximate intervals—for example, "forever," "immediately," "soon," "right away," or "as soon as possible." Informal time expressions create the most communication problems because the terms have different meanings for different people.

ON THE JOB

Workplace Promptness

You're supervising six junior members of your firm, four of whom are prompt in arriving at work and in getting their work done. Two, however, are always late; they arrive late and their work is often late. You realize that you're a bit of a stickler for time, but these two members are clearly not doing their share in terms of moving the projects along. What are some of the things you might do to encourage greater promptness?

Monochronism and Polychronism

Another important cultural distinction exists between monochronic and polychronic time orientations (Hall, 1959, 1976; Hall & Hall, 1987). **Monochronic** peoples or cultures such as those of the United States, Germany, Scandinavia, and Switzerland schedule one thing at a time. These cultures compartmentalize time and set sequential times for different activities.

Polychronic peoples or cultures such as those of Latin America, the Mediterranean, and the Arab world, on the other hand, schedule multiple things at the same time. Eating, conducting business with several different people, and taking care of family matters may all go on at once.

It's interesting to note that social media and perhaps especially the smartphone has brought multitasking (essentially a polychronic activity) to a new level and has turned normally monochronic cultures into polychronic cultures. For example, at meetings, at dinner, and even in many classrooms, members are multitasking with their smartphones and tablets. And, perhaps not so surprising, women are generally more polychronic than are men (Hall, 1983).

In what ways do you multitask? Are you offended in any way when someone—say, in a face-to-face conversation—surfs the Internet or talks on their cell?

ON THE JOB

Multitasking

You're leading a task group charged with improving company morale. The problem is that two of the six group members multitask throughout the meetings. They make dinner appointments, talk to their kids on the phone, and answer their e-mail when you need them to concentrate on the task at hand. What are some of the things you can do to improve this group's focus?

No culture is entirely monochronic or polychronic; rather, these are general or preponderant tendencies. Some cultures combine both time orientations; in Japan and in parts of American culture, for example, both orientations can be found. Table 9.2 identifies some of the distinctions between these two time orientations.

Displaced and Diffused Orientation

Closely related to monochronic and polychronic time is the distinction between displaced and diffused time orientation. A **displaced time** orientation views time exactly and precisely. A person with this orientation views an appointment at 5:00 P.M. to mean exactly that: 5:00 P.M. A **diffused time** orientation, however, views time in more approximate terms. An appointment at 5:00 P.M. means that one should arrive sometime around 5:00 P.M., say between 4:50 and 5:10. In some cases, there would be much greater latitude.

In some cultures, Japan is often cited as an example—time is displaced, things are done exactly on time. Time must not be wasted. In other cultures—Indonesia is a good example as are many Mediterranean countries—time is diffused, things are done on an approximate, loose time schedule. In fact, when researchers compared the accuracy of clocks in Japan, Indonesia, the United States, Italy, England, and Taiwan, they found that the clocks were most accurate in Japan and least accurate in Indonesia. Interestingly enough, when the speed with which citizens of these countries walk was measured, it was found that the Japanese walked the fastest and the Indonesians the slowest (LeVine & Bartlett, 1984).

TABLE 9.2 Monochronic and Polychronic Time

As you read down this table, based on Hall (1983) and Hall and Hall (1987), note the potential for miscommunication that might develop when M-time and P-time people interact. Have any of these differences ever created interpersonal misunderstandings for you?

The Monochronic-Time Person	The Polychronic-Time Person
Does one thing at a time; full attention is given to a specific task.	Does several things at once; multitasks where attention is spread over several tasks.
Treats time schedules and plans very seriously; feels they may be broken only for the most serious of reasons; promptness/punctuality is extremely important.	Treats time schedules and plans as useful, not sacred); feels they may be broken for a variety of purposes; promptness/punctuality is viewed in more flexible terms.
Considers the job the most important part of a person's life, ahead of even family.	Considers the family and interpersonal relationships more important than the job.
Considers privacy extremely important; seldom borrows or lends to others; works independently.	Is actively involved with others; works in the presence of and with lots of people at the same time.

The Social Clock

An especially interesting aspect of cultural time is the **social clock** (Neugarten, 1979). Your culture, and your more specific society within that culture, maintains a schedule that dictates the right times to do a variety of important things; for example, the right times to start dating, to finish college, to buy your own home, to have a child. You also may feel that you should be making a certain salary and working at a particular level of management by a certain age. Most people learn about and internalize this clock as they grow up. On the basis of your social clock, you evaluate your own social and professional development. If you're on time relative to the rest of your peers—for example, if you all started dating at around the same age or you're

EXERCISE

MAKING SELF-DISCLOSURE DECISIONS

Examining your own feelings about disclosing personal information will enable you to think more objectively about impending self-disclosures away from any interpersonal pressure. In Column 1 are listed a variety of messages you might communicate over the course of a relationship. Columns 2 and 3 indicate when in the course of the relationships you would communicate these messages. After completing this table, formulate, in 140 characters or fewer, the rule you followed in deciding when (if ever) to self-disclose. This exercise can easily be expanded to include a wider variety of relationships; some useful ones to explore might be work colleagues, acquaintances in your class, neighbors, and siblings.

Message	Romantic Relationship	Virtual Friendship
Your annual salary and financial worth	*The relationship would have to be a potentially serious one for me to reveal this.*	*Probably no reason to ever reveal this; then again, if I never see the person, it wouldn't matter*
Your sexual fantasies		
Your attitudes toward other religions, nationalities, or races		
Your health status		
Your self-concept		

General Rule: ____

____.

all finishing college at around the same age—then you will feel well adjusted, competent, and a part of the group. If you're late, you will probably experience feelings of dissatisfaction and inadequacy.

BIOLOGICAL TIME

Biological time orientation often refers to our body clocks, the ways in which our bodies respond at different times. Here we can discuss a popular approach to biological time known as biorhythms and then look at time preferences for morning or evening.

Biorhythms

According to **biorhythm** research, you function in three different cycles (physical, emotional, and intellectual). Each cycle begins at birth and continues throughout life, repeating itself periodically. Each of these three cycles has (1) an up-side, during which you are particularly sharp—approximately the first half of the cycle; (2) a down-side, during which you are particularly dull—approximately the second half of the cycle; and (3) a crucial period during which you are at your absolute worst—when the cycle changes from up to down.

- **Physical cycle.** The physical cycle is concerned with strength, energy, coordination, and resistance to disease. It lasts 23 days. During the up-side you are in good health, have coordinated balance, are hyperactive, and are especially good athletically. During the down-side, you are tired and lazy, you lack coordination, you have low endurance, and you are especially prone to accidents and ailments. See Figure 9.1A.
- **Emotional cycle.** The emotional cycle is concerned with mood, you optimism and pessimism, and your ability to work effectively with others. It lasts 28 days. During the up-side you are calm, cheerful, cooperative, understanding, and creative. During the down-side, you are moody, negative, irritable, and hypersensitive. See Figure 9.1B.
- **Intellectual cycle.** The intellectual cycle is concerned with your intellectual abilities and activities. It lasts 33 days. During the up-side you are intellectually driven and efficient; you have good memory power and can make rapid and accurate decisions. During the down-side your thinking capacity is diminished, your mental abilities are low, your memory is poor, and your reactions are slower. See Figure 9.1C.

There is little valid and reliable research to substantiate the claims made by proponents of biorhythmic analysis. Nevertheless, it does raise the important issue of body clock cycles and how these may influence behaviors, moods, and abilities.

Daytime Preferences

Another aspect of biological time is your orientation to day or evening, frequently referred to as the lark and the owl. For example, respond to the following statements by indicating morning (let's say, between getting up and noon) or evening (let's say,

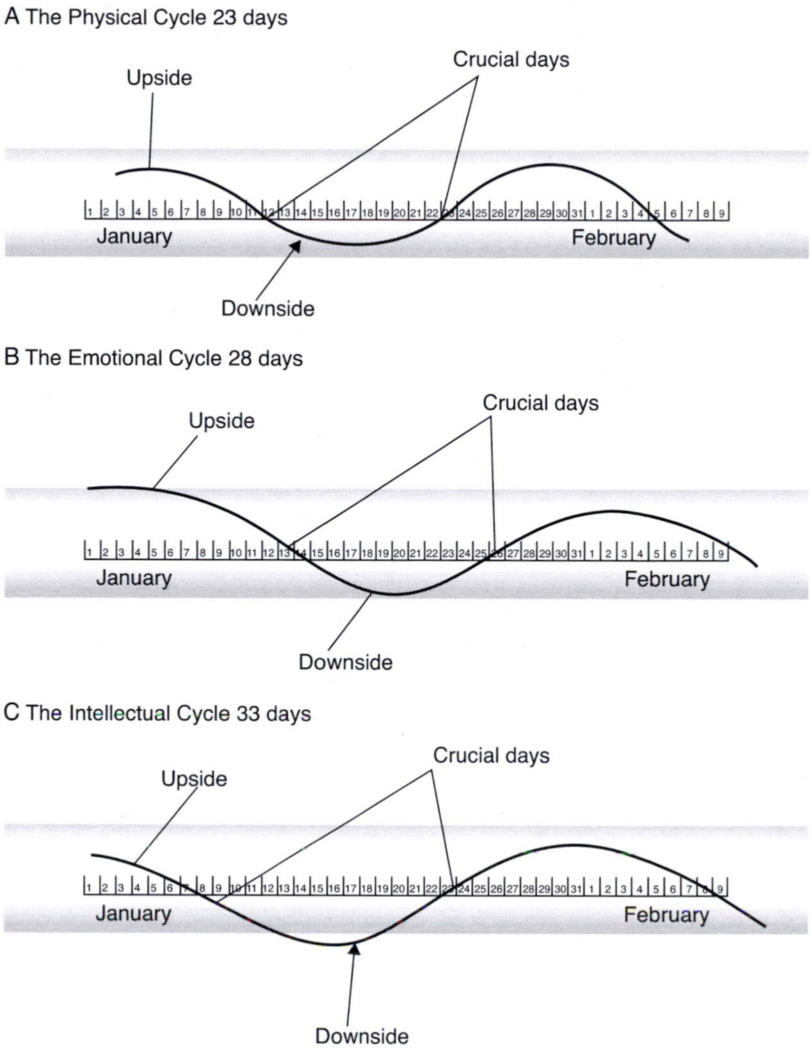

Figure 9.1 Biorhythm Charts

from 4:00 to 8:00): (The idea for this type of test comes from the Owl and Sparrow from Rosenfeld [1990] and the Measure of Time Orientation from Richmond, McCroskey, and Hickson [2010].)

- I prefer (morning, evening) classes.
- I'm at my best in the (morning, evening).
- I like doing things in the (morning, evening).
- I'm less easily annoyed in the (morning, evening).
- I exercise in the (morning, evening).
- I enjoy social networking in the (morning, evening).
- I feel healthiest/most robust in the (morning, evening).
- I seem happiest in the (morning, evening).
- I enjoy interacting with people more in the (morning, evening).
- I'm most creative in the (morning, evening).

EXERCISE

CHARTING YOUR BIORHYTHMS

The easiest way to construct your own biorhythm chart, since you have to count the number of days since you were born, is to use a computer program. Simply search for *biorhythm calculator*—you'll find several—put in your date of birth and the program will chart your biorhythms. You can then look back on significant events in you life—good and bad—and see if these match the predictions made by the biorhythm calculator. The following table may help you structure your responses. In Column 1 are listed the three major cycles. In Column 2 record one or two predictions that biorhythm analysis makes for each of the three cycles. In Column 3 indicate what really happened and whether or not the biorhythm prediction was accurate.

Cycles	Biorhythm Prediction (e.g., up-side, down-side, or crucial days)	What Really Happened/ Accuracy
Physical	*October 4 = crucial day*	*Tripped and broke my toe/too accurate*
Emotional		
Intellectual		

Given your time preferences, what would be the ideal job for you? Why?

These statements are simply meant to highlight some of the differences in our preferences for doing different things during different times of the day. In fact, you no doubt have spoken of *morning people* or *evening people* in recognition of this difference.

As you can appreciate, these differences can cause a variety of problems. For example, consider the romantic couple who are in totally different time preferences;

one wants to be quiet and contemplative in the morning while the other wants to talk and debate national issues. Or consider the irritability of people during different parts of the day; some people are extremely touchy in the morning but quite easy to get along with later in the day. These differences can also cause problems for the college student—having to take chemistry at 8:00 in the morning may be ideal for some and absolutely horrible for others. And, of course, professors are in the same situation; teaching chemistry at 8:00 in the morning may be great for some but not for others.

TIME MANAGEMENT

Time is one of the things you never have enough of—there's always more to see, more to read, more to write, more to do. Oddly enough, and despite its importance, there are no courses in time management in the curricula of most colleges. Consequently, the student, especially the beginning student, is often left adrift—having more to do than time will allow. Here then are a dozen suggestions especially for the college student, though the principles are relevant and useful to anyone concerned with making more effective use of one's time.

1. **Understand your use of time.** This has got to be the first step—if you don't do this then you won't have a firm grasp on how you now use your time or how you can possibly change it. Take a look at what takes up most of your time. In a 24-hour day, what takes up the largest block of time (aside from sleeping)? Ideally, you'd chart your use of time for at least a week and categorize the major uses, for example, talking on the phone, eating, studying, taking classes, commuting to classes, working, and so on. Once you know how you spend your time, you'll be able to see what can be and should be cut back. Analyze what needs to be done. Look over your time chart and examine the major categories and see which can be eliminated or at least cut back.
2. **Attack your time-wasters.** Very likely you'll find lots of time-wasters—things that take up your time but you can easily do without—whether it's watching Jerry Springer or always arriving early for appointments and waiting for others to arrive or playing Spider Solitaire. Identify these and add up or estimate the time these wasters take up in one work week. Begin by getting rid of the one time-waster that you can most easily do without.

What are your three greatest time-wasters? How do you feel about this? © 2013, jcjgphotography, Shutterstock, Inc.

3. **Attack your self-defeating beliefs.** Most people, it seems, have beliefs that are unproductive and in fact often self-defeating. These are beliefs that you need to do things that are actually impossible to do. For example, you may have the belief that you have to be loved by everyone and so you attend every function of just about every family member or friend, keep in touch with people you hardly know through your social media communication—fearful that they will not like you if you don't and, in the process, neglect to do things that would benefit you in more important ways. Well, the truth is you can't be loved by everyone; it's a totally unrealistic belief. Perhaps even more important is that even if you could be loved by everyone, it isn't vital that you are so loved. It's nice to be loved but it isn't essential. Another belief is that you must do everything in the shortest possible time. These beliefs prevent the wise use of time.
4. **Avoid self-handicapping strategies.** These strategies are designed to give you an excuse for failing. One self-handicapping strategy that college students have been known to use is to party the night before a test so that if they don't do well on the test, they have a ready excuse. Of course, this strategy simply makes your task all the more difficult and wastes the time you could have used more productively.
5. **Avoid procrastination.** Avoid the tendency to delay things to the last minute, another strategy that college students often use in the mistaken belief that they work better under pressure. It's highly unlikely that you will do a better job when you're rushed than when you have the available and necessary time to complete a task.
6. **Use tools.** You wouldn't think of cooking without using the appropriate utensils and yet many go about "organizing" their lives without the multitude of organizing tools. Whether you use the low-tech schedule book or the Google Calendar or Rescue Time's app on your smartphone, use a tool. Everyone needs help and you can't keep everything in short-term memory. In selecting an organizing tool, do consider the great search advantages of electronic schedules over the traditional schedule book.
7. **Prioritize.** Make lists. Generally, time management experts recommend some ABC type system. So, for example, you'd list all the tasks you want to accomplish for a day or a week and then prioritize them: A = tasks that should definitely be done today or this week; B = tasks that it would be nice to complete but could be delayed; and C = tasks that aren't essential; only do these if you have the time. Or you might prioritize the tasks in the order in which you want to accomplish them. The objective here is to put some order into your list. And, depending on the system you use, it may enable you to distinguish between necessary and unnecessary tasks.
8. **Break up large tasks.** Often a large task seems so daunting that it's put at the end of the priority list—not because it's not important but just because it's so large an undertaking. This is a mistake that many people make. In actual practice,

most large tasks can be divided into small steps and broken up to accomplish during our work day. So, for example, if you have a speech to prepare there's no reason to prepare it from beginning to end at one sitting. In fact, that would probably be a mistake for lots of reasons—for example, you need time to simply let some of the ideas gel. You can break up the speech preparation process very easily in steps, for example, selecting the topic, purpose, and thesis might be the first step. Do this and then move on to another task, say completing the first two exercises in the chemistry manual.

9. **Set realistic time limits**. Whether the task is large or small, it often helps to set time limits, especially when the task is unpleasant, like doing your income tax or reading a boring but important textbook. If you set time limits, it will be easier to get into the task. So, if you set yourself 30 minutes to read the text, it won't seem like such an onerous task but, rather, it will seem (and be) something you can do with ease. Of course, the time limit you'd set would depend on a variety of factors—how much there is to accomplish, how comfortable you are with sticking with one task, how onerous you feel the task is, and so on. If the time periods are too short, you'll waste lots of time—after all, getting into a task takes time; if the time periods are too long, you'll resist the task and perhaps view it as overly difficult.
10. **Reward yourself**. It often helps, especially with unpleasant tasks, to plan to reward yourself after completing a unit of work. It doesn't have to be only for completing a task in totality but could also be for completing 1 hour's textbook reading or completing the research portion of your speech. Do be careful to keep the reward in proportion. You don't want to reward yourself with unhealthy food or "breaks" that last longer than the work task itself.
11. **Do things once rather than twice.** For example, one of the popular rules for time management is to look only once at a piece of paper, act on it, and then file or get rid of it. Today, this would concern such things as reading your e-mail when you aren't ready to answer it or opening bills when you aren't ready to pay them or record them. Instead, read your e-mail when you have the time to answer it; open your bills when you're ready to pay or record them.
12. **Avoid distractions**. Distractions are often not controllable and so you're not going to be able to work without any distractions. However, you can attempt to minimize them. You don't have to answer every phone call exactly when it comes in; you don't have to leave your office or dorm door open, which invites others to come in to chat. If you do find yourself easily distracted, ask yourself if you're actually looking for and encouraging distractions. One clue to this is to analyze the distractions you do encounter; if they come more frequently with the more unpleasant tasks—rather than at random—then you're likely encouraging them as a way to get out of the unpleasant task you now face.

EXERCISE

ANALYZING YOUR OWN TIME MANAGEMENT

Analyze and improve your own time management by reexamining the time management rules just discussed and listed here in Column 1. In Column 2 indicate whether or not you follow this rule generally with a simple yes or no. In Column 2—for those you answered no, indicate what you can do to improve your efficient use of time.

Time Management Rule Questions	Yes/No	If no, what can you do about it?
Do you understand your own use of time?	*No*	*Need to keep a time log for 2 or 3 days to understand better where my time goes*
Do you attack your time-wasters?		
Do you attack your self-defeating beliefs?		
Do you avoid self-handicapping strategies?		
Do you avoid procrastination?		
Do you use the available time management tools?		
Do you prioritize tasks?		
Do you break up large tasks into more manageable units?		
Do you set time limits?		
Do you reward yourself periodically?		
Do you do things once rather than twice?		
Do you avoid distractions?		

Summary

1. Chronemics is the study of time or temporal communication.
2. Psychological time refers to the emphasis one puts on the past, present, and future.
3. Interpersonal time refers to such factors as punctuality, wait time (the time you wait for someone), lead time (the time interval for making decisions), the time devoted to an event (duration), and simultaneity (the number of activities done at the same time).
4. Cultural time refers to the ways in which a culture treats time, for example, how important time is considered to be.
5. Monochronism refers to doing one thing at a time, whereas polychronism refers to doing more than one thing at the same time. Cultures vary in their tendencies toward one or the other orientation.
6. Biological time refers to the physical, emotional, and intellectual cycles that some theorists claim exert influence on your behaving, feeling, and thinking.
7. Time management refers to the efficient and effective use of time and can be aided with time management tools, by avoiding common pitfalls, and by apply some well-proven strategies.

Key Terms

Supply a definition for each of the following terms. Once you've formulated these "standard" definitions, consider the following ideas for further defining and understanding. Not all will work for all key terms, but some will work for some terms and some will work for others.

- Find a quotation that illustrates the term.
- Provide an example from personal interaction, television, film, novels, or plays.
- Create a short dialogue to illustrate the operation of the key term.
- Locate a research study investigating the key term and report its findings.
- Illustrate the concept nonverbally.
- Find a video that illustrates the key term.
- Find images—photos or graphics, abstract or specific, literal or metaphorical.
- Diagram the concept.
- Explain the negative, what the concept is not.
- State a skill that centers on the concept.

Key Concept	Definition
Chronemics	
Psychological time	
Interpersonal time	
Cultural time	
Formal time	
Informal time	
Monochronism	
Polychronism	
Social clock	
Biological time	
Biorhythms	
Time management	

AND IN ADDITION

Using your favorite search engine (in addition, use Google Scholar or the databases in your college library for the more scientific research articles), search for time, social clock, **time and culture, biological time, time management, daytime preferences, monochronism and polychronism,** or any of the other terms and topics considered in this chapter and add to the chapter contents. Depending on the structure of the course and the facilities available, you may want to post these additions to a course website; to a social media site such as Twitter, Facebook, or Google+; or to a listserv or through e-mail, for example. Here are a few ways in which you might make your addition:

- Write a paragraph that adds to the discussion of a particular concept.
- Provide a new, contradictory, or intercultural example of a concept.
- Create a figure or table to illustrate or organize a particular topic.
- Illustrate with an image or two or a 10- to 15-second video a particular concept of nonverbal behavior.
- Summarize and evaluate the results of a scientific study on a topic relevant to this chapter.
- Summarize and evaluate an online article that focuses on one of the topics considered here.

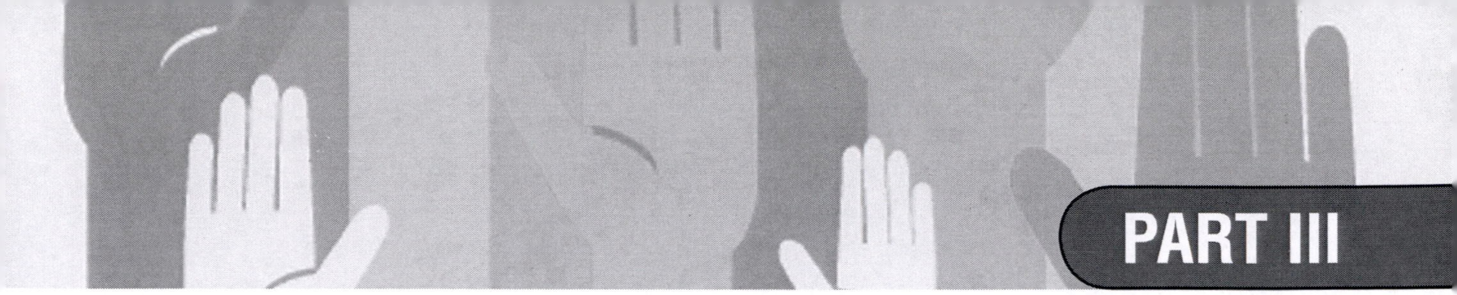

PART III

Putting It All Together

Throughout this book we've approached nonverbal communication in terms of the specific codes or channels through which nonverbal signals are sent, for example, face and eye messages. But, in reality, nonverbal signals occur in packages—messages from the eye, for example, will likely be accompanied by facial and spatial messages as well as by verbal messages. Here, then, we try to put it all together by selecting certain topics on which nonverbal researchers have focused and examining them in terms of the variety of signals (verbal and nonverbal) that are used in communicating messages. So, we're putting this all together in two ways: combining the various nonverbal channels and combining the nonverbal with the verbal channel. We focus here on four topics:

- *Attraction.* What is attractiveness? What makes one person more attractive than another? How can you increase your own attractiveness?
- *Lying.* What is lying? Why and how do people lie? How can you tell if someone is lying?
- *Immediacy.* What is immediacy? What are its benefits? How can you increase your own immediacy?
- *Power.* What is power? How does power operate? How can you increase your power?

Chapter 10

Attraction, Deception, Immediacy, and Power

© 2013, skyfotostock, Shutterstock, Inc.

CHAPTER TOPICS

CHAPTER EXERCISES

Describing Attraction **In Your Life**
Describing Lying **In Your Life**
Describing Immediacy **In Your Life**
Describing Power **In Your Life**

CHAPTER OBJECTIVES

After reading this chapter, you should be able to:

1. Define *attraction*, identify the factors influencing perceptions of attractiveness, and describe attraction in your own life.
2. Define *lying* and identify the types of lies, the general behavior of liars, and describe lying in your own life.
3. Define *immediacy* and explain the responses to immediacy, apply the ways to increase immediacy, and describe immediacy in your own life.
4. Define *power* and paraphrase the four principles of power, apply the suggestions for increasing power nonverbally and verbally, and describe power in your own life.

This chapter focuses on four topics: attraction, lying, immediacy, and power. For each topic, we consider its nature and relevant principles and the signals (verbal and nonverbal) that help you achieve it and provide an exercise to stimulate you to look at the concept in terms of your own life. These exercises should also help emphasize that nonverbal (and verbal) elements work together in communication.

ATTRACTION

Most people (perhaps all) want to be thought attractive. After all, our perceived attractiveness will influence us throughout our lives, in the friends we make, in the romantic partners we meet, in the job we get, and in the success we have with all our relationships. Here we look at some basic principles of attraction that will help explain what attraction is and how it operates.

Principles of Attraction

Let's look into attraction and attractiveness a bit more closely and examine the major principles of attraction. If you're like most people, then you're attracted to others on the basis of a variety of factors: similarity, proximity, reinforcement, physical attractiveness and personality, socioeconomic and educational status, and reciprocity of liking.

Similarity Increases Attraction

If you could construct your mate, according to the **similarity** principle, it's likely that your mate would look, act, and think very much like you (Burleson, Kunkel, & Birch, 1994; Burleson, Samter, & Luccetti, 1992). Generally, people like those who are similar to them in nationality, race, abilities, physical characteristics, intelligence, and attitudes (Pornpitakpan, 2003). In some cases, people are attracted to their opposites, a pattern called **complementarity**; for example, a dominant person might be attracted to someone who is more submissive. Generally, however, people prefer those who are similar to them.

Do you find this principle of similarity operating in your own choice of romantic and friendship relationships?

In this connection, consider the matching hypothesis. This hypothesis states that you date and mate those people who are similar to you in attractiveness. That is, you select persons for dating and ultimately mating who are neither much more attractive nor much less attractive than you are. You may wish to see if this is true in the relationships with which you're familiar or in relationships of public figures.

Sometimes, an unattractive person and an attractive person do date and mate. When you see this you probably wonder why this attractive person is dating the unattractive person. You already know why the unattractive person is dating the more attractive. What can account for this unmatched pairing? And so you look for compensating factors, factors that would account for the attractive person pairing up with the much less attractive person. Money probably comes to mind most quickly. Power and status probably come next in importance. Personality, a sense of humor, warmth, supportiveness, and all the other qualities we consider significant in a relational partner are also important.

Proximity Increases Attraction

If you look around at people you find attractive, you will probably find that they are the people who live or work close to you. People who become friends are the people who have the greatest opportunity to interact with each other. **Proximity**, or physical closeness, is most important in the early stages of interaction—for example, during the first days of school (in class or in dormitories). The importance of proximity as a factor in attraction decreases, though always remaining significant, as the opportunity to interact with more distant others increases.

Reinforcement Increases Attraction

Not surprisingly, you're attracted to people who give rewards or reinforcements, which can range from a simple compliment to an expensive cruise. You're also attracted to people you reward (Aronson, Wilson, & Akert, 2013; Jecker & Landy, 1969). That is, you come to like people for whom you do favors; for example, you've probably increased your liking for persons after buying them an expensive present or going out of your way to do them a special favor. In these situations you justify your behavior by believing that the person was worth your efforts; otherwise, you'd have to admit to spending effort on people who don't deserve it.

Physical and Personality Factors Increase Attraction

It's easily appreciated that people like physically attractive people more than they like physically unattractive people. Although we normally think that attractiveness is culturally determined—and to some degree it is—some research shows that definitions of attractiveness are becoming universal. A person rated as attractive in one culture is likely to be rated as attractive in other cultures—even in cultures in which people are generally quite different in appearance from people in the first culture.

One nonverbal researcher synthesizes the research on what makes for physical attractiveness with five principles (Remland, 2009):

- *The principle of youthfulness.* Youth is prized. To this other researchers add sexual maturity (Burgoon et al., 2010).
- *The principle of straightness.* Straight teeth with the jaw and the forehead aligned are preferred features.
- *The principle of proportionality.* Facial and bodily features should be in proportion to each other. The extra-large nose is perhaps the best example of a feature that is not in proportion and perhaps the reason for the popularity of rhinoplasty.
- *The principle of symmetry.* Both sides of the face should be symmetrical, a situation which is usually but not always the case (e.g., people who have one "lazy" eye or uneven lips).
- *The principle of averageness.* Average faces, perhaps because they are more familiar to us, are generally preferred over those faces with features very different from most faces.

And, of course, you are attracted to people who have a pleasant personality. Although what is and what is not a pleasant personality will vary from one person to another,

What other qualities do you consider important in contributing to an "attractive personality?" © 2013, Paul Matthew Photography, Shutterstock, Inc.

most people would include such qualities as these in their definition of an attractive personality:

- *Good listener*. Listens more than talks.
- *Optimistic*. Sees good rather than bad around the corner.
- *Focused on the other person*. Avoids self-focus or "me-ness."
- *Positive*. Avoids negativity and even neutrality; sees light rather than darkness, hope rather than despair.
- *Friendly*. Open and outgoing people seem to be thought more attractive than those who are standoffish or loners.
- *Helpful*. Is willing to do favors for others (even without getting "paid back").

To the degree that you can demonstrate such qualities nonverbally, you're likely to be thought to have an attractive personality.

Socioeconomic and Educational Status Affect Attraction

Popular belief holds that among heterosexual men and women, men are more interested in a woman's physical attributes than in her socioeconomic status. And indeed, research shows that women flirt on the Internet by stressing their physical attributes, whereas men stress their socioeconomic status (Whitty, 2003). Interestingly, there is evidence that men too consider a woman's socioeconomic status in making romantic relationship decisions—but whereas women find higher socioeconomic status more attractive, men find just the opposite. Men report greater likelihood of a romantic relationship with a woman lower in socioeconomic status than they are. Furthermore, men find women with a higher educational level (which is often responsible for the higher socioeconomic status) less likable and less faithful and as a result see less likelihood of a romantic relationship with such women (Greitemeyer, 2007).

Reciprocity of Liking Increases Attraction

It will come as no surprise that research supports what you already know from your own experience: you tend to be attracted to people you think are attracted to you; you come to like those who you think like you. This tendency, also known as

reciprocity of attraction or **reciprocal liking**, is seen in a variety of situations. We initiate potential friendships and romantic relationships with people who we think like us, certainly not with those we think dislike us. There is even evidence to show that people like "likers"—people who like others generally—more than they like people who don't express such liking (Eastwick & Finkel, 2009).

Increasing Attractiveness

From the above factors that can influence attractiveness, five main suggestions for increasing your own attractiveness may be derived.

- **Express similarities.** People like people and are attracted to those who are like them, who have similar attitudes and beliefs. Emphasize the similarities; play down the differences.
- **Keep in touch.** Allow the proximity principle to operate. Social media have made this extremely easy and keeping in touch is now intermeshed with most people's interactional lives. Being there physically will generally add to the perception of attractiveness.
- **Reinforce.** We enjoy being complimented, supported, thought highly of. We're attracted to people who reward us, who give us things—whether social or material.
- **Stress the positive.** We like positive people, people who have a pleasant, upbeat personality rather than those who are all doom and gloom.
- **Be liking.** If you like someone and express this liking in appropriate ways, you're likely to be thought more attractive and to be liked more.

In addition, there are a variety of specific behaviors that are likely to get you perceived as more attractive. Here are some dos and don'ts:

- Gesture to show liveliness and animation in ways that are appropriate to the situation and to the message. However, don't gesture for the sake of gesturing or gesture in ways that may prove offensive to members of other cultures.
- Nod and lean forward to signal that you're listening and are interested. However, avoid going on automatic pilot, nodding without any coordination with what is being said, or lean forward so much that you intrude on the other's space.
- Smile and otherwise show your interest, attention, and positiveness facially. However, be careful that you don't overdo it; inappropriate smiling is likely to be perceived negatively.
- Make eye contact in moderation. Don't stare, ogle, glare, or otherwise make the person feel that he or she is under scrutiny.
- Touch in moderation when appropriate. Avoid touching excessively or too intimately. When it doubt, avoid touching another.
- Use vocal variation in rate, rhythm, pitch, and volume to communicate your animation and involvement in what you're saying. However, don't fall into the pattern where, for example, your voice goes up and down, up and down, up and down without any relationship to what you're saying.
- Use silence to listen the same amount of time as you speak. Show that you're listening with appropriate facial reactions, posture, and backchanneling cues, for example. Avoid listening motionlessly or in ways that suggest you're only listening half-heartedly.

What do you consider the single most unattractive conversational behavior?

- Stand reasonably close to show a connectedness. However, be careful that you don't exceed the other person's comfort zone. Stand and sit tall; don't slouch.
- Present a pleasant smell and be careful to camouflage onions, garlic, or smoke, which are scents you're so used to that you can't smell them. Avoid overdoing cologne or perfume or wearing your body sweat as a sign of a heavy workout.
- Dress appropriately to the situation. Avoid clothing that proves uncomfortable or that calls attention to itself and hence away from your message.

EXERCISE

DESCRIBING ATTRACTION IN YOUR LIFE

To understand attractiveness in your own life, consider the six influences on attractiveness just considered and listed in Column 1. For each of these factors provide a paraphrase or explanation in your own words in Column 2. In Column 3 provide an example illustrating how one, two, three, or all of the factors in Column 1 influenced your perception of someone else's attractiveness or an example where you think it may have influenced someone else's perception of your attractiveness (this will not be easy).

Influences on Attractiveness	Paraphrase	Influence Examples of Others, of Self
Similarity	*People are generally attracted to others who are similar to them in attitudes, appearance, and thinking.*	*Jane's love of animals (similar to mine) makes her seem more attractive to me.*
Proximity		
Reinforcement		
Physical and personality attractiveness		
Socioeconomic and educational status		
Reciprocity of liking		

LYING

One of the reasons that nonverbal communication is so often in the news and so popular generally is that it's thought that, with a knowledge of nonverbal communication, you can read a person like a book and particularly tell whether someone is lying or telling the truth. As already noted, we cannot read a person like a book and, research tells us, detecting lying is not as easy as you might like. Here we note a few principles of lying and offer some suggestions for increasing your deception detection abilities.

Principles of Lying

The following principles should help explain the nature of lying.

Lying Involves Both Sender and Receiver

Although you can lie to yourself and engage in a variety of self-deception strategies, here we are concerned with *interpersonal* lying, with lying to another person; lying must involve both a sender and a receiver. More formally, we may define **lying** as the act of (1) sending messages (2) with the intention of giving another person information you believe to be false and (3) when that person expects you to tell the truth (Frank & Suetieva, 2013).

1. Lying involves sending some kind of verbal and/or nonverbal message (and remember that the absence of facial expression or the absence of verbal comment also communicates); it also requires reception by another person.
2. The message must be sent to deceive intentionally. If you give false information to someone but you believe it to be true, then you haven't lied. You do lie when you send information that you believe to be untrue and you intend to mislead the other person.
3. The person must expect you to be telling the truth. For example, the poker player who bluffs—trying to deceive the others at the table into thinking he or she had a winning hand—is not lying because the people playing poker expect you to attempt deception; it's part of the game.

Lies Vary in Type

Lies vary greatly in type; each lie seems a bit different from every other lie. Here is one useful system that classifies lies into four types (McGinley, 2000).

Prosocial deception: To achieve some good. These are lies that are designed to benefit the person lied to or lied about. For example, praising a person's effort to give him or her more confidence or to tell someone they look great to simply make them feel good would be examples of prosocial lies.

Self-enhancement deception: To make yourself look good. These are lies designed to make yourself seem a lot better than you are. When you write your profile on a dating website and lie about your financial status, your attractiveness, or your age, for example, you're engaging in self-enhancement deception. Another way in which people engage in self-enhancement lying is through the use of a "beard." Much like a beard helps a man disguise himself, an interpersonal beard is a person who enables you to appear to be something you're not, to disguise who you really are.

For example, not so many years ago—and in many parts of the world today—gay men and lesbians would enlist the aid of a beard—someone to pose as a heterosexual romantic partner—to appear heterosexual oneself. Among celebrities this is still a common practice—often extending to marriage. Another type of beard, to use an example from Morris (1977), is the adult daughter or son who is passed off as one's sister or brother so as to give a younger image.

Selfish deception: To protect yourself. These lies are designed to protect yourself. Sometimes it's something as simple as not answering the phone because you want some time to do something else. Or you might conceal certain facts to protect yourself—previous failed relationships, an unsavory family history, or being fired. Hiding an extrarelational affair is perhaps the classic example of selfish deception.

Anti-social deception: To harm someone. These lies are designed to hurt another person. For example, such lies might include spreading false rumors about someone you dislike or falsely accusing an opposing candidate of some wrongdoing (something you see regularly in political debates).

Liars Lie in Different Ways

As you can imagine people lie in various ways (Burgoon et al., 2010; Knapp, 2008). Here are some of the ways which you'll recognize from your own observations.

Exaggeration. Here you lead people to believe that, for example, you earn more money than you do, your grades are better than they are, or your relationship is more satisfying than it really is.

Minimization. Instead of exaggerating the facts, here you minimize them. You can minimize your lack of money (we have more than enough), the consequences of poor grades, or your relationship dissatisfaction.

Substitution. In this method you exchange the truth for a lie—for example, *I wasn't at the bar, I stopped in at Starbucks for coffee.*

Equivocation. When you equivocate, your message is sufficiently ambiguous to lead people to think something different from your intention. *That outfit really is something, very interesting* instead of *Ugh!*

Omission. And, of course, you can lie by not sending certain messages. So, when your romantic partner asks where you were last night, you might omit those things your partner would frown on and just include the positives.

Lies Are Viewed Differently in Different Cultures

Not surprisingly, cultural differences exist with lying—in the way lying is defined and in the way lying is treated. For example, as children get older, Chinese and Taiwanese (but not Canadians) see lying to minimize the good deeds that they do as positive (as we'd expect for cultures that emphasize modesty) but taking honest credit for these same good deeds is seen negatively (Lee, Xu, Fu, Cameron, & Chen, 2001).

Some cultures consider lying to be more important than others—in one study, for example, European Americans considered lies less negatively than did Ecuadorians. Both, however, felt that lying to an out-group member was more acceptable than lying to an in-group member (Mealy, Stephan, & Urritia, 2007).

Lying Has Ethical Implications

Not surprisingly, lies have ethical implications. In fact, one of the earliest cultural rules children are taught is that lying is wrong. At the same time, children also learn that in some cases lying is effective—in gaining some reward or in avoiding some punishment.

Some prosocial, self-enhancement, and selfish-deception lies are considered ethical (e.g., publicly agreeing with someone you really disagree with to enable the person to save face, saying that someone will get well despite medical evidence to the contrary, or simply bragging about your accomplishments). Some lies are considered not only ethical but required (e.g., lying to protect someone from harm or telling the proud parents that their child is beautiful). Other lies (largely those in the antisocial category) are considered unethical (e.g., lying to defraud investors or to falsely accuse someone).

However, a large group of lies are not that easy to classify as ethical or unethical, for example:

- *Is it ethical to lie to get what you deserved but couldn't get any other way?* For example, would you lie to get a well-earned promotion or raise? Would it matter if you hurt a colleague's chances of advancement in the process?
- *Is it ethical to lie to your relationship partner to avoid a conflict and perhaps splitting up?* In this situation, would it be ethical to lie if the issue was a minor one (you were late for an appointment because you wanted to see the end of the football game) or a major one (say, continued infidelity)?
- *Is it ethical to lie to get yourself out of an unpleasant situation?* For example, would you lie to get out of an unwanted date, an extra office chore, or a boring conversation?
- *Is it ethical to lie about the reasons for breaking up a relationship to make it easier for you and the other person?* For example, would you conceal that you've fallen in love with another person (or that you're simply bored with the relationship or that the physical attraction is gone) in your breakup speech?
- *Is it ethical to exaggerate the consequences of an act in order to discourage it?* For example, would you lie about the bad effects of marijuana in order to prevent your children or your students from using it?
- *Is it ethical to lie about yourself in order to appear more appealing—for example, saying you were younger or richer or more honest than you really are?* For example, would you lie in your profile on Facebook or MySpace or on a dating website to increase your chances of meeting someone really special?

Increasing Lie Detection Ability

One of the more interesting questions about lying is how liars act. Do they act differently from those telling the truth? And, if they do act differently, how can you tell when someone is lying to you? These questions are not easy to answer and we are far from having complete answers to such questions. However, we have learned a great deal. Before reading what research has found, consider these cautions.

None of the behaviors to be discussed below, taken alone or in a group, is proof that a person is lying. Liars can be especially adept at learning to hide any signs that they might be lying. Nor is an absence of these features proof that the person is telling the truth.

Research shows that it's very difficult to detect when a person is lying or telling the truth. The hundreds of research studies conducted on this topic find that in most instances people judge lying accurately in less than 60 percent of the cases, only slightly better than chance (Knapp, 2008). And these percentages are even lower when you try to detect lying in a person from a culture very different from your own (Sabourin, 2007).

And there is some evidence to show that lie detection is even more difficult (i.e., less accurate) in long-standing romantic relationships—the very relationships in which the most significant lying occurs (Guerrero, Andersen, & Afifi, 2007). One of the most important reasons for this is the **truth bias**. In most situations you assume that the person is telling the truth; you normally operate under the principle that assumes that what a person says is the truth. This truth bias is especially strong in long-term relationships where it's simply expected that each person tells the truth. There are situations where there is a **deception bias**. For example, in prison where lying is so prevalent and where lie detection is a crucial survival skill, prisoners often operate with a lie bias and assume that what the speaker is saying is a lie (Knapp, 2008).

At the same time, you need to know something about the person to be able to interpret his or her nonverbals. For example, if a person is normally apprehensive in most communication situations, then you need to take this into consideration in using apprehension cues as indicators of lying. In other words, you need to see the cues to possible lying against a baseline of normal behavior (i.e., truth-telling behavior).

Another reason that makes lie detection so difficult in close relationships is that the liar knows how to lie, largely because he or she knows how you think and can therefore tailor lies that you'll fall for. And, of course, the liar often has considerable time to rehearse the lie, which generally makes lying more effective (i.e., less easy to detect).

To complicate things just a bit further: Lie detection, as you'd expect, is more difficult in *inter*cultural situations than in *intra*cultural situations. One reason for this greater difficulty is that in intercultural situations the display rules for eye contact, let's say, are different. So, whereas in one culture eye avoidance may be taken as a sign of lying (a popular but not very reliable indication of lying); in another culture, eye

Before reading about the behaviors that research finds often accompany lying, think about your own lie-detection theories—what behaviors do you think characterize/accompany lying?

avoidance may be a sign of respect and have nothing at all to do with lying. Another reason is that people are often more guarded and restrained in intercultural situations. Consequently, they may give off cues that may be interpreted as lying when they are simply exhibiting discomfort because of the interculturalness of the situation.

With these cautions in mind, and from a combination of research studies, the following behaviors were found to most often accompany lying (Andersen, 2004; Burgoon, 2005; DePaulo et al., 2003; Knapp, 2008; Leathers & Eaves, 2008):

- **Liars hold back.** They speak more slowly (perhaps to monitor what they're saying), take longer to respond to questions (again, perhaps monitoring their messages), and generally give less information and elaboration.
- **Liars leak.** Very slight facial and eye movements (what we referred to earlier as micromomentary movements) may reveal the person's real feelings, a process referred to as leakage. Often this is the result of what has come to be called "duping delight"—the pleasure you get when you feel you're putting over a lie. Here you may leak your lying through slight movements in your lips or eyes.
- **Liars make less sense.** Liars' messages contain more discrepancies, more inconsistencies.
- **Liars give a more negative impression.** Generally, liars are seen as less willing to be cooperative, smile less than truth-tellers, and are more defensive.
- **Liars are tense.** The tension may be revealed by their higher-pitched voices and their excessive body movements.
- **Liars exhibit greater pupil dilation, more eyeblinks, and more gaze aversion.**
- **Liars speak with a higher vocal pitch**. Their voices often sound as if they were under stress.

EXERCISE

DESCRIBING LYING IN YOUR LIFE

To understand lying and lie detection in your own life, consider the two deception behavior tendencies noted in Column 1. In Column 2 list at least one situation (and the people involved) where you would be likely to operate with the truth bias. In Column 3 identify the reasons why you are likely to operate with a truth or a deception bias. After you've completed this chart, consider what would lead you to change from a truth bias to a deception bias and what would lead you to change from a deception bias to a truth bias.

Deception Behavior Tendencies	Likely Situations and Likely Other People or Types of People	Reasons
Truth bias	*My communication instructor in student–teacher conferences*	*She has no reason to lie and has always told the truth in the past*
Deception bias		

- **Liars make more errors and use more hesitations in their speech.** They pause more and for longer periods of time;
- **Liars make more hand, leg, and foot movements.**
- **Liars engage in more self-touching movements.** For example, liars touch their face or hair more and engage in more object touching, for example, playing with a coffee cup or pen.

In detecting lying be especially careful that you formulate any conclusions with a clear understanding that you can be wrong and that accusations of lying (especially when untrue but even when true) can often damage a relationship to the point where it's beyond repair.

IMMEDIACY

Immediacy is the creation of closeness, a sense of togetherness, of oneness, between speaker and listener. When you communicate immediacy you convey a sense of interest and attention, a liking for and an attraction to the other person. You communicate immediacy with both verbal and nonverbal messages.

Principles of Immediacy

Here are just a few principles of immediacy to clarify its nature and importance in communication generally and in nonverbal communication in particular.

Immediacy Behaviors Are Generally Perceived Positively

Not surprisingly, people respond to communication that is immediate more favorably than to communication that is not. You like people who are immediate, who demonstrate a closeness to you, an interest in you, and a liking for you.

Immediacy behaviors will generally increase your perceived attractiveness and so in your relationship world, immediacy behaviors will generally prove helpful. In addition, there is considerable evidence to show that immediacy behaviors are also effective in workplace communication, especially between supervisors and subordinates (Richmond et al., 2012). For example, when a supervisor uses immediacy behaviors, he or she is seen by subordinates as interested and concerned; subordinates are therefore likely to communicate more freely and honestly about issues that can benefit the supervisor and the organization. Also, workers with supervisors who communicate immediacy behaviors have higher job satisfaction and motivation.

Immediacy behaviors of teachers have been found to contribute to the student having more positive feelings about the class, learning more, and evaluating their instructor more highly (Richmond et al., 2012).

But, there are cautions to be observed here; there are potential disadvantages. Immediacy researchers note two important ones (Richmond et al., 2012).

First, Immediacy generates increased communication, which not everyone wants. For example, your smile may encourage your colleague to come into your office to chat when all you wanted to do was be friendly but left alone. Also, recognize that because immediacy behaviors prolong and encourage in-depth communication, they may not be responded to favorably by people who are fearful about communication and/or who want to get the interaction over with as soon as possible.

Second, immediacy behaviors are ambiguous and can lead to false perceptions. For example, you may find yourself in trouble when you intend your smile as friendly, as a way of saying "hello," but your colleague interprets it as flirting.

Immediacy Varies from Culture to Culture

Not all cultures or all people respond in the same way to immediacy messages. For example, in the United States immediacy behaviors are generally seen as friendly and appropriate. In other cultures, however, the same immediacy behaviors may be viewed as overly familiar——as presuming that a relationship is close when only an acquaintanceship exists (Richmond, McCroskey, & Powell, 2013).

Similarly, in intercultural situations, the normal ambiguity of nonverbal behaviors is compounded, making it even more important that you determine the culture's view of immediacy behaviors before demonstrating them yourself. Observing members of the culture is probably your best strategy. The smile that your U.S. colleague misinterprets can be a minor problem in comparison to those that may happen in an intercultural situation.

Increasing Immediacy

Here are a few suggestions for communicating immediacy verbally and nonverbally (Mottet & Richmond, 1998; Richmond et al., 2012):

- Self-disclose; reveal something significant about yourself.
- Refer to the other person's good qualities of, say, dependability, intelligence, or character ("You're always so reliable").
- Express your positive view of the other person and of your relationship ("I'm sure glad you're my roommate; you know everyone").
- Talk about commonalities, things you and the other person have done together or share.
- Demonstrate your responsiveness by giving feedback cues that indicate you want to listen more and that you're interested ("And what else happened?").
- Express psychological closeness and openness by, for example, maintaining physical closeness and arranging your body to exclude third parties.
- Maintain appropriate eye contact and limit looking around at others.
- Smile and express your interest in the other person.
- Focus on the other person's remarks. Make the speaker know that you heard and understood what was said and give the speaker appropriate verbal and nonverbal feedback.
- Express positiveness through your facial expressions.

At the same time that you'll want to demonstrate these immediacy messages, try also to avoid nonimmediacy messages such as speaking in a monotone, looking away from the person you're talking to, frowning while talking, having a tense body posture, or avoiding gestures.

EXERCISE

DESCRIBING IMMEDIACY IN YOUR LIFE

To appreciate the role of immediacy in your life, identify one, two, or three situations in which you are likely to profit (in terms of being liked or thought attractive, for example) from increased immediacy. Record these in Column 1. In Column 2 indicate the nonverbal immediacy behaviors you might use and in Column 3 indicate the likely accompanying verbal behaviors that will help you achieve increased immediacy.

Situations	Nonverbal Immediacy Behaviors	Verbal Immediacy Behaviors
1. Asking my roommate to borrow the car.	*Look really needy with a sad facial expression; touch her hand as I'm making the request.*	*Use her name; explain my need but respect her need for negative face.*
2.		
3.		

POWER

Power is the ability of one person to influence what another person thinks or does. You have power over another person to the extent that you can influence what this person thinks or what this person does. And, conversely, another person has power over you to the extent that he or she can influence what you think or do. Perhaps the most important aspect of power to recognize is that power is asymmetrical: If one person has greater power, the other person must have less. If you are stronger than another person, then this person is weaker than you. If you are richer, then the other person must be poorer. In any one area—for example, strength or financial wealth—one person has more and, inevitably and by definition, the other person has less (is weaker or poorer).

Principles of Power

Here are just a few principles of power that impact on nonverbal communication.

Power Can Increase and Decrease

Although people differ greatly in the amount of power they wield at any time and in any specific area, everyone can increase their power in some way. You can lift weights and increase your physical power. You can learn the techniques of negotiation and increase your power in group situations. You can learn the principles of communication and increase your persuasive power. Power can also be decreased. Probably the most common way to lose power is by unsuccessfully trying to control another's behavior. For example, the person who threatens you with punishment and then fails to carry out the threat loses power. Another way to lose power is to allow others to control you; for example, to allow others to take unfair advantage of you. When you don't confront these power tactics of others, you lose power yourself.

Power Follows the Principle of Less Interest

The more a person needs a relationship, the less power that person has in it. The less a person needs a relationship, the greater is that person's power. In a love relationship, for example, the person who maintains greater power is the one who would find it easier to break up the relationship. The person who is unwilling (or unable) to break up has little power, precisely because he or she is dependent on the relationship and the rewards provided by the other person.

Power Generates Privilege

When one person has power over another person, the person with power is generally assumed to have certain privileges, many of which are communication privileges. And the greater the power difference, the greater is the license of the more powerful individual. Sometimes we're mindful of the privilege or license that comes with power. Most often, however, we seem to operate mindlessly, with no one questioning the power structure. For example, those with power may encroach on the territory of those with little power (a supervisor can enter the cubicle of a trainee but the trainee cannot enter the office of the supervisor—at least not without being invited or before knocking). Similarly, a supervisor may touch the arm or rearrange the collar of a subordinate, but not the other way around. The general may touch the corporal, but not the other way around. The doctor may put his or her arm on a patient, but the patient would not do that to a doctor. Similarly, the one with power can ignore the markers of those with less power, but not vice versa.

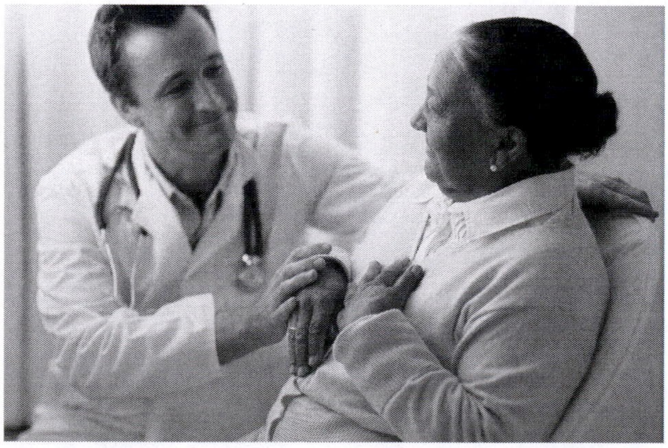

What kinds of power can you identify in this photo? © 2013, Reflekta, Shutterstock, Inc.

Power Comes in Different Types

Research has identified six types of power: legitimate, referent, reward, coercive, expert, and information or persuasion (French & Raven, 1968; Raven, Centers, & Rodrigues, 1975). You hold **legitimate power** when others believe you have a right—by virtue of your position—to influence or control others' behaviors. For example, as an employer, judge, manager, or police officer, you'd have legitimate power by virtue of your role. You have **referent power** when others wish to be like you. Referent power holders often are attractive, have considerable prestige, and are well liked and well respected. For example, you may have referent power over a younger brother because he wants to be like you.

You have **reward power** when you control the rewards that others want. Rewards may be material (money, promotion, jewelry) or social (love, friendship, respect). For example, teachers have reward power over students because they control grades, letters of recommendation, and social approval. You have **coercive power** when you have the ability to administer punishments to or remove rewards from others if they do not do as you wish. Usually, people who have reward power also have coercive power. For example, teachers may give poor grades or withhold recommendations. But be careful: Coercive power may reduce your other power bases. It can have a negative impact when used, for example, by supervisors on subordinates in business (Richmond et al., 1984).

You have **expert power** when others see you as having expertise or special knowledge. Your expert power increases when you're perceived as being unbiased and as having nothing personally to gain from exerting this power. For example, judges have expert power in legal matters and doctors have expert power in medical matters. You have **information power**—also called "persuasion power"—when others see you as having the ability to communicate logically and persuasively. For example, researchers and scientists may acquire information power because people perceive them as informed and critical thinkers.

Increasing Power

Much research has focused on the nonverbal factors related to your ability to persuade and influence others (Burgoon et al., 2010). For example, clothing and other artifactual symbols of authority help people to influence others. Research shows that others will be more easily influenced by someone in, for example, a respected uniform (such as that of a police officer or doctor) than by someone in civilian clothes. Affirmative nodding, facial expressions, and gestures help you express your concern for the other person and for the interaction and thus help you establish your charisma, an essential component of credibility. Self-manipulations (playing with your hair or touching your face, for example) and backward leaning will damage your power, making your appear uncomfortable and ill at ease.

Here are some popular suggestions for communicating power nonverbally.

- **Respond to the eyebrow flash.** Be sure to respond in kind to another's eyebrow flash (raising the eyebrow as a way of acknowledging another person).
- **Avoid adaptors.** Self, other, and object adaptors may make you appear uncomfortable and hence without power. Avoid these, especially when you wish to communicate confidence and control.

- **Use consistent packaging.** Be especially careful that your verbal and nonverbal messages don't contradict each other.
- **Select the right chairs.** When sitting, select chairs you can get in and out of easily; avoid deep plush chairs that you will sink into and will have trouble getting out of.
- **Shake.** To communicate confidence with your handshake, exert more pressure than usual and hold the grip a bit longer than normal.
- **Dress conservatively.** Other things being equal, dress relatively conservatively if you want to influence others; conservative clothing is usually associated with power and status. Trendy and fad clothing usually communicates a lack of power and status. And, of course, expensive clothing is more powerful than inexpensive clothing.
- **Use facial expressions and gestures as appropriate.** These help you express your concern for the other person as well as your comfort and control of the communication situation. Smile to show approval and that you're enjoying yourself but avoid excessive or purposeless smiling.
- **Walk slowly and deliberately.** To appear hurried is to appear as without power, as if you were rushing to meet the expectations of another person who had power over you.
- **Maintain eye contact.** People who maintain eye contact are judged to be more at ease and less afraid to engage in meaningful interaction than those who avoid eye contact. Be aware, however, that in some contexts, if you use excessive or protracted direct eye contact, you may be seen as exercising coercive power (Aquinis & Henle, 2001). When you break eye contact, direct your gaze downward; otherwise, you'll communicate a lack of interest in the other person.
- **Avoid vocalized pauses.** Avoid the "er's" and "ah's" that frequently punctuate conversations when you're not quite sure of what to say next.
- **Maintain reasonably close distances between yourself and those with whom you interact.** If the distance is too far, you may be seen as fearful or uninvolved. If the distance is too close, you may be seen as pushy or overly aggressive.
- **Relax.** A relaxed posture communicates confidence and control—qualities of power. A tense body posture can easily signal fear and discomfort—qualities of the powerless.
- **Vary your speech rate, volume, and pitch as appropriate to the conversation.** Be careful to avoid a monotone speaking style.
- **Accommodate.** Accommodate to the communication style of the other person if you want to increase your likeability, which can easily translate into influence and power. When you accommodate, you imitate the speaking style of the other person. Usually, this is effective when it's done to a small degree and goes unnoticed on a conscious level. If done too much, it may appear as mocking and insulting.
- **Move and gesture purposefully.** Avoid gestures and movements that can appear random and without purpose. This will generally signal discomfort.
- **Take up your space.** If you crouch in the corner of a couch, for example, you're going to appear less powerful than if you take up your allotted space. If you take up too much space, for example, spreading your legs apart and in effect taking up two spaces, you're likely to be seen as impolite.
- **Still your feet.** Excessive foot movement usually signals a discomfort and hence little power.

Of the various suggestions for increasing power nonverbally, how many can you observe in this one photo? Do any of the other photos in this chapter illustrate power? How (specifically) do this do this? © 2013, auremar, Shutterstock, Inc.

Here are a few verbal suggestions (Dillard & Marshall, 2003; Guerrero et al., 2007; Johnson, 1987; Kleinke, 1986; Molloy, 1981):

- **Avoid hesitations**; for example, "I, er, want to say that, ah, this one is, er, the best, you know?" (Hesitations make you sound unprepared and uncertain.)
- **Avoid too many intensifiers**; for example, "Really, this was the greatest; it was truly phenomenal." (Too many intensifiers make everything sound the same and don't allow you to intensify what should be emphasized.)
- **Avoid disqualifiers**; for example, "I didn't read the entire article, but . . ." or "I didn't actually see the accident, but. . . ." (Disqualifiers signal a lack of competence and a feeling of uncertainty.)
- **Avoid tag questions**; for example, "That was a great movie, wasn't it?" "She's brilliant, don't you think?" (Tag questions ask for another's agreement and therefore may signal your need for agreement and your own uncertainty.)
- **Avoid self-critical statements**; for example, "I'm not very good at this" or "This is my first interview." (Self-critical statements signal a lack of confidence and may make public your own inadequacies.)
- **Avoid slang and vulgar expressions**; slang and vulgarity signal low social class and hence little power).

EXERCISE

DESCRIBING POWER IN YOUR LIFE

To understand the role of power in your life, consider the six types of power discussed above and listed in Column 1. In Column 2 explain in your own words the nature of each of these types of power the ways in which you possess this type of power. In Column 3 indicate some of the ways in which you might go about increasing each of these types of power.

Type of Power	Explanation	Nonverbal and Verbal Ways in which You Might Increase This Type of Power
Legitimate power	*Power that comes from a person's position or job.*	*Dress more professionally and hang my degrees on the wall.*
Referent power		
Reward		
Coercive		
Expert		
Informational		

Summary

1. Attraction depends on a variety of factors, most notably similarity, proximity, reinforcement, physical attractiveness and personality, socioeconomic and educational status, and reciprocity of liking.
2. Lying is the act of sending messages with the intention of giving another person information you believe to be false. Detecting deception is a lot more difficult than popular books and television shows would indicate.
3. Immediacy is the creation of closeness, a sense of oneness, of togetherness. It is one of the major factors in appearing likeable.
4. Power is the ability of one person to control or influence the behavior of another. Power can be increased and decreased, follows the principle of less interest, generates privilege, and comes in a variety of types (legitimate, referent, reward, coercive, expert, and information).

Key Terms

Supply a definition for each of the following terms. Once you've formulated these "standard" definitions, consider the following ideas for further defining and understanding. Not all will work for all key terms, but some will work for some terms and some will work for others.

- Find a quotation that illustrates the term.
- Provide an example from personal interaction, television, film, novels, or plays.
- Create a short dialogue to illustrate the operation of the key term.
- Locate a research study investigating the key term and report its findings.
- Illustrate the concept nonverbally.
- Find a video that illustrates the key term.
- Find images—photos or graphics, abstract or specific, literal or metaphorical.
- Diagram the concept.
- Explain the negative, what the concept is not.
- State a skill that centers on the concept.

Key Concept	Definition
Attraction	
Similarity	
Complementarity	
Proximity	
Reinforcement	
Physical attractiveness and personality	

(Continued)

Key Concept	Definition
Socioeconomic and educational status	
Reciprocity of liking	
Lying	
Prosocial deception	
Self-enhancement deception	
Selfish deception	
Antisocial deception	
How people lie	
Truth bias	
Leakage	
Immediacy	
Power	
Ingratiation	
Disqualifiers	
Tag questions	

AND IN ADDITION

Using your favorite search engine (in addition, use Google Scholar or the databases in your college library for the more scientific research articles), search for **attraction**, **lying**, **deception**, **immediacy**, **power**, or any of the other terms and topics considered in this chapter and add to the chapter contents. Depending on the structure of the course and the facilities available, you may want to post these additions to a course website; to a social media site such as Twitter, Facebook, or Google+; or to a listserv or through e-mail, for example. Here are a few ways in which you might make your addition:

- Write a paragraph that adds to the discussion of a particular concept.
- Provide a new, contradictory, or intercultural example of a concept.
- Create a figure or table to illustrate or organize a particular topic.
- Illustrate with an image or two or a 10- to 15-second video a particular concept of nonverbal behavior.
- Summarize and evaluate the results of a scientific study on a topic relevant to this chapter.
- Summarize and evaluate an online article that focuses on one of the topics considered here.

Appendix A

Researching Nonverbal Communication

This appendix is not a research discussion in the sense that it covers the methods and procedures of communication research. That's covered in other courses and textbooks. Here, our aim is much more modest and it's simply to encourage you to work with some of the essential concepts in nonverbal communication as might some researchers. In this way you'll learn about nonverbal communication from a different perspective.

There are, of course, many ways of conducting research. And, again, covering these types of research is not the aim here. The discussions presented here represent just a small part of the research process and generally focus on the major steps you'd take to conduct research in nonverbal communication.

OPERATIONAL DEFINITION

One of the first steps you'd take in conducting research in nonverbal communication is to define the concepts you're going to study. And here your best route to take is to define the variable or concept operationally. An **operational definition** identifies how the variables will be identified and measured. The most often used example to illustrate the operational definition is the definition of weight—an operational definition of weight would consist of the numbers that show up on a scale when the item is weighted. Consider a nonverbal communication example. You'll recall from an earlier chapter that Edward Hall defined the four interpersonal distances operationally as follows: intimate distance = touching to 18 inches; personal distance = 1½–4 feet; social distance = 4–12 feet; and public distance = 12 feet to more than 25 feet. Each of these distances is defined operationally—you can identify and measure the distance and thereby identify the interpersonal distance type. You can observe any interaction and easily observe intimate, personal, social, or public distances according to the operational definitions given by Hall.

As you can appreciate, defining variables operationally enables you to communicate what you find in our research very precisely and enables others to replicate your findings. It also ensures that your findings will prove reliable. **Reliability** refers to the degree to which other people will agree with what is and what is not, say, touching or smiling. Findings that are highly reliable are those that different researchers—using the same methods of study—agree upon and findings that are unreliable are those that other researchers would not agree upon or that other research are not able to replicate. A related and often confused concept is validity. **Validity** refers to the degree to which a test or measuring instrument measures what it purports to measure.

RESEARCH HYPOTHESES

At the heart of a research study is the hypothesis, often several hypotheses. On one level a hypothesis is a guess about how something works. So, I might guess that if I smile, others will smile in response. In a research study/framework, the hypothesis is stated more formally and may be in one of two basic forms:

- A **null hypothesis** states that no relationship exists between the two items you're testing. In the above example, the two items would be your smiling behavior and the smiling behavior of others. A null hypothesis, then, might be stated as follows: *Smiling by one person in a group does not increase the smiling behavior of other members.* A more technically accurate phrasing might be: *Smiling by one person in a group does not influence the smiling behavior of other members.* As an experimenter/researcher you'd want to *disprove* this hypothesis; you want to show that this null hypothesis is incorrect and that smiling by one person in a group does increase (or perhaps even decrease) the smiling of others.
- A **directional hypothesis** states that a relationship does exist and that it predicts the relationship that the experimenter expects to find. Continuing with the above example, a directional hypothesis might be phrased as follows: *Smiling by one person in a group increases the smiling behavior of others.*

Generally, you'd set up a null hypothesis when you don't have any good reason for thinking that the relationship will go one way or another; that is, when you have no theory that makes predictions. On the other hand, you'd set up a directional hypothesis when you do have good reason (theoretical predictions) for stating the direction of the relationship.

RESEARCH DESIGN

Let's continue with the smiling example and assume that we're going to research the null hypothesis that smiling by one person in a group does not influence the smiling of others; it does not increase it or decrease it. With this hypothesis in mind, your next step is to decide how you'll test it, to design the study that will enable you to disprove your null hypothesis. Two general methods are especially useful: self-reports and observation.

If you use the **self-report strategy** you would develop a set of questions to help you collect information relevant to your hypothesis. So, sticking with the smiling example, you might construct a questionnaire asking people to describe their own smiling behaviors or to describe the smiling behavior of another person. You might, for example, ask such questions as the following:

When are you most likely to smile?
What factors influence your smiling behavior?
What kinds of messages do you communicate when you smile?

Or, you might ask questions that contain alternatives that force your respondents to put their responses into a specific category. For example, you might ask:
What factors influence your smiling behavior?

_______ 1. You recall a funny story
_______ 2. You smile in return to someone else's smiling
_______ 3. You look in the mirror
_______ 4. You see a cute dog or cat or baby
_______ 5. Other

And you can specify some kind of rating. For example, you might ask: How often do you smile as a result of the following circumstances (5 = always or almost always; 4 = usually; 3 = sometimes yes, sometimes no; 4 = rarely; 5 = never or almost never):

_____ When alone thinking about something funny
_____ When someone else smiles
_____ When I see something cute or humorous
_____ When I want to show affection and liking for someone
_____ When I want to ask someone for a favor

Or, you might ask them to rate it on a scale of, say, 7 points such as:

Check along the following scale to indicate how often do you smile in response to another person's smile.

Always _____: _____: _____: _____: _____: _____: _____ Never

In addition to the self-report type of research, you might use controlled observation. One simple way to do this might be to get a confederate (someone working with you, the experimenter, without the knowledge of others) to join a group of fellow students. The confederate would smile and you'd observe whether or not others in the group smiled in response. This, then, essentially is the barebones of the research design. With a bit of tweaking, we can build this skeleton into a respectable research study.

Here are a few questions you'd need to consider as you design your study, whether you use the self-report or observation method.

Informants

Informants (or subjects) is the term used by many researchers to identify the people they are studying. If you want to study college students then you'd obviously need to have college student informants in the group. Realize, of course, that if you limit your sample to college students, these results are not necessarily going to apply to young children or to much older people. And if you do the study in the United States, the results may not apply to cultures in which smiling is viewed differently. Of course, you can't do everything and it's better to focus on a clearly identifiable group and limit your findings and conclusions than to try to have your findings apply universally. As we've seen throughout this book, there is so much gender and cultural variation in nonverbal communication that findings with men are not easily generalizable to women and findings from students at the University of Michigan, for example, are not easily generalizable to students from Peking University.

With this in mind, you need to decide if you want your findings to apply to both men and women or if you want limit your study to one sex. If you want your conclusions to apply to both men and women, then you'd need to include both in the study. And, while thinking about the male–female issue, you need to consider (in observation research) who will be your confederate: a male or a female. Again, if you want your conclusions to apply to both male and female smilers and to both male and female smiling-responders, then you're going to need to have both male and female smilers and groups consisting of both males and females.

Observers

In an observational study, you'll need to give consideration to your observers. Since you are setting up the study and know what you hope to find, you would not be a good observer. You'd need to enlist someone to function as the observer. Perhaps you'd want to use both male and female observers. And then you'd need to consider if one male and one female observer is enough. Probably not. In fact, you'd probably want several observers. If you videotape the group interaction, you could easily have a number of observers view the video and identify the smiling or nonsmiling responses.

One of the important considerations with observers is to ensure that they are all looking for the same thing, and this is where your operational definition of smiling comes in. The observers must all have the same definition of smiling and you expect a high degree of agreement among the observers. If there is little or no agreement, then your observers are not observing the same thing and that doesn't enable you to test effectively your hypothesis. In fact, you'll probably need to train your observers as to what constitutes smiling.

A related question concerns how the observers will record their observations. One way might be to construct a simple diagram of the group members and have the observers record the behavior of each member (as smiling or nonsmiling) after the confederate smiles.

Data Analysis

After the observers have recorded their observations or the respondents have answered your questionnaire, you'd collect their responses and tally them. Here, you'd need some statistical sophistication to analyze your data scientifically. Because you're learning about the process of nonverbal communication research—not statistics—it will be sufficient to deal with raw numbers, something like this:

- For the self-report study: When asked what factors influenced their smiling behavior, 8 out of 12 men and 11 out of 12 women indicated that they smile in response to another's smile.
- For the observation study: Among males, an average of 4 (out of groups of 6) members smiled in response to the confederate's smiling. Among females, an average of 5 (out of groups of 6) members smiled in response to the confederate's smiling.

Conclusions

To be able to reject the null hypothesis that smiling by one member does not influence other members of a group, you'd need to analyze the data statistically. But, again, for our purposes, we can simply present the raw data and let it speak for itself. For example, you might conclude:

- For the self-report study: From the questionnaire responses we may conclude that both men and women smile in response to another's smile, but this effect is stronger for women. Put more scientifically, you might say something like this: On the basis of the questionnaire responses, the null hypothesis that smiling by one member in a group does not influence the smiling behavior of others is rejected and the alternative (directional) hypothesis that smiling by one member increases the smiling behavior of others is accepted.
- For the observation study: Or you might note that on the basis of the average number of returned smiles observed, it would seem that smiling by one member does in fact influence the smiling behaviors of other group members and specifically that it influences them in the direction of returning the smile. Put more scientifically, you might say something like this: On the basis of the data, the null hypothesis that smiling by one member in a group does not influence the smiling behaviors of others is rejected and the alternative (directional) hypothesis that smiling by one member increases the smiling behavior of others is accepted.

Results and Directions for Future Research

Here you would identify the ways in which your results are limited. Some of these things we've already mentioned—that the results would apply to students in the United States and not necessarily to much younger or much older people. Of course, these results might be the same for different age and cultural groups, but this specific study does not provide the evidence necessary to make that claim. And so, for starters, you might mention that future research should look at this question among different age and cultural groups.

Write-up

Once all the above questions are dealt with, you can devote yourself to writing up the study. Here is a simple outline with a few suggestions:

- ***Title.*** Give your study a title. The title should identify the behavior being studied and perhaps something about the informants used. An appropriate title for our smiling study might be: Factors that Influence Smiling or Responses to Smiling in Groups of College Students.
- ***Abstract.*** Summarize the purpose of the study, the basic design, and the major findings in approximately 150 words.
- ***Background and Hypotheses.*** Here you'd state the general nature of the area under investigation, something about previous research on smiling, and perhaps its significance to communication and to human behavior generally. You don't need to review all the research on smiling in this paper, but you

should demonstrate a familiarity with relevant research. The more similar previous research is to your present study, the more important it is that you cover it in this section of the research paper. Here you'd also state your hypothesis or hypotheses. Generally, researchers also include the reasons that led them to formulate the hypothesis or hypotheses they did. Most appropriate are reasons derived from well-grounded theory and previous research studies.

- ***Methods and Procedures.*** Briefly but completely state the methods and procedures you used to investigate your hypothesis. Here you'd talk about the questionnaire you developed, the groups you established, the observers you used, how you trained your observers, how you defined smiling, and just about everything that would be relevant if someone wanted to repeat your study.
- ***Findings and Results.*** Present your findings in numerical form in some kind of table or chart. The easier it is for people to grasp your results, the better.
- ***Conclusions.*** Given your findings, what do you conclude? What do your data tell us about nonverbal communication? Relate these conclusions to your hypothesis or hypotheses. You might even offer some practical results or conclusions that we can draw from your findings, for example, to break tension or to be liked. This practical application, however, is not an essential part of the academic research paper, although it's often appreciated by readers.
- ***References.*** Append a list of all those references that are directly relevant to your study and that you have used and referred to in your paper. Do not list sources that you may have consulted but not used in the actual paper. Use the APA Style Manual for writing up the paper and for bibliographic references. Numerous websites will help you format your references in appropriate form; just search for "APA style" or "bibliography format" and you'll find plenty of help for this tedious task.

Appendix B

Creating a Video on Nonverbal Communication

An excellent experience for learning about nonverbal communication is to teach it. Consequently, a popular assignment in many nonverbal communication courses is to create a video to teach some aspect of nonverbal communication. You might then upload it to YouTube or some similar site, exchange videos with others, and critique each other's productions.

There are numerous websites that illustrate and demonstrate the ways to go about making a video. For example, *www.youtube.com/create* offers suggestions for creating a video. And, of course, there are a variety of websites that will help you film, design, and edit your video. Just search for "video design," "create video," or similar terms and you'll find the most recent videos on creating videos. These websites and their accompanying videos—as well as all the videos you've already watched—will provide a lot better instruction than any print description could.

In addition to the suggestions you'll find online, consider these as well.

1. **Keep your video short**—aim for about 2 minutes. This will force you to compact your ideas but still treat a single idea in some depth.
2. **Clarify the purpose you want to achieve.** Do you want to illustrate specific gestures or an interaction? Do you want to compare nonverbals in different cultures? Once you've formulated your purpose, you'll be better able to select appropriate ways of creating your video.
3. **Select the appropriate means for achieving your purpose.** So, for example, if you want to illustrate different gestures in different cultures, then you'll likely need members of both cultures to demonstrate the gestures or you'll need photos or graphics.
4. **Keep your subject limited.** Don't try to cover too much. For your first nonverbal communication video, consider focusing on one code and illustrating one aspect of that code—for example, if you want to focus on touch, then you might limit your video to, say, relationship touching. Or, if you want to focus on gestures, you might limit your video to adaptors or illustrators. The idea here is to cover a limited topic but in some depth rather than a broad topic in only general terms.
5. **Keep any slides simple.** If you use PowerPoint or Prezi slides, keep them simple. Viewers are not likely to read slides with too much information on them. Similarly, don't crowd the slides with visual images. Use additional slides rather than crowd them.

6. **Keep it professional.** You may find it useful to add this video to your resumé should you want employers to see it. Of course, if it's on a public site, prospective employers are very likely to see it whether you want them to or not.
7. **Research.** Here is a list of nonverbal communication videos that you can use as examples of the varied types of videos you might create. It should prove useful to review some of these with the idea of doing your own video. What are some of the pitfalls that you'd want to avoid? What are some clever techniques that you might want to adapt?

SAMPLE NONVERBAL COMMUNICATION VIDEOS

These videos vary widely in just about every conceivable way. Some are quite professional and sophisticated in terms of production whereas others are the works of beginners with little technical equipment. Some are basically informational—those produced by colleges and narrated by professors, for example—whereas others are promotional for books or seminars. Some are designed to sell a product and others are designed to fulfill a requirement in a communication course. Some of the videos make well-substantiated claims, the kinds of conclusions you find in your nonverbal communication textbooks and research articles. Others, however, make claims beyond what most academics would accept. For example, if you just watched the videos you'd come away with the idea that you can read a person like a book. Of course, you can't.

I've tried to group these into a few categories, though most of the videos vary over several nonverbal codes. The categories used here simply reflect the videos I found that I thought would be useful. Most of the videos are short—the longest is 11 minutes, 23 seconds and the shortest is 32 seconds. The average is probably around 4 minutes.

General

General introduction to nonverbal communication,
www.youtube.com/watch?v=VfDWQG47pAQ

What is nonverbal communication? Nonverbal communication, vocal cues, and facial expressions, 3.01
www.youtube.com/watch?v=pMhvtA2QvqU

Movie clips showing varied forms of nonverbal communication, 2.58
www.youtube.com/watch?v=VfDWQG47pAQ

Deborah Borisoff and others on nonverbal communication—general, 3.01
www.youtube.com/watch?v=07AufHZygjs

Doctor–patient nonverbal communication, 7.19
www.youtube.com/watch?v=MRE7f52bS7w

Candidates/campaigning and body language effectiveness
www.youtube.com/watch?v=d3yy5eIJW2Y&feature=related

Power and nonverbal communication
www.youtube.com/watch?v=cS1LI_ut3fs

Interpersonal conflict, 4.32
www.youtube.com/watch?v=joVSUPkWTGg

Perception/Attraction/First Impressions

Perception of beauty, 1.15
www.youtube.com/watch?v=dAnRQncZ_uk

The factors that make for attraction, 11.23
www.youtube.com/watch?v=gfizpfBwYng

What makes a man attractive to women?
www.youtube.com/watch?v=PoKA-a5vEEc

Body language and attraction, a series of images depicting various forms of body language that communicate attraction, 2.25
www.youtube.com/watch?v=3E-qu2rtCgo

Measuring beauty, 2.58
www.youtube.com/watch?v=mVVroi8q0Y0

Culture

For a discussion of cultural differences in gestures, 5.19
www.youtube.com/watch?v=fRQSRed58XM&feature=related

The use of silence in Japan, 7.11
www.youtube.com/watch?v=QyjenhfSnFU

Cultural dimensions, Hofstede, 2.09
www.youtube.com/watch?v=6gJzRS0I7tA

A discussion of Hofstede's cultural dimensions
www.youtube.com/watch?v=9JJnkM0h6uQ

Touch behavior in different cultures, 3.39
www.youtube.com/watch?v=5PGCkSoy5nk

NVC in Greek culture, 4.47
www.youtube.com/watch?v=IEps2bzE0u8

NVC in Brazilian culture, 3.09
www.youtube.com/watch?v=zTgPMkFWDlQ

NVC and culture, 4.43
www.youtube.com/watch?v=kn3NwMtAEHs

NVC and culture—general, 5.24
www.youtube.com/watch?v=LyPhAeZcsvY

NVC and South Korean culture, 4.31
www.youtube.com/watch?v=cFQFp05Twww

NVC gestures and cultures, 5.17
www.youtube.com/watch?v=BM9Iu4OQXAw

Body language in high- and low-context cultures, 3.58
www.youtube.com/watch?v=8tIUilYX56E&feature=results_main&playnext=1&list=PLCE91F207FC0B2098

NVC and culture, 4.24
www.youtube.com/watch?v=CS1diUo42UQ

Russian gestures, 6.26
www.youtube.com/watch?v=1uSw_JC_xOw

Polish and Japanese gestures, 1.41
www.youtube.com/watch?v=Mi6h8zktO1s

Colombian hand gestures, 1.12
www.youtube.com/watch?v=QDEAPV73v4s

Hand gestures in various cultures with subtitles identifying the varied meanings, 3.24
www.youtube.com/watch?v=xHSe1ogHYUw

Maria Baltar talks about greeting rituals in different cultures, 7.30
www.youtube.com/watch?v=vMskROH6v6U

Dan Fishel from the Columbia Business School talks about the American handshake, 4.42
www.youtube.com/watch?v=yDhXD25fmMo

Deception

NVC and deception, 4.45
www.youtube.com/watch?v=3IQgpPjiV70

Lying, spotting deception, 8.15
www.youtube.com/watch?v=6WFvcZnokKE

Lying in the beginning of relationships, 3.28
www.youtube.com/watch?v=FcBsRbT4vLQ

James Pennebaker on deception and words—a useful addition to most of the nonverbal stuff on deception—(discusses and shows tapes of Representative Anthony Weiner who lied and then told the truth about sending sexual photos), 2.33
www.youtube.com/watch?v=Vc073RIC7_M

Suggests there are three ways to tell if someone is lying to you, 7.22
www.youtube.com/watch?v=MWQtuXSnXtU

Social behavior and etiquette—signs of lying (discusses some of the popular beliefs about deception detection), 1.59
www.youtube.com/watch?v=Qt_cvMRIGC4

Jan Hargrave talks about deception and aims to teach you how to tell what others are thinking through observing nonverbal communication, 9.34
www.youtube.com/watch?v=5X7fKZTmZa4&feature=results_main&playnext=1&list=PLD0D3AA38EE11B8D4

Effectiveness in Interviewing and Dating

Simple word charts with voiceover on first impressions (both verbal and nonverbal), offers the standard advice but very well phrased, 1.23
www.youtube.com/watch?v=XqiIXOpH-BA

Staged interactions of job interviews with some good advice on nonverbal communication, 9.28
www.youtube.com/watch?v=I5Cy1yf9wwQ

Suggestions for speed dating, both verbal and nonverbal, 2.28
www.youtube.com/watch?v=P43aALpN1UY

Suggestions for making a good first impression, 1.19
www.youtube.com/watch?v=IOGFmFRJ2xA

Discussion of suggestions for more effective body language in dating, 5.44
www.youtube.com/watch?v=WKx–9CG0fY

Interview with Barbara Roberts on face reading, especially if you can tell when someone is dangerous solely from face reading, 5.47
www.youtube.com/watch?v=gpgM2tbCUMQ&feature=results_video&playnext=1&list=PLD0D3AA38EE11B8D4

Professor Gary Deaton talks about posture and gesture in a job interview, 3.52
www.youtube.com/watch?v=_bNSsfDfy2Q

Nick Morgan talks about how speakers are evaluated by the way they stand and walk to the stage, 2.20
www.youtube.com/watch?v=tIdttrC0xtM

Specific Codes (Touch, Gestures, Smell, etc.)

A short video on tracking eye movements to study consumer behavior, 2.44
www.youtube.com/watch?v=L7m3liNrvrs

Touch avoidance, 1. 29
www.youtube.com/watch?v=EMSdfqJWPT4&feature=results_video&playnext=1&list=PL32CB04D75ACCFCE8

On color communication, 1.56
www.youtube.com/watch?v=0nCsVt_vilw

Silence—puts forth examples of when silence is destructive
www.youtube.com/watch?v=ED008VqMDJU&feature=fvst

Chronemics: Polychronic versus monochronic time orientations (shows a variety of people with different time orientations), 10.41
www.youtube.com/watch?v=uzTDdru1GwM

Monochronicity versus polychronicity, 3.07
www.youtube.com/watch?v=UOE4nuivNKI

Proxemics—the close talker from Seinfeld, .47
www.youtube.com/watch?v=tgO8V6TdAKM

Nonverbal proxemic violations, 4.54
www.youtube.com/watch?v=Pmc9JItJ0C4

Eye contact, 1.44
www.youtube.com/watch?v=QwxtGzI2xVI

On the silent treatment, cartoon character talks about the problems with the silent treatment, 5.53
www.youtube.com/watch?v=0IwEnZPa0N8

Rate of speech from a sales training point of view, "listenable rate of speech," 6.13
www.youtube.com/watch?v=CKABu6rXbAM

A humorous monotone speaker, 1.16
www.youtube.com/watch?v=ZLQ8kEg8vfc

Clothing and communication, 2.02
www.youtube.com/watch?v=cNJ7zfMd2fw

Clothing—do clothes make the man?, with some good historical notes, 3.05
www.youtube.com/watch?v=Wg7eqQ3QTYI

Sales tips on dressing for your prospects, 2.20
www.youtube.com/watch?v=feMK9Kr1yDc

Cathrine Hatcher talks about color as communication, 5.48
www.youtube.com/watch?v=pUefDi65d6I

An ad for Old Spice that illustrates the importance of smell, .32
www.youtube.com/watch?v=FgGVXhya6hk

Glossary of 200 Nonverbal Communication Concepts

Listed here are definitions of the technical terms in nonverbal communication—the words that are peculiar or unique to this discipline. All boldface terms within the definitions appear as separate entries in the glossary.

accommodation The process of adjusting your communication patterns to those with whom you're interacting.

active listening The process by which a listener expresses his or her understanding of the speaker's total message, including the verbal and nonverbal, the thoughts and feelings.

adaptors Nonverbal behaviors that satisfy some personal need and usually occur without awareness; for example, scratching to relieve an itch or moistening your lips to relieve dryness. Three types of adaptors are often distinguished: **self-adaptors**, **alter-adaptors**, and **object-adaptors**.

affect blends Facial expressions that are a combination of two or more primary emotions.

affect displays Movements of the facial area that convey emotional meaning—for example, expressions showing anger, fear, or surprise.

alter-adaptors Body movements you make in response to your current interactions; for example, crossing your arms over your chest when someone unpleasant approaches or moving closer to someone you like.

ambiguity The condition in which a message or relationship may be interpreted as having more than one meaning.

apology An expression of regret or sorrow for having done what you did or for what happened.

artifactual communication Communication that takes place through the wearing and arrangement of various items—for example, clothing, jewelry, buttons, or the furniture in your house and its arrangement.

assertiveness A willingness to stand up for your rights but with respect for the rights of others.

asynchronous communication Communication in which the sending and receiving of messages do not take place simultaneously (messages are sent and received at different times); opposed to **synchronous communication**.

attraction The state or process by which one individual is drawn to another and forms a highly positive evaluation of that other person.

backchanneling cues Listener responses to a speaker that do not ask for the speaking role.

batons A type of **illustrator**; like the conductor's baton, illustrator batons emphasize a particular word or phrase with, say, a hand movement.

beard A person who is used to hide something about another person, for example, having a friend pose as a spouse to give the impression that you're married.

behavioral constraint Restriction on your movements; a major contributor to **crowding**.

behavioral synchrony The similarity in the behavior, usually nonverbal, of two persons, and generally interpreted as an index of mutual liking. Also see **mirroring**.

biological time One's preference for different times of the day and also to one's biological cycles.

biorhythms Cycles that the body goes through in a pattern; physical, emotional, and intellectual cycles are often distinguished.

body adornment A general term for jewelry, tattoos, and similar body ornaments.

body language A popular term for nonverbal communication.

body posture The positioning of the body in interaction with others; **inclusiveness/noninclusiveness**, **face-to-face/parallel**, and **congruence/incongruence** positions are usually identified.

body territory The area around you that you need to have to do what you want to do.

boundary marker An object that divides one person's territory from another's—for example, a fence.

central marker An item that is placed in a territory to reserve it for a specific person—for example, the sweater thrown over a library chair to signal that the chair is taken.

channel The vehicle or medium through which signals are sent.

chronemics The study of the communicative nature of time—of the way you treat time and use it to communicate.

civil inattention Polite ignoring of others so as not to invade their privacy.

code A set of symbols used to translate a message from one form to another.

color communication The meanings that different colors communicate in various cultures.

communication (1) The process or act of communicating; (2) the actual message or messages sent and received; (3) the study of the processes involved in the sending and receiving of messages.

complementarity A principle of **attraction** stating that you are attracted by qualities that you do not possess or that you wish to possess and to people who are opposite or different from yourself; opposed to **similarity**.

congruence/incongruence A **body posture** referring to the degree of **mirroring** of one person's body posture by another person.

connotation The feeling or emotional aspect of a word's meaning; generally viewed as consisting of evaluation (e.g., good–bad), potency (strong–weak), and activity (fast–slow) dimensions. Opposed to **denotation**.

contamination Rendering a territory impure; a form of **territorial encroachment**.

context The physical, social–psychological, temporal, and cultural environment in which communication takes place.

conversational management The conduct of a conversation by means of **conversational turns**.

conversational turns The process of exchanging the speaker and listener roles during conversation.

crowding The psychological perception that there are too many people around and a consciousness of restrictions on your spatial freedom; distinguished from **density**.

cultural display Signs that communicate a person's cultural identification, for example, clothing or religious jewelry.

cultural rules Rules that are specific to a given cultural group.

cultural time The perspective on time shared by members of a particular culture.

culture The relatively specialized lifestyle of a group of people—consisting of their values, beliefs, artifacts, ways of behaving, and ways of communicating—that is passed on from one generation to the next.

deception bias The assumption that the other person is lying; opposed to a **truth bias**.

deception cues Verbal or nonverbal cues that reveal the person is lying.

decoding The process of extracting a message from a code—for example, translating speech sounds into nerve impulses. See also **encoding**.

deictic movements A type of **illustrator** that points to a person or thing that you want someone else to focus on.

denotation The objective or descriptive aspect of a word's meaning; the meaning you'd find in a dictionary. Opposed to **connotation**.

density The number of people within an area of space; distinguished from **crowding**.

display rules Cultural norms for what is and what is not appropriate to display in public.

double-bind message A special type of ambiguous message in which verbal and nonverbal signals contradict each other; if you do what the verbal message asks you to do you violate what the nonverbal message tells you to do and vice versa.

Duchenne smile A genuine smile; a smile that is a reflection of your real feelings.

duping delight Nonverbal **leakage** that occurs when someone takes satisfaction and pleasure at fooling someone.

dyadic communication Two-person communication.

dyadic effect The tendency to reciprocate, to imitate (in some way) what the other person does or says.

earmarker A physical sign that identifies an item as belonging to a specific person—for example, a nameplate on a desk or initials on an attaché case.

emblems Nonverbal behaviors that directly translate words or phrases—for example, the signs for "OK" and "peace."

emoticon A written symbol to indicate an emotion.

emotional contagion The process by which the strong emotions of one person are taken on by another person; the assumption that, like the flu, emotions may be contagious.

encoding The process of putting a message into a code—for example, translating nerve impulses into speech sounds. See also **decoding**.

equilibrium theory A theory that attempts to explain the relationship between intimacy and space and holds that intimacy and distance vary together; the greater the intimacy, the closer the distance; the lower the intimacy, the greater the distance.

expectancy violations theory A theory of **proxemics** holding that people have a certain expectancy for space relationships. When that expectancy is violated (e.g., when a person stands too close to you or a romantic partner maintains abnormally large distances from you), the relationship comes into clearer focus and you wonder why this "normal distance" is being violated.

eye movements Use eye movements to seek feedback, exchange conversational turns, signal the nature of your relationship with others, and compensate for increased physical distance. At the same time, look for such meanings in the eye movements of others.

eye roll Moving the eyes upward as a condescending gesture.

eyebrow flash A raising of the eyebrows, often a sign of acknowledgment.

face-to-face/parallel A **body posture** referring to the degree to which two people face each other directly or indirectly.

facial feedback hypothesis The theory that your facial expressions can produce physiological and emotional effects.

facial management techniques Techniques used to mask certain emotions and to emphasize others; for example, intensifying your expression of happiness to make a friend feel good about a promotion.

facial messages Use facial expressions to communicate that you're involved in the interaction. As a listener, look to the emotional expressions of others as additional cues to their meaning.

facial recognition The process of identifying a person from facial cues.

facial style A person's normal and usual form of facial expression, thought to be a part of a person's personality.

feedback Information that is given back to the source. Feedback may come from the source's own messages (as when we hear what we are saying) or may come from the receiver(s) in the form of applause, yawning, puzzled looks, questions, comments on a blog post or letters to the editor of a newspaper, increased or decreased subscriptions to a magazine, and so forth.

feedforward Information that is sent prior to a regular message telling the listener something about what is to follow.

feng shui The principles of living in a harmonious relationship with one's environment and surroundings, including principles for furniture arrangement.

flirt The process of sending nonverbal (and verbal) signals to indicate a romantic interest.

formal time Time units that are established and that have precise meanings, for example, hour or day. See also **informal time**.

gaze Looking at another person. See also **mutual gaze**, **gaze omission**, and **gaze aversion**.

gaze aversion Intentional avoidance of making eye contact. Opposed to **gaze omission**. See also **gaze** and **mutual gaze**.

gaze omission Unintentional avoidance of making eye contact. Opposed to **gaze aversion**. See also **gaze** and **mutual gaze**.

home-field advantage The increased power that comes from being in your own territory.

home territories Territories about which individuals have a sense of intimacy and over which they exercise control—for example, a professor's office.

ideographs. A type of **illustrator**; ideographs trace the path of an idea or thought.

illustrators Nonverbal gestures that enhance (literally illustrate the verbal message that they accompany), for example, moving your head to the left when you refer to something on the left.

image management The process and strategies of using communication to convey a particular image of yourself to others.

immediacy A quality of interpersonal effectiveness that creates a sense of contact and togetherness and conveys interest in and liking for the other person.

inclusiveness/noninclusiveness A **body posture** indicating the degree to which your body position includes or excludes others.

informal time Approximate rather than exact time, denoted in terms such as "soon," "early," and "in a while." See also **formal time**.

information power Power that a person possesses because others see that individual as having significant information and the ability to communicate logically and persuasively. Also called "persuasion power."

insulation A reaction to **territorial encroachment** in which you erect some sort of barrier between yourself and the invaders.

interactional territories Areas where people gather and interact with each other, for example, the dinner table or a park bench.

interpersonal time The time dimension of interpersonal interaction, for example, punctuality, response time, and relationship time.

interruptions In conversation, attempts to take over the role of the speaker.

intimate distance The closest **proxemic distance**, ranging from touching to 18 inches.

invasion The unwarranted entrance into another's territory that changes the meaning of the territory; a form of **territorial encroachment**.

irreversibility A principle of communication holding that communication cannot be reversed; once something has been communicated, it cannot be uncommunicated.

kinesics The study of the communicative dimensions of facial and bodily movements.

kinetographs. A type of **illustrator** that imitates or depicts bodily movements.

leakage The process whereby slight nonverbal movements (often around the lips and eyes) reveal one's true feelings.

leave-taking cues Verbal and nonverbal cues that indicate a desire to terminate a conversation.

linguistic collusion A response to **territorial encroachment** in which the members of the in-group use a language unknown to the invaders.

lying The act of deliberately trying to mislead another person by communicating information you believe to be false.

markers Devices that signify that a certain territory belongs to a particular person. See also **boundary marker**, **central marker**, and **earmarker**.

masking The process of replacing or substituting a felt expression for one that is more appropriate to the situation.

matching hypothesis An assumption that you date and mate people who are comparable to yourself—who match you—in physical attractiveness.

metacommunication Communication about communication.

metamessage A message that refers to another message.

mirroring The process of imitating or mimicking the nonverbal behaviors of another person, often considered to promote perceived attractiveness.

monochronic time orientation A view of time in which things are done sequentially; one thing is scheduled at a time; opposed to **polychronic time orientation**.

multitasking Doing more than one thing at one time; a pattern of those with a **polychronic time orientation**.

mutual gaze The situation in which two people look at each other at the same time.

negative face need The desire to be autonomous, to have the right to do as you wish.

negative face strategies Messages that recognize a person's right to autonomy.

noise Anything that distorts the message; noise is present to the extent that the message received is not the message sent.

nonverbal communication Communication without words; communication by means of space, gestures, facial expressions, touching, vocal variation, and silence, for example.

nonverbal dominance Nonverbal behavior through which one person exercises psychological dominance over another.

object-adaptors Movements that involve manipulation of some object; for example, punching holes in or drawing on a Styrofoam coffee cup, clicking a ballpoint pen, or chewing on a pencil.

oculesis A technical term for the study of eye movements.

olfactory communication Communication by smell.

paralanguage The vocal but nonverbal aspect of speech. Paralanguage consists of voice qualities (e.g., pitch range, resonance, tempo); vocal characterizers (laughing or crying, yelling or whispering); vocal qualifiers (intensity, pitch height); and vocal segregates ("uh-uh," meaning "no," or "sh," meaning "silence").

pauses Silent periods in the normally fluent stream of speech. Pauses are of two major types: filled pauses (interruptions in speech that are filled with such vocalizations as "er" or "um") and unfilled pauses (silences of unusually long duration).

personal distance The second-closest **proxemic distance**, ranging from 18 inches to 4 feet.

pictographs A type of **illustrator** that draws a picture of the thing talked about.

pitch The highness or lowness of the vocal tone.

politeness Civility, consideration, refinement, respect, and regard for others as expressed verbally and nonverbally; interaction that follows the socially accepted rules for interpersonal interaction.

politeness strategies Strategies that support another's face needs and may be used as a strategy to appear likeable.

Pollyanna effect The tendency to see the positive side of things rather than the negative.

polychronic time orientation A view of time in which several things may be scheduled or engaged in at the same time; opposed to **monochronic time orientation**.

positive face need The desire to be viewed positively by others, to be thought of favorably.

positive face strategies Messages that compliment and praise another. *Use these as appropriate.*

positiveness A characteristic of effective communication involving positive attitudes toward the self and toward the interpersonal interaction. Also can mean complimenting another and expressing acceptance and approval.

posture The way in which one stands or sits.

power The ability to control or influence the attitudes, beliefs, or behaviors of others.

primacy effect The condition in which what comes first exerts greater influence in our perceptions than what comes later. See also **recency effect**.

primary affect displays Facial displays of the primary emotions.

primary emotions The basic or pure emotions, often considered to be happiness, anger, sadness, disgust, fear, surprise, and contempt.

primary territories Areas that a person can consider his or her own exclusive preserve—for example, someone's room or office.

privacy The degree to which one perceives oneself (and one's messages) to be free from surveillance.

protection theory A theory of **proxemics** referring to the fact that people establish a body-buffer zone to protect themselves from unwanted closeness, touching, or attack.

proxemic distances The spatial distances that people maintain in communication and social interaction: four distances are generally distinguished: **intimate distance**, **personal distance**, **social distance**, and **public distance**.

proxemics The study of the communicative function of space; the study of how people unconsciously structure their space—the distances between people in their interactions, the organization of spaces in homes and offices, and even the design of cities.

proximity Physical closeness; one of the qualities influencing **attraction**. Also, as a principle of **perception**, the tendency to perceive people or events that are physically close as belonging together or representing some unit.

psychological time The importance you place on past, present, or future time.

public distance The longest proxemic distance, ranging from 12 to more than 25 feet.

public territories Areas that are open to all people (e.g., restaurants or parks).

pupil dilation The widening of the pupils of the eyes, often a sign of interest.

pupillometrics The study of communication through changes in the size of the pupils of the eyes.

rate The speed with which you speak, generally measured in words per minute.

receiver Any person or thing that takes in messages. Receivers may be individuals listening to or reading a message, a group of people hearing a speech, a scattered television audience, or machines that store information.

recency effect The condition in which what comes last (i.e., most recently) exerts greater influence in our perceptions than what comes first. See also **primacy effect**.

reciprocity of liking Liking someone as a response to your perceiving that they like you.

regulators Nonverbal behaviors that regulate, monitor, or control the communications of another person, such as nods or changes in body posture.

reinforcement One of the factors contributing to **attraction**; the giving of a reward or the removal of an aversive stimulus.

reliability A quality of research or support that can be counted on as accurate and trustworthy.

secondary territories Areas that do not belong to a particular person but that have been occupied by that person and are therefore associated with her or him—for example, the seat you normally take in class.

self-adaptors Movements that usually satisfy a physical need, especially a need to be more comfortable; for example, scratching your head to relieve an itch, moistening your lips because they feel dry, or pushing your hair out of your eyes.

shrug A body gesture in which the shoulders are raised, often accompanied by a bewildered expression, and often designed to communicate a lack of concern or knowledge.

silence The absence of vocal communication. Often mistakenly thought to be the absence of any and all communication, silence actually can communicate feelings or can serve to prevent communication about certain topics.

similarity A theory of attraction that holds that people are attracted to those who are similar to them; opposed to **complementarity**.

smell The sense by which you receive olfactory signals.

smell adaptation The situation in which you gradually lose the distinctiveness of a smell due to overexposure to it.

smell blindness The inability to identify and distinguish among smells.

smell discrimination The ability to distinguish one smell from another.

smell memory The ability to recall previous events through smell and to recall the smells themselves.

smell overload The situation in which your sense of smell is overloaded, bombarded by too many smells or smells that are too intense.

smell satiation The situation in which a smell becomes difficult to perceive because of overexposure to it.

smile A facial expression usually indicating pleasure, though other emotions may be signed by slightly different smiles, for example, annoyance. See also **Duchenne smile**.

social clock The cultural time table for the accomplishment of a variety of life's milestones.

somatotyping Classifying people's personality and temperament on the basis of their body type, whether tall and thin, short and stout, or muscular.

source Any person or thing that creates messages. A source may be an individual speaking, writing, or gesturing or a computer sending an error message.

spatial distance Physical distance that signals the type of relationship you are in: intimate, personal, social, or public.

spatial movements A type of **illustrator** that indicates spatial relationships or size, for example.

spiral of silence The theory that holds that you are more likely to voice agreement with others than disagreement. The result is that this spirals, with the majority position becoming stronger and the minority positions becoming weaker.

stimulus overload The situation that occurs when the stimuli around you exceed your comfort zone; a major contributor to **crowding.**

surveillance Being watched by another; a major contributor to **crowding**.

synchronous communication Communication in which the sending and receiving of a message takes place at the same time; opposed to **asynchronous communication**.

taboo Forbidden; culturally censored; frowned upon by "polite society." Taboos may include entire topics as well as specific words—for example, death, sex, certain forms of illness, and various words denoting sexual activities and excretory functions.

tag questions Questions that ask for another's agreement and often signal weakness or uncertainty, for example, "That dinner was fine, don't you think?"

temporal communication The messages communicated by a person's time orientation and treatment of time.

territorial encroachment An intrusion into your territory.

territoriality A possessive or ownership reaction to an area of space or to particular objects.

theory A general statement or principle applicable to related phenomena.

tie signs Nonverbal (and verbal) cues that two people are somehow connected in some significant relational way.

time management The efficient use of time.

touch avoidance The tendency to avoid touching and being touched by others.

touch communication Communication through tactile means.

touch deprivation The psychological reaction to the absence of touch.

truth bias The assumption that the other person is telling the truth; opposed to a **deception bias.**

turf defense A response to **territorial encroachment** in which you defend your territory against intruders.

turn-denying cues Verbal or nonverbal cues indicating that the listener does not want to assume the role of speaker.

turn-maintaining cues Verbal or nonverbal cues that communicate your wish to maintain the role of speaker.

turn-requesting cues Verbal or nonverbal cues that indicate a desire to assume the speaker's turn.

turn-taking cues A general term for verbal and/or nonverbal cues indicating a desire to exchange speaking/listening turns.

turn-yielding cues Verbal or nonverbal cues indicating the speaker's desire to give up the speaker's role.

unrepeatability Principle of communication stating that no communication can ever be re-created in quite the same way because circumstances are never the same.

violation The unwarranted use of another's territory; a form of **territorial encroachment**.

visual dominance The use of the eyes to maintain a superior or controlling position; for example, when making an especially important point, you might look intently at the other person.

vocalics The study of the vocal (but nonverbal) dimension of speech, for example, **pitch**, **rate**, or **volume**.

voice qualities Aspects of **paralanguage**, for example, **pitch**, **rate**, and **volume**.

volume The relative loudness of the voice.

withdrawal A reaction to **territorial encroachment** in which we leave the territory.

References

Acor, A. A. (2001). Employers' perceptions of persons with body art and an experimental test regarding eyebrow piercing. *Dissertation Abstracts International: Section B. The Sciences and Engineering, 61,* 3885.

Addington, D. W. (1968). The relationship of selected vocal characteristics to personality perception. *Communication Monographs,* 35, 492–503.

Adler, R. B., Rosenfeld, L. B., & Proctor, R. F. (2012). *Interplay: The process of interpersonal communication.* New York: Oxford University Press.

Afifi, W. A. (2007). Nonverbal communication. In B. B. Whaley & W. Samter (Eds.), *Explaining communication: Contemporary theories and exemplars* (pp. 39–60). Mahwah, NJ: Erlbaum.

Afifi, W. A., & Johnson, M. L. (2005). The nature and function of tie-signs. In V. Manusov (Ed.), *The sourcebook of nonverbal measures: Going beyond words* (pp. 189–198). Mahwah, NJ: Erlbaum.

Altman, I. (1975). *The environment and social behavior.* Monterey, CA: Brooks/Cole.

Andersen, P. (2005). The touch avoidance measure. In V. Manusov (Ed.), *The sourcebook of nonverbal measures* (pp. 57–66). Mahwah, NJ: Erlbaum.

Andersen, P. A. (2009). *The complete idiot's guide to body language.* New York: Alpha/Penguin.

Andersen, P. A., & Leibowitz, K. (1978). The development and nature of the construct touch avoidance. *Environmental Psychology and Nonverbal Behavior, 3,* 89–106.

Andersen, P. A., Guerrero, L. K., & Jones, S. M. (2006). Nonverbal behavior in intimate interactions and intimate relationships. In V. Manusov & M. L. Patterson (Eds.), *The Sage handbook of nonverbal communication* (pp. 259–278). Los Angeles, CA: Sage.

Anderson, K. J., & Leaper, C. (1998). Meta-analyses of gender effects on conversational interruption: Who, what, when, where, and how. *Sex Roles, 39,* 225–252.

Angier, N. (1995, February 14). Powerhouse of senses: Smell, at last, gets its due. *New York Times,* pp. C1, C6.

Aquinis, H., & Henle, C. A. (2001). Effects of nonverbal behavior on perceptions of a female employee's power bases. *Journal of Social Psychology* 141 (August), 537–549.

Argyle, M. (1988). *Bodily communication* (2nd ed.). New York: Methuen.

Argyle, M., & Dean, J. (1965). Eye contact, distance and affiliation. *Sociometry, 28,* 289–304.

Argyle, M., & Ingham, R. (1972). Gaze, mutual gaze, and distance. *Semiotica, 1,* 32–49.

Aronson, E., Wilson, T. D., & Akert, R. M. (2013). *Social psychology: The heart and the mind,* 8th ed. Boston, MA: Pearson

Aronson, E., Wilson, T. D., & Akert, R. M. (2013). *Social psychology: The heart and the mind,* 8th ed. Boston: Pearson.

Ashcraft, M. H. (1998). *Fundamentals of cognition.* New York: Longman.

Axtell, R. E. (1991). *Do's and taboos of public speaking: How to get those butterflies flying in formation.* Hoboken, NJ: Wiley.

Axtell, R. E. (2007). *Essential do's and taboos: The complete guide to international business and leisure travel.* Hoboken, NJ: Wiley.

Bach, G. R., & Deutsch, R. M. (1990). *Stop! You're driving me crazy.* Boston: Berkley.

Barnlund, D. C. (1975). Communicative styles in two cultures: Japan and the United States. In A. Kendon, R. M. Harris, & M. R. Key (Eds.), *Organization of behavior in face-to-face interaction* (pp. 427–456). The Hague, Netherlands: Mouton.

Basso, K. H. (1972). To give up on words: Silence in Apache culture. In P. P. Giglioli (Ed.), *Language and social context.* New York, NY: Penguin.

Beach, W. A. (1990–91). Avoiding ownership for alleged wrongdoings. *Research on Language and Social Interaction, 24,* 1–36.

Behzadi, K. G. (1994). Interpersonal conflict and emotions in an Iranian cultural practice: QAHR and ASHTI. *Culture, Medicine, and Psychiatry, 18,* 321–359.

Beier, E. (1974). How we send emotional messages. *Psychology Today, 8,* 53–56.

Birren, F. (1963). *Color: A survey in words and pictures.* Secaucus, NJ: Citadel Press.

Brown, P., & Levinson, S. C. (1987). *Politeness: Some universals of language usage.* Cambridge, England: Cambridge University Press.

Bruneau, T. (1990). Chronemics: The study of time in human interaction. In J. A. DeVito & M. L. Hecht (Eds.), *The nonverbal communication reader* (pp. 301–311). Prospect Heights, IL: Waveland Press.

Bruneau, T. (2009/2010). Chronemics: Time-binding and the construction of personal time. *General Semantics Bulletin, 76,* 82–94.

Burgoon, J., Guerrero, L., & Floyd, K. (2010). *Nonverbal communication.* Boston: Allyn & Bacon.

Burgoon, J. K. (1982). Privacy and communication. In M. Burgoon (Ed), *Communiation Yearbook 6* (pp. 206–249). Los Angeles, CA: Sage.

Burgoon, J. K. (2005). Measuring nonverbal indicators of deceit. In V. Manusov (Ed.), *The sourcebook of nonverbal measures: Going beyond words* (pp. 237–250). Mahwah, NJ: Erlbaum.

Burgoon, J. K., & Bacue, A. E. (2003). Nonverbal communication skills. In J. O. Greene & B. R. Burleson (Eds.), *Handbook of communication and social interaction skills* (pp. 179–220). Mahwah, NJ: Erlbaum.

Burgoon, J. K., & Dunbar, N. E. (2006). Nonverbal expressions of dominance and power in human relationships. In V. Manusov, & M. L. Patterson (Eds.), *The Sage handbook of nonverbal communication* (pp. 279–298). Los Angeles, CA: Sage.

Burleson, B. R., Kunkel, A. W., & Birch, J. D. (1994). Thoughts about talk in romantic relationships: Similarity makes for attraction (and happiness, too). *Communication Quarterly, 42*, 259–273.

Burleson, B. R., Samter, W., & Luccetti, A. E. (1992). Similarity in communication values as a predictor of friendship choices: Studies of friends and best friends. *Southern Communication Journal, 57*, 260–276.

Butler, J., Pryor, B., & Grieder, M. (1998). Impression formation as a function of male baldness. *Perceptual and Motor Skills, 86,* 347–350.

Cappella, J. N. (1993). The facial feedback hypothesis in human interaction: Review and speculation. *Journal of Language and Social Psychology, 12*, 13–29.

Cappella, J. N., & Schreiber, D. M. (2006). The interaction management function of nonverbal cues. In *The Sage handbook of nonverbal communication* (pp. 361–379), V. Manusov & M. L. Patterson (Eds.). Thousand Oaks: Sage Publications.

Carroll, D. W. (1994). Psychology of language, 2d ed. Pacific Grove, CA: Brooks/Cole.

Carré, J. M., & McCormick, C. M. (2008). In your face: facial metrics predict aggressive behaviour in the laboratory and in varsity and professional hockey players. *Proceedings of the Royal Society B. Biological Sciences, 275*, 2651–2656.

Chaney, R. H., Givens, C. A., Aoki, M. F., & Gombiner, M. L. (1989). Pupillary responses in recognizing awareness in persons with profound mental retardation. *Perceptual and Motor Skills*, 69 (October), 523–528.

Connor-Greene, P. A. (1988). Gender differences in body weight perception and weight-loss strategies of college students. *Women & Health, 14*, 27–42.

Cortes, J. B., & Gatti, F. M. (1965). Physique and self-description of temperament. *Journal of Consulting Psychology, 29*, 432–439.

Crawford, M. (1994). Rethinking the romance: Teaching the content and function of gender stereotypes in the Psychology of Women course. *Teaching of Psychology, 21,* 151–153.

Crown, C. L., & Cummins, D. A. (1998). Objective versus perceived vocal interruptions in the dialogues of unacquainted pairs, friends, and couples. *Journal of Language and Social Psychology, 17*, 372–389.

Crusco, A. H., & Wetzel, C. G. (1984). The Midas touch: The effects of interpersonal touch on restaurant tipping. *Personality and social Psychology Bulletin*, *10*, 512–517.

Davitz, J. R. (Ed.). (1964). *The communication of emotional meaning.* New York: McGraw-Hill.

DePaulo, B. M., Lindsay, J. J., Malone, B. E., Muhlenbruck, L., Charlton, K., & Cooper, H. (2003). Cues to deception. *Psychological Bulletin, 129,* 74–118.

Dillard, J. P., & Marshall, L. J. (2003). Persuasion as a social skill. In J. O. Greene & B. R. Burleson (Eds.), *Handbook of communication and social interaction skills* (pp. 479–514). Mahwah, NJ: Erlbaum.

Doherty, R. W., Orimoto, L., Singelis, T. M., Hatfield, E., & Hebb, J. (1995). Emotional contagion: Gender and occupational differences. *Psychology of Women Quarterly,* 19, 355–371.

Donaldson, S. (1992). Gender and discourse: The case of interruptions. *Carleton Papers in Applied Language Studies, 9*, 47–66.

Drass, K. A. (1986). The effect of gender identity on conversation. Social *Psychology Quarterly, 49,* 294–301.

Dresser, N. (1996). *Multicultural manners: New rules of etiquette for a changing society.* Hoboken, NJ: Wiley.

Drews, D. R., Allison, C. K., & Probst, J. R. (2000). Behavioral and self-concept differences in tattooed and nontattooed college students. *Psychological Reports, 86,* 475–481.

Dreyfuss, H. (1971). *Symbol sourcebook.* New York: McGraw-Hill.

Duncan, S. D., Jr. (1972). Some signals and rules for taking speaking turns in conversation. *Journal of Personality and Social Psychology, 23*, 283–292.

Eastwick, P. W. & Finkel, E. J. (2009). Reciprocity of liking. In H. T. Reis & S. Sprecher (Eds.), *Encyclopedia of human relationships* (pp. 1333–1336). Los Angeles, CA: Sage.

Ehrenhaus, P. (1988). Silence and symbolic expression. *Communication Monographs, 55,* 41–57.

Ekman, P. (2009). *Telling lies: Clues to deceit in the marketplace, politics, and marriage* (3rd ed.). New York: Norton.

Ekman, P., & Friesen, W. V. (1969). The repertoire of nonverbal behavior: Categories, origins, usage, and coding. *Semiotica, 1,* 49–98.

Ekman, P., & Friesen, W. V. (2003). *Unmasking the face: A guide to recognizing emotions from facial expressions.* Cambridge, MA: Malor Book. (Original work published 1975)

Ekman, P., Friesen, W. V., & Ellsworth, P. (1972). *Emotion in the human face: Guidelines for research and an integration of findings.* New York: Pergamon Press.

Elliot, A. J., & Niesta, D. 2008). Romantic red: Red enhances men's attraction to women. *Journal of Personality and Social Psychology, 95*, 1150–1164.

Erceau, D., & Guéguen, N. (2007) Tactile contact and evaluation of the toucher. *Journal of Social Psychology*, *147*, 441–444.

Exline, R. V., Ellyson, S. L., & Long, B. (1975). Visual behavior as an aspect of power role relationships. In P. Pliner, L. Krames, & T. Alloway (Eds.), *Nonverbal communication of aggression*. New York: Plenum Press.

Forbes, G. B. (2001). College students with tattoos and piercings: Motives, family experiences, personality factors, and perception by others. *Psychological Reports, 89,* 774–786.

Frank, M. G., & Suetieva, E. (2013). Deception. In D. Matsumoto, M. G. Frank, & H. S. Hwang (Eds.), *Nonverbal communication: Science and applications* (pp. 121–144). Los Angeles, CA: Sage.

French, J. R. P., Jr., & Raven, B. (1968). The bases of social power. In D. Cartwright & A. Zander (Eds.), *Group dynamics: Research and theory* (3rd ed., pp. 259–269). New York: Harper & Row.

Furlow, F. B. (1996). The smell of love. *Psychology Today,* 29, 38–45.

Galin, D., & Ornstein, R. (1974). Individual differences in cognitive style. I. Reflective eye movements. *Neuropsychologia, 12*, 367–376.

Gladstone, G. L., & Parker, G. B. (2002). When you're smiling, does the whole world smile for you? *Australasian Psychiatry, 10,* 144–146.

Goffman, E. (1967). *Interaction ritual: Essays on face-to-face behavior.* New York: Pantheon.

Goffman, E. (1971). *Relations in public: Microstudies of the public order.* New York: HarperCollins.

Goldin-Meadow, S., Nusbaum, H., Kelly, S. D., & Wagner, S. (2001). Gesture—psychological aspects. *Psychological Science, 12*, 516–522.

Gonzalez, A., & Zimbardo, P. G. (1985). Time in perspective. *Psychology Today, 19*, 20–26.

Gonzenbach, W. J., King, C., & Jablonski, P. (1999). Homosexuals and the military: An analysis of the spiral of silence. *Howard Journal of Communication, 10*, 281–296.

Gosling, S. D., Ko, S. J., Mannarelli, T., & Morris, M. E. (2002). A room with a cue: Personality judgments based on offices and bedrooms. *Journal of Personality and Social Psychology, 82*, 379–398.

Graham, J. A., & Argyle, M. (1975). The effects of different patterns of gaze combined with different facial expressions on impression formation. *Journal of Movement Studies, 1,* 178–182.

Graham, J. A., Bitti, P. R., & Argyle, M. (1975). A cross-cultural study of the communication of emotion by facial and gestural cues. *Journal of Human Movement Studies, 1*, 68–77.

Greif, E. B. (1980). Sex differences in parent-child conversations. *Women's Studies International Quarterly, 3,* 253–258.

Greitemeyer, T. (2007). What do men and women want in a partner? Are educated partners always more desirable? *Journal of Experimental Social Psychology, 43*, 180–194.

Grossin, W. (1987). Monochronic time, polychronic time and policies for development. *Studi di Sociologia, 25*, 18–25.

Guerrero, L. K., & Andersen, P. A. (1991). The waxing and waning of relational intimacy: Touch as a function of relational stage, gender and touch avoidance. *Journal of Social and Personal Relationships, 8,* 147–165.

Guerrero, L. K., Andersen, P. A., & Afifi, W. A. (2007). *Close encounters: Communication in relationships* (2nd ed.). Los Angeles, CA: Sage.

Guéguen, N., & Fischer-Lokou, J. (2004). Hitchhikers smiles and receipt of help. *Psychological Reports, 94*, 756–760.

Guéguen, N., & Vion, M. (2009). The effect of a practitioner's touch on a patient's medication compliance. *Psychology, Health, and Medicine, 14*, 689–694.

Guéguen, N., Fischer-Lokou, J. (2002). An evaluation of touch on a large request: a field setting. *Psychological Reports, 90*, 267–269.

Guéguen, N., Fischer-Lokou, J. (2003). Another evaluation of touch and helping behavior. *Psychological Reports, 92*, 62–64.

Guéguen N. (2002). Touch, awareness of touch, and compliance with a request. *Perceptual and Motor Skills, 95*, 355–360.

Haga, Y. (1988). Traits de langage et caractere Japonais. *Cahiers de Sociologie Economique et Culturelle, 9*, 105–109.

Hagen, S. (2011). *The everything body language book*, 2nd ed. Avon, MA: Adams Media.

Hall, E. T. (1959). *The silent language.* Garden City, NY: Doubleday.

Hall, E. T. (1963). A system for the notation of proxemic behavior. *American Anthropologist, 65*, 1003–1026.

Hall, E. T. (1966). *The hidden dimension.* Garden City, NY: Doubleday.

Hall, E. T. (1976). *Beyond culture.* New York: Anchor Books.

Hall, E. T. (1983). *The dance of life: The other dimension of time.* New York: Anchor Books/Doubleday.

Hall, E. T., & Hall, M. R. (1987). *Hidden differences: Doing business with the Japanese.* New York, NY: Doubleday.

Hall, J. A. (1984). *Nonverbal sex differences.* Baltimore: Johns Hopkins University Press.

Hall, J. A. (1996). Touch, status, and gender at professional meetings. *Journal of Nonverbal Behavior, 20*, 23–44.

Haselhuhn, M. P., & Wong, E. M. (2011). Bad to the bone: Facial structure predicts unethical behaviour. *Proceedings of the Royal Society B. Biological Sciences.*

Heap, J. L. (1992). Seeing snubs: An introduction to sequential analysis of classroom interaction. *Journal of Classroom Interaction, 27*, 23–28.

Helgeson, V. S. (2009). *Psychology of gender,* 3rd ed. Upper Saddle River, NJ: Prentice-Hall.

Henley, N. M. (1977). *Body politics: Power, sex, and nonverbal communication.* Englewood Cliffs, NJ: Prentice-Hall.

Hertenstein, M. J., Holmes, R., McCullough, M., & Keltner, D. (2009). The communication of emotion via touch. *Emotion, 9*, 566–573.

Hesegawa, T., & Gudykunst, W. B. (1998). Silence in Japan and the United States. *Journal of Cross-Cultural Psychology, 29*, 668–684.

Hess, E. H. (1975). *The tell-tale eye.* New York: Van Nostrand Reinhold.

Hess, E. H., Seltzer, A. L., & Schlien, J. M. (1965). Pupil response of hetero- and homosexual males to pictures of men and women: A pilot study. Journal of Abnormal Psychology, 70, 165–168.

Hoft, N. L. (1995). *International technical communication: How to export information about high technology.* Hoboken, NJ: Wiley.

Hogue, M. E., McDuff, D. J., & Picard, R. W. (2012). Exploring temporal patterns in classifying frustrated and delighted smiles. *IEEE Transactions on Affective Computing.*

Holmes, J. (1995). *Women, men and politeness.* New York, NY: Longman.

Iizuka, Y. (1993). Regulators in Japanese conversation. *Psychological Reports, 72*, 203–209.

Infante, D. A., Rancer, A. S., & Avtgis, T. A. (2010). *Contemporary communication theory.* Dubuque, IA: Kendall Hunt.

Ingegneri, R. (2008). How should you handle tattoos and body piercing during a job interview. Http://ezinearticles.com/?expert=Rachel_Ingegneri.

Ivy, D. K., & Wahl, S. T. (2009). *The nonverbal self: Communication for a lifetime.* Boston, MA: Allyn & Bacon.

Jaworski, A. (1993). *The power of silence: Social and pragmatic perspectives.* Thousand Oaks, CA: Sage.

Jecker, J., & Landy, D. (1969). Liking a person as a function of doing him a favor. *Human Relations, 22,* 371–378.

Jeffres, L. W., Neuendorf, K. A., & Atkin, D. (1999). Spirals of silence: Expressing opinions when the climate of opinion is unambiguous. *Political Communication, 16,* 115–131.

Johnson, C. E. (1987). An introduction to powerful and powerless talk in the classroom. *Communication Education, 36,* 167–172.

Joiner, T. E. (1994). Contagious depression: Existence, specificity to depressed symptoms, and the role of reassurance seeking. *Journal of Personality and Social Psychology,* 67, 287–296.

Jones, S., & Yarbrough, A. E. (1985). A naturalistic study of the meanings of touch. *Communication Monographs, 52,* 19–56.

Joule, R.V., & Guéguen N. (2007). Touch, compliance, and awareness of tactile contact. *Perceptual and Motor Skills, 104,* 581–588.

Kanner, B. (1989, April 3). Color schemes. *New York Magazine,* pp. 22–23.

Kennedy, C. W., & Camden, C. T. (1988). A new look at interruptions. *Western Journal of Speech Communication, 47,* 45–58.

Ketcham, H. (1958). *Color planning for business and industry.* New York: Harper.

Keyes, R. (1980). *The height of your life.* New York: Warner Books.

Kleinke, C. L. (1986). *Meeting and understanding people.* New York: W. H. Freeman.

Kluger, J. (2008, January 28). Why we love. *Time,* pp. 54–61.

Knapp, M. L. (2008). *Lying and deception in human interaction.* Boston: Pearson.

Knapp, M. L., & Hall, J. (2010). *Nonverbal behavior in human interaction* (7th ed.). Belmont, CA: Thompson/Wadsworth.

Kuhnke, E. (2007). *Body language for dummies.* Hoboken, NJ: Wiley.

Lanzetta, J. T., Cartwright-Smith, J., & Kleck, R. E. (1976). Effects of nonverbal dissimulations on emotional experience and autonomic arousal. Journal of Personality and Social Psychology, 33, 354–370.

Larsen, R. J., Kasimatis, M., & Frey, K. (1992). Facilitating the furrowed brow: An unobtrusive test of the facial feedback hypothesis applied to unpleasant affect. *Cognition and Emotion,* 6, 321–338.

Leathers, D., & Eaves, M. H. (2008). *Successful nonverbal communication: Principles and applications* (4th ed.). Boston: Allyn & Bacon.

Lee, H. O., & Boster, F. J. (1992). Collectivism–individualism in perceptions of speech rate: A cross-cultural comparison. *Journal of Cross-Cultural Psychology, 23,* 377–388.

Lee, K., Xu, F., Fu, G., Cameron, C. A., & Chen, S. (2001). Taiwan and mainland China and Canadian children's categorization and evaluation of lie- and truth-telling: A modest effect. *British Journal of Developmental Psychology, 19,* 525–542.

Lee, R. L. M. (1984). Malaysian queue culture: An ethnography of urban public behavior. *Southeast Asian Journal of Social Science, 12,* 36–50.

LeVine, R., & Bartlett, K. (1984). Pace of life, punctuality, and coronary heart disease in six countries. *Journal of Cross-Cultural Psychology, 15,* 233–255.

Luscher, M. (1969). *The Luscher color test* (I. A. Scott, Trans. & Ed.). New York: Random House.

Lyman, S. M., & Scott, M. B. (1967). Territoriality: A neglected sociological dimension. *Social Problems, 15,* 236–249.

Ma, K. (1996). *The modern Madame Butterfly: Fantasy and reality in Japanese cross-cultural relationships.* Rutland, VT: Charles E. Tuttle.

MacLachlan, J. (1979). What people really think of fast talkers. *Psychology Today, 13,* 113–117.

Malandro, L. A., Barker, L., & Barker, D. A. (1989). *Nonverbal communication* (2nd ed.). New York: Random House.

Mannes, A. (2012). Shorn scalps and perceptions of male dominance. *Social Psychology and Personality Science.*

Manusov, V. (Ed.). (2005). *The sourcebook of nonverbal measures: Going beyond words.* Mahwah, NJ: Erlbaum.

Manusov, V., & Patterson, M. L. (Eds.). (2006). *The Sage handbook of nonverbal communication.* Los Angeles, CA: Sage.

Maricchiolo, F., Livi, S., Bonaiuto, M., & Gnisci, A. (2011). Hand gestures and perceived influence in small group interaction. *Spanish Journal of Psychology, 14,* 755–764.

Marsh, P. (1988). *Eye to eye: How people interact.* Topfield, MA: Salem House.

Marshall, E. (1983). *Eye language: Understanding the eloquent eye.* New York: New Trend.

Martin, G. N. (1998). Human electroencephalographic (EEG) response to olfactory stimulation: Two experiments using the aroma of food. *International Journal of Psychophysiology, 30,* 287–302.

Massachusetts Institute of Technology. (2012, May 28). People smile when they are frustrated, and the computer knows the difference. *ScienceDaily.* Retrieved December 30, 2012, from *www.sciencedaily.com /releases/2012/05/120528152736.htm.*

Matsumoto, D. (1991). Cultural influences on facial expressions of emotion. *Southern Communication Journal, 56,* 128–137.

Matsumoto, D., & Hwang, H. S. (2013a). Body and gestures. In D. Matsumoto, M. G. Frank, & H. S. Hwang, H. S. (Eds.), *Nonverbal communication: Science and applications* (pp. 75–96). Los Angeles, CA: Sage.

Matsumoto, D., & Hwang, H. S. (2013b). Cultural influences on nonverbal behavior. In D. Matsumoto, M. G. Frank, & H. S. Hwang, H. S. (Eds.), *Nonverbal communication: Science and applications* (pp. 97–120). Los Angeles, CA: Sage.

Matsumoto, D., & Kudoh, T. (1993). American-Japanese cultural differences in attributions of personality based on smiles. *Journal of Nonverbal Behavior, 17*, 231–243.

Matsumoto, D., Frank, M. G., & Hwang, H. S. (Eds.). (2013). *Nonverbal communication: Science and applications.* Los Angeles, CA: Sage.

Matsumoto, D., Frank, M. G., & Hwang, H. S. (Eds.). (2013). *Nonverbal communication: Science and applications.* Los Angeles, CA: Sage.

McGinley, S. (2000). Children and lying. Available at *www.ag.arizona.edu/pubs/general/resrpt2000/childrenlying.pdf.*

Mealy, M., Stephan, W., & Urritia, C. (2007). The acceptability of lies: A comparison of Ecuadorians and Euro-Americans. *International Journal of Intercultural Relations, 31*, 689–702.

Metts, S., & Planalp, S. (2002). Emotional communication. In M. L. Knapp & J. A. Daly (Eds.), *Handbook of Interpersonal Communication* (3rd ed., pp. 339–373). Los Angeles, CA: Sage.

Molloy, J. (1981). *Molloy's live for success.* New York: Bantam.

Montagu, A. (1971). *Touching: The human significance of the skin.* New York: Harper & Row.

Morris, D. (1977). *Manwatching: A field guide to human behavior.* New York: Abrams.

Morris, D. (2002). *Peoplewatching.* New York: Vintage.

Mottet, T., & Richmond, V. P. (1998). Verbal approach and avoidance items. *Communication Quarterly, 46*, 25–40.

Neugarten, B. (1979). Time, age, and the life cycle. *American Journal of Psychiatry, 136*, 887–894.

Ng, S. H., Loong, C. S. F., He, A. P., Liu, J. H., & Weatherall, A. (2000). Communication correlates of individualism and collectivism: Talk directed at one or more addressees in family conversations. *Journal of Language and Social Psychology*, *19*, 26–45.

Noelle-Neumann, E. (1973). Return to the concept of powerful mass media. In H. Eguchi & K. Sata (Eds.), *Studies in broadcasting: An international annual of broadcasting science* (pp. 67–112). Tokyo, Japan: Nippon Hoso Kyokai.

Noelle-Neumann, E. (1980). Mass media and social change in developed societies. In G. C. Wilhoit & H. de Bock (Eds.), *Mass communication review yearbook* (Vol. 1, pp. 657–678). Los Angeles, CA: Sage.

Noelle-Neumann, E. (1991). The theory of public opinion: The concept of the spiral of silence. In J. A. Anderson (Ed.), *Communication yearbook 14* (pp. 256–287). Los Angeles, CA: Sage.

Ober, C., Weitkamp, L. R., Cox, N., Dytch, H., Kostyu, D., & Elias, S. (1997). *American Journal of Human Genetics, 61*, 494–496.

Pearson, J. C., & Spitzberg, B. H. (1990). *Interpersonal communication: Concepts, components, and contexts* (2nd ed.). Dubuque, IA: William C. Brown.

Pearson, J. C., Nelson, P. E., Titsworth. S., & Harter, L.(2008). *Human communication.* New York: McGraw-Hill.

Place, K. S., & Becker, J. A. (1991). The influence of pragmatic competence on the likeability of grade school children. *Discourse Processes, 14*, 227–241.

Pornpitakpan, C. (2003). The effect of personality traits and perceived cultural similarity on attraction. *Journal of International Consumer Marketing, 15*, 5–30.

Porter, R. H., & Moore, J. D. (1981). Human kin recognition by olfactory cues. *Physiology and Behavior* 27, 493-495.

Rabin, R. C. (2009, May 26). A memory for faces, extreme version. *New York Times*, p. D6.

Rapsa, R., & Cusack, J. (1990). Psychiatric implications of tattoos. *American Family Physician 41*, 1481–1486.

Raven, R., Centers, C., & Rodrigues, A. (1975). The bases of conjugal power. In R. E. Cromwell & D. H. Olson (Eds.), *Power in families* (pp. 217–234). New York: Halsted Press.

Remland, M. S. (2009). *Nonverbal communication in everyday life.* Boston, MA: Allyn & Bacon.

Richmond, V., McCroskey, J. C., & Hickson, M. (2012). *Nonverbal behavior in interpersonal relations* (7th ed.). Boston: Allyn & Bacon.

Richmond, V. P., Davis, L. M., Saylor, K., & McCroskey, J. C. (1984). Power strategies in organizations: Communication techniques and messages. *Human Communication Research, 11*, 85–108.

Rosenfeld, L. B. (1990). *Communicating with competency.* New York: Scott, Foresman.

Rubin, D. C., Groth, E., & Goldsmith, D. J. (1984). Olfactory cues of autobiographical memory. *American Journal of Psychology, 97*, 493–507.

Sabourin, M. (2007). The assessment of credibility: An analysis of truth and deception in a multiethnic environment. *Canadian Psychology, 48*, 24-31.

Scheflen, A. (1964). The significance of posture in communication systems. *Psychiatry, 27*, 316–331.

Scheflen, A. (1974). *How behavior means.* New York: Gordon and Breach.

Scherer, K. R. (1986). Vocal affect expression. *Psychological Bulletin, 99*, 143–165.

Scheufele, D. A., & Moy, P. (2000). Twenty-five years of the spiral of silence: A conceptual review and empirical outlook. *International Journal of Public Opinion Research, 12*, 3–28.

Sheldon, W. H. (1940). *The varieties of human physique: An introduction to constitutional psychology.* New York: Harper & Row.

Sheldon, W. H. (1954). *Atlas of men: A guide for somatotyping the adult male of all ages.* New York: Harper & Row.

Singh, N., & Pereira, A. (2005). *The culturally customized web site.* Oxford, UK: Elsevier Butterworth-Heinemann.

Smith, M. H. (2003). Body adornment: Know the limits. *Nursing Management, 34*, 22–23.

Smith-Lovin, L., & Brody, C. (1989). Interruptions in group discussions: The effects of gender and group composition. *American Sociological Review, 54*, 424–435.

Spillman, D. M., & Everington, C. (1989). Somatotypes revisited: Have the media changed our peception of the female body image? *Psychological Reports, 64*, 887–890.

Stirrat, M., & Perrett, D. I. (2012). Face structure predicts cooperation. *Psychological Science 23*, 718–722.

Storrs, D., & Kleinke, C. L. (1990). Evaluation of high and equal status male and female touchers. *Journal of Nonverbal Behavior, 14*, 87–95.

Stratford, J. (1998). Women and men in conversation: A consideration of therapists' interruptions in therapeutic discourse. *Journal of Family Therapy, 20*, 383–394.

Swanbrow, D. (2011, May 16). Persuasive speech: The way we, um, talk sways our listeners. *ISR Sampler*. Available at *www.umich.edu/.../persuasive-speech-the-way-we-um-talk-sways-our-listeners.*

Trager, G. L. (1958). Paralanguage: A first approximation. *Studies in Linguistics, 13*, 1–12.

Trager, G. L. (1961). The typology of paralanguage. *Anthropological Linguistics, 3*, 17–21.

Tyler, J. J., Feldman, R. S., & Reichert, A. (2006). The price of deceptive behavior: Disliking and lying to peole who lie to us. *Journal of Experimental Social Psychology, 42*, 69–77.

Vainiomaki, T. (2004). Silence as a cultural sign. *Semiotica, 150*, 347–361.

Valla, J. M., Ceci, S. J., & Williams, W. M. (2011). The accuracy of inferences about criminality based on facial appearance. *Journal of Social, Evolutionary, and Cultural Psychology, 5*, 66–91.

Varenik, T. (2010). How tattoos and body piercing affect your career. http://www.resumark.com/blog/tatiana/how-tattoos-and-body-piercing-affect-your-career.

Wade, N. (2002, January 22). Scent of a man is linked to a woman's selection. *New York Times*, p. F2.

Wennerstrom, A., & Siegel, A. F. (2003). Keeping the floor in multiparty conversation: Intonation, syntax, and pause. Discourse Processes, 36 (September), 77–107.

Whitty, M. (2003). Cyber-flirting. *Theory and Psychology, 13*, 339–355.

Willis, J., & Todorov, A. (2006). First impressions: Making up your mind after a 100-ms exposure to a face. *Psychological Science, 17*, 592–598.

Windahl, S., & Signitzer, B. (with Olson, J. T.). (1992). *Using communication theory: An introduction to planned communication.* Los Angeles, CA: Sage.

Wood, J. T. (1994). *Gendered lives: Communication, gender, and culture.* Belmont, CA: Wadsworth.

Wood, J. T. (2012). *Interpersonal communication: Everyday encounters*, 5th ed. Belmont, CA: Thompson/Wadsworth.

Zaleski, Z., Cycon, A., & Kurc, A. (2001). Future time perspective and subjective well-being in adolescent samples. In P. Schmuck & K. M. Sheldon (Eds.), *Life goals and well-being: Towards a positive psychology of human striving* (pp. 58–67). Cambridge, MA: Hogrefe & Huber.

Zuckerman, M., Klorman, R., Larrance, D. T., & Spiegel, N. H. (1981). Facial, autonomic, and subjective components of emotion: The facial feedback hypothesis versus the externalizer–internalizer distinction. *Journal of Personality and Social Psychology, 41*, 929–944.

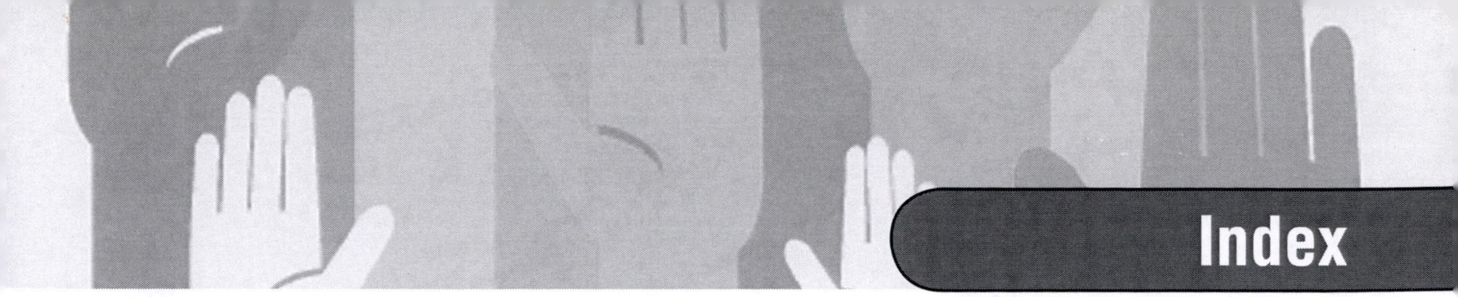

Index

D

E

F